BY THE SECOND SPRING

BY THE
SECOND SPRING

*Seven Lives and One Year
of the War in Ukraine*

Danielle Leavitt

Farrar, Straus and Giroux
New York

Farrar, Straus and Giroux
120 Broadway, New York 10271

The map on page viii is copyright © 2025 by Jeffrey L. Ward.
The photograph on page 142 is from Wikimedia Commons.
The photograph and drawing on page 282 are used with the
permission of the artist.

Library of Congress Cataloging-in-Publication Data
Names: Leavitt, Danielle, 1992– author.
Title: By the second spring : seven lives and one year of the war in
    Ukraine / Danielle Leavitt.
Other titles: Seven lives and one year of the war in Ukraine
Description: New York : Farrar, Straus and Giroux, 2025.
Identifiers: LCCN 2024052366 | ISBN 9780374614331 (hardcover)
Subjects: LCSH: Russian Invasion of Ukraine, 2022—Biography. | Russian
    Invasion of Ukraine, 2022—Personal narratives, Ukrainian. |
    Russian Invasion of Ukraine, 2022—Social aspects. | Ukraine—Social
    conditions—21st century. | Ukraine—Social life and customs—
    21st century.
Classification: LCC DK5429 .L438 2025 | DDC 947.706/210922—dc23/
    eng/20250203
LC record available at https://lccn.loc.gov/2024052366

Designed by Patrice Sheridan

Our books may be purchased in bulk for promotional, educational, or business
use. Please contact your local bookseller or the Macmillan Corporate and
Premium Sales Department at 1-800-221-7945, extension 5442, or by email at
MacmillanSpecialMarkets@macmillan.com.

www.fsgbooks.com
Follow us on social media at @fsgbooks

1   3   5   7   9   10   8   6   4   2

The names of some persons described in this book have been changed.

Anna,

Maria,

Polina,

Tania,

Vitaly,

Volodymyr,

and Yulia—

and the millions of Ukrainians they represent,

each of whom deserves a book of their own

CONTENTS

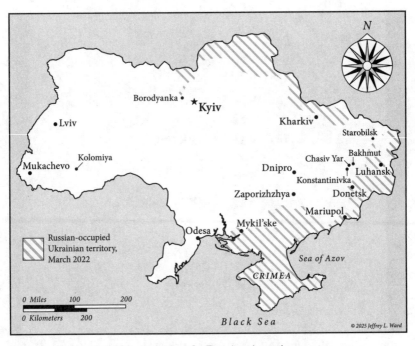

Ukraine in March 2022, just after the Russian invasion

PREFACE

IN THE WEEKS following Russia's full-scale invasion of Ukraine in February 2022, individual demonstrations of Ukrainian resilience became international folklore: there were the Ukrainian farmers who harvested Russian tanks with their tractors, the grandma who brought down a drone from her window with a jar of pickled tomatoes, and the border guard who, when told to surrender Ukraine's Snake Island, replied "Russian warship, go fuck yourself"—the last communication before the island was captured. These stories traveled far and wide and helped rally support for the Ukrainian cause.

And yet, even today, despite the richness of these anecdotes, most Ukrainians remain unknown and faceless, represented only abstractly in diminishing news coverage and political discourse.

While much has been written about the Russo-Ukrainian war that's informative, moving, and insightful, I've been perplexed to see that portrayals of the Ukrainian experience itself are often flattening. In popular understanding, Ukrainians can become one-dimensional characters—either desperate victims or nearly superhuman heroes, rebuffing Russian aggression and stunning the world with their courageous will to resist. Both characterizations have validity, but on their own they fail to adequately describe the people and society.

In the first months of the war, I was often surprised by how many people, knowing of my connection to the country, asked me to tell them about these people—the Ukrainians—the ones they were reading about every day in the news, who were fleeing and fighting and forging ahead with their lives. In the early 2000s, my family moved from the United States to Ukraine, where my parents ran legal education programs, and from the time I was twelve years old, I spent a portion of nearly every year there. From my earliest exposure to Ukraine, I was fascinated by it all: the smart and dark sense of humor, minor-key folk songs, old women selling lingerie in underground walkways, how people regard long walks as a primary form of entertainment. Ask any Ukrainian what they like to do for fun, and they will likely say "*huliati*"—to stroll around.

And yet, apart from President Volodymyr Zelenskyy, who seems the only Ukrainian most people around the world can name or recognize, Ukrainians have become relatively nameless, faceless *war people*. I have wondered: Is it possible for readers abroad to truly know Ukrainians beyond Zelenskyy, BBC sound bites, and the occasional blue-and-yellow flag hanging from a window?

My answer is yes, and this book joins others in taking up that task. Here I have sought to bring names, faces, personality, and identity to the often anonymous Ukrainians we read about daily in the news. In this book, I seek to know them not as war people or superheroes but as mere humans confronted with what was for many the unimaginable. Just like all of us, they are often brave, and they are sometimes not. As the book proceeds from the Russian invasion of February 2022 through the first tumultuous year of war, we'll follow them deep inside war-torn Ukraine, exploring their personal histories and families, elucidating the context and conundrums that define modern Ukraine and its relationship with Russia, all while exploring the incomprehensible and deeply human task of believing in the future while destruction rages on.

In the early days of the invasion, I was completing a PhD in Ukrainian history. I soon became involved as well in a humanitarian project run by my parents' institute—the Leavitt Institute for International Development—and funded by the Dell Loy Hansen Family Foundation, which provided financial assistance to several hundred families, most from Southern and Eastern Ukraine. Along with the aid, the team set up a very simple online platform that Ukrainians could use to record their experiences and thoughts—anything they wanted, in the form of a diary—as they lived through war. I was trained as a historian and knew that these are exactly the kinds of records that future historians and scholars can employ to make sense of the past. It felt imperative to give as many Ukrainians as possible a chance to write their stories and play a role in defining how the history of this war might be written in future decades.

Many received the diary project enthusiastically. It turned out that people were quite motivated to share their experiences, and within a few months the database had several hundred unique entries. Some wrote just one or two individual posts, but many wrote consistently, week after week, sometimes a few entries a week. In time, their stories became robust, and nuanced. I did not help to administer the diary project, but I was granted unique access to the database, and I read what people were writing, following their stories as they evolved over time. I became invested in how certain people fared, how particular problems resolved or didn't, and I wanted to know more, more about where they came from, their families, their ideas. They had become real to me, and their fates felt personal.

As the war entered its first summer, in 2022, I knew that other people needed to read these stories, too, and that if they could, they might come to know Ukraine more fully. Using WhatsApp, I contacted several of the diarists and asked if I could follow them in real time, for many months, in order to better understand the realities of life in war. They all agreed—in fact more wanted to participate than I could feasibly interview. In the end, I chose to focus on seven individuals and their families. Of these, one is a friend I've known since childhood, two were introduced to me by mutual friends, and four I came to know through the diary project. They come from across Ukraine and are of various ages and political persuasions, representing together a cross section of modern Ukrainian society, though each of them is of Slavic origin, and most are ethnically Ukrainian while some are ethnically Russian. For well over a year, I was in near-constant contact with the people featured in this book, and they sent me detailed accounts of their circumstances through messages and voice recordings, photos and videos. In February 2023, one of these people, Vitaly, messaged me: "You know, Danielle, I'm not a master writer. But I'm trying, I'm really trying." When I began my interviews with another—Maria—she said after just a few questions: "You know, it's very important for me to remember these things and to talk about them. It helps me to continue living, to move forward."

I followed their stories from the full-scale Russian invasion in February 2022, organizing their experiences into distinct episodes and arranging them by seasons, beginning with the first winter in the war, and ending in the spring of 2023—the second spring. They would recount, in intimate detail, their first reactions to the invasion, why opposition to Russia was so fierce, and why and how such a sudden and shocking spirit of mass volunteerism arose. I concern myself less with the movement of military forces and more with exploring the daily realities of war in a relatively developed country.

Of course, we all watched closely as the Ukrainians' unrelenting will to resist repelled Russian forces in the first months of the war, and we've continued to watch as the war has settled into an increasingly protracted grind that has prompted weariness in the West and sometimes among Ukrainians themselves. My hope is that here, in this book, the everyday lives of a few individuals and families become palpable and resonant, shedding new light on what's at stake for average Ukrainians and what it means to live inside the madness of an unwanted and brutal modern war.

DRAMATIS PERSONAE

ANNA: An eighteen-year-old police cadet originally from the eastern city of Luhansk. She is left alone in Western Ukraine.

MARIA: A woman in her midtwenties from Mariupol, where she lived with her husband, Leonid, and young son, David. Leonid joins the defense of Mariupol.

POLINA: A young Ukrainian woman living in LA. Polina is married to John, an American. They return to Ukraine to help.

TANIA: A woman from Southern Ukraine who runs a small pig farm with her husband, Viktor. As the Russians invade, Tania and Viktor decide to stay in their village.

VITALY: A middle-aged man who owns a coffee shop in a suburb of Kyiv. Vitaly makes his money in recycling.

VOLODYMYR: An engineer at the Chernobyl nuclear plant who became a writer and filmmaker in the late 1980s.

YULIA: A middle-aged woman from Konstantinivka, a small town in the eastern region of Donetsk. Yulia and her husband, Oleg, have two daughters. Yulia is skilled in handicrafts.

PART 1

THE
FIRST WINTER

VITALY

Borodyanka, Ukraine

SOON AFTER VITALY was born, the Soviet housing administration assigned his family a three-room apartment. It was a relatively cushy reward for his father's work constructing their small town, Borodyanka, thirty miles northwest of Kyiv. His father helped build at least half the structures along Borodyanka's central street in the 1970s and early '80s as the town rapidly expanded to accommodate new residents, who'd come to work at a large excavator manufacturing plant.

After years of creating new apartments for factory workers, Vitaly's family were finally granted keys to one of their own. A topographer by trade, Vitaly's father had spent his career making dozens of identical Soviet apartment buildings. He surveyed land, its elevation and contours, studied all the features of the terrain, the gentle slopes of the tract, and created detailed maps of each site before passing them off to architects and construction workers. In the late Soviet period, the USSR's housing authority fashioned hundreds of thousands of new apartments, all with standardized layouts and configurations. In the end, the land mapped by Vitaly's dad was inevitably covered by nine-story concrete buildings, each unit within following the classic Brezhnev-era layout—a narrow corridor connecting the rooms, isolated toilet and shower spaces, and a small square kitchen with an enclosed balcony attached to its side. From the balcony, the units overlooked a community courtyard with benches, concrete flowerpots, and a small playground. Though invisible from the street, a back alleyway led to this courtyard, which was the vibrant hub of that small universe.

It was in such a courtyard that Vitaly started to make sense of the world. In a small kindergarten at the ground level, Vitaly learned to sound out the letters in his name. He and his best friend, Serhiy, turned the open space of the yard into a soccer stadium and played sports while they waited for their parents to come home from work. In the courtyard, Vitaly fell in love with a pretty neighbor named Natalka, who was a disciplined student. Vitaly did not do well in school—he was energetic and unfocused—but Natalka tutored him. Though they were never in a romantic relationship, they remained close friends, and forty-five years later, Vitaly said "I trust her more than I trust myself."

When they were thirteen, Natalka got a baby brother—Artem. Vitaly showered the baby with affection to impress Natalka, a performance that quickly turned into real fondness for the baby. Artem grew into a bright-eyed tagalong whose cheery disposition, huge front teeth, and mop of blond hair made him the darling of the courtyard.

The Soviet Union collapsed in 1991, but the courtyard remained, and all the children who first saw the world from that small plot of land grew up. Vitaly, Serhiy, Natalka, and Artem went away to school or did their military service, found spouses, had children, picked up hobbies, got divorced, and watched their own children grow up in identical courtyards. They all remained friends, and for forty years they trod across the worn path from the street to their apartments, passing through that common space where Vitaly's mother became an old woman, and where other children made their first best friends and learned to fight and swear and forgive. All of them, crisscrossing through time and space, sharing that place once constructed by Vitaly's dad, where the complex spectrum of human life and love and loss took form.

Coming of age in the post-Soviet 1990s was formative for Vitaly. For him and many others of his generation, with the arrival of McDonald's, Nirvana, and acid-wash jeans, "the West" became synonymous with cool. Despite job insecurity and catastrophic inflation, most young people rejected the ideologies of the past in favor of the rickety, dysfunctional market capitalism taking root. Disney images and posters of Sylvester Stallone sprang up throughout post-Soviet Ukraine, as did modern, "Western" methods to manage old realities—for example, tampons. New coffee shops, bars, and pizzerias proliferated. A taxi driver in Kyiv once pointed out to me a small basement café in the center of the city. It was the site of the first pizzeria that opened in Kyiv in the late 1980s, and everyone who knew anything about being cool wanted to spend even just a few minutes taking in what they imagined were the smells and tastes of the United States.

Much of Vitaly's wardrobe referenced America. In one mid-2000s photo, he stands on the banks of the Dnieper River in Kyiv, wearing shorts emblazoned with the American flag, a shirt with an NBA star superimposed onto the New York City skyline, a Yankees hat, and flip-flops. He exuded a distinctive Eastern European machismo, and in photos poses with a serious, unflinching expression—not happy, not sad, unquestionably alpha. And yet, at moments, a tenderness peeked through his tough exterior. He loved to draw, he sometimes recited poetry, and he wore his heart on his sleeve, pining on occasion for Natalka, who moved with her children to the United States in 2015. As a young man in the 1990s, Vitaly had developed two dreams: to own his own coffee shop and to see the Statue of Liberty. When Natalka moved to New York City, he decided he wasn't going to wait anymore. He would save all his money and open his coffee shop. In time, he'd make enough money to buy a ticket to the Big Apple and see the Statue of Liberty.

Seeing America was a common dream for his generation, if only because the country represented the opposite of where they came from. It was the citadel of global capitalism. From the perspective of a young Ukrainian kid living in Borodyanka in the aftermath of the Soviet Union's collapse, it glittered. He and many of his generation were quick to disavow the Soviet past: in the late 1980s and early '90s, as the Soviet Union spiraled into collapse, they criticized their grandparents for being so stupid as to follow Stalin, made fun of Communist tropes, bought and sold clothes and music and drugs on the black market, and waved blue-and-yellow Ukrainian flags in the streets. For many of these kids, such gestures were only in part about their own nationality. It is difficult to parse what was nationalism based on conviction and what was an angry reaction against the Soviet regime, under which their parents and grandparents had suffered hunger, repression, and fear for so long. The nationalist movement that preceded the fall of the Soviet Union was generally led by intellectuals, artists, and writers, but its strength in numbers came largely from youth, who, throughout those final years, did not mince words about their disdain for Soviet authority and their desire to be independent from it.

Following Mikhail Gorbachev's ascent to the top of the Soviet system in 1985, many ethnic and national groups in the USSR sought greater autonomy and cultural recognition. The Baltic republics—

Lithuania, Latvia, and Estonia—as well as Ukraine and Georgia led movements for independence. Historians have attributed the Soviet collapse to many factors—economic stagnation and decline, bureaucratic gridlock, military overextension in Afghanistan—and the demise of the USSR was a multifaceted event. But the role of national movements, which challenged Soviet authority and sparked new political entities and ideologies, cannot be overstated.

The Ukrainian national movement that gained new strength in the late 1980s had existed for many decades. In the nineteenth century, intellectuals influenced by a Europe-wide fervor for national self-determination based on linguistic, cultural, and historical commonalities began canonizing ideas about Ukrainian identity and history, distinct from Russia's. Who were these people living on the frontier borderlands between the Eurasian Steppe and Eastern European parklands? Although they had different names in different times (Ruthenians and Rusyns, among others), nineteenth-century nation builders chose the word *Ukrainian* to describe themselves. It meant literally "those from the borderland." Fundamental to their identity was that they were not the center—not the empire but the edge.

Positioned on the edge of many empires—Poland, Hungary, and Lithuania to the west, Russia to the east—Ukrainians acquired a nonconformity and a sense of independence that became a major thorn in the side of anyone who tried to rule them. The steppe brought together communities of Slavic peasants, Jews, Crimean Tatars, Poles, Greeks, and other ethnic groups. Starting in the fifteenth century, Ukrainian Cossacks, a group of seminomadic people in the central and southeastern regions of contemporary Ukraine, established self-governing states with elected rulers and led uprisings against overlords. According to the historian Serhii Plokhy, the Cossacks ruled the steppe in a manner akin to the pirates of the Mediterranean and the frontiersmen of the American

West. They generally lived up to their name, which was derived from the Turkic word *qazaq*, meaning "adventurer" or "free man."

In the mid-1600s, after the Polish-Lithuanian Commonwealth limited Cossack authority, imposed heavy taxes, and suppressed Orthodox Christianity, a Cossack leader named Bohdan Khmelnytsky led a successful revolt, quickly gaining support from other Cossack groups as well as Ukrainian peasants and townspeople. Claiming to fight in defense of Orthodox Christianity, the Cossacks unleashed a violent series of attacks on the region's Jews, ransacking many Jewish communities and towns and forcing the conversion to Christianity of hundreds, if not thousands.

The Khmelnytsky Uprising fundamentally shifted the order of the region. In 1654, seeking an ally against Poland, Khmelnytsky entered into a treaty with Tsar Alexis of Muscovy that established a Ukrainian polity under Muscovy's protection. The unintended result: an arrangement that Khmelnytsky and other Cossack leaders hoped would bring greater autonomy and freedom from Polish dominion marked instead the beginning of Ukraine's subjugation to Moscow and the expanding Russian Empire.

Over time, Cossack states—or hetmanates—were dismantled, and Cossack leaders were absorbed into the Russian aristocracy. Ukrainian land was, over time, incorporated into a burgeoning Russian Empire that spread a narrative of a shared fatherland. Russian imperial administrative structures and policies were imposed in Ukraine, and the empire encouraged the settlement of ethnic Russians, particularly in regions that had an ethnic Ukrainian majority.

For centuries, the Russian Empire expanded, conquering territory and assimilating new peoples. By the early twentieth century, Russia ruled a vast multiethnic, multireligious territory, comprised not just of Slavic groups—Russians, Ukrainians, and Belarussians—but Georgians, Jews, Armenians, Azerbaijanis, Bashkirs, Tatars, Chuvash, Chechens, Kazakhs, Uzbeks, Kyrgyz, Turkmen, Latvians,

Lithuanians, Estonians, Finns, and more. In both the Russian Empire and the USSR, maintaining authority and control over so many peoples required carefully constructed narratives of unity and brotherhood. These narratives, especially those about Ukraine and Russia, knitted conquered peoples together with the imperial center with myths of primordial connection. The stories were invented by eighteenth- and nineteenth-century imperial thinkers who sought to legitimize Russia's imperial reach. To quell nationalist unrest and keep Ukraine firmly within its dominion, the Russian imperial center exercised immense control over how Ukrainians understood their national identity. Russia twisted historical evidence, arguing that Ukrainians and Russians were historically the same people, and that Khmelnytsky had not been seeking a reciprocal alliance but had voluntarily subordinated his people to Russia.

Ukrainian intellectuals in the nineteenth century began to push against imperial narratives about Ukrainian and Russian sameness. They began writing in particular about the original Cossacks from previous centuries, whom they regarded as the true fathers of the nation. The Cossacks' dark history of violence against other ethnic and national groups was whitewashed in this reinvention, and over time, the hetmans grew into central figures of Ukrainian mythology: rough-and-tumble freedom fighters who resisted foreign domination and symbolized national identity. The most prominent of these Ukrainian intellectuals was a poet named Taras Shevchenko, who wrote, in classical Ukrainian, about his homeland and the Cossacks, using them as symbols of freedom, independence, and resistance against oppression. As he and other Ukrainian nationalists developed their ideas, Ukraine's national movement gained some strength, but Russian imperial authorities cracked down hard. Shevchenko was exiled to St. Petersburg, where he died in 1861 at the age of forty-seven. Eventually, Russian authorities outlawed the use of the Ukrainian language in print, Russifying Ukrainians by force, and punishing those who resisted.

When the Russian Empire fell in 1917, Ukraine's national movement was sufficiently strong that activists in Kyiv declared independence and created their own state, the Ukrainian People's Republic. The republic, however, was short lived. Within months, its sovereignty was challenged by various external powers, and Ukraine lost its western territories to Poland. In the east, the war raged as several factions vied for control of the region, including Ukrainian nationalists, Bolsheviks, White (Russian imperial) forces, anarchists, and foreign interventionists. The complex nature of the civil war left Ukraine ravaged. Jews suffered numerous pogroms, leading to overwhelming destruction of their communities and significant emigration from the region. Eventually, the Bolsheviks prevailed and eliminated the independent Ukrainian government. They established Soviet power in Ukraine, and in 1922, Ukraine became a founding member of the Union of Soviet Socialist Republics—the USSR—of which it remained a part until 1991.

In the 1920s, Bolshevik leaders of the new USSR tried to demonstrate their egalitarianism by granting limited freedoms of expression to non-Russian national groups, implementing a type of "Affirmative Action" for minority ethnic and national groups, as the historian Terry Martin has called it. In a movement called *korenizatsiya*, or literally "indigenization," they encouraged Georgians, Kazakhs, Belorussians, Armenians, and Ukrainians, among others, to use their native languages, wear traditional dress, and celebrate their unique national heritage. But fearing the potential for national groups to undermine the power of central authority, Stalin largely reversed these policies in the late 1930s, ensuring that central authority in Moscow had direct control over all aspects of governance, including cultural and linguistic affairs. A new slogan prevailed—"The Friendship of the Peoples"—which was meant to promote unity and cooperation among various ethnic and national groups. And yet the Soviet state and society became, throughout the 1930s, increasingly Russified, with Russian history and culture sitting at the center of education curriculums, state-controlled media operating predominantly in Russian, and a widespread purge of nationalists.

Even after the destructive upheaval of the civil war, the 1930s and '40s are regularly cited as the most traumatic decades in Ukrainian history. In those years, the ideological projects of two neo-empires, as the historian Timothy Snyder calls the Soviet Union and Nazi Germany, converged on the territory of Ukraine. In the late 1920s, under Stalin, the Soviet Union embarked on its first Five-Year Plan, establishing targets and production quotas for Soviet industry. The aims of these centralized economic plans, which continued in several-year increments until the Soviet collapse, ruled Soviet society. To accomplish Stalin's ambitious goals of transforming a predominantly agrarian society into a powerful industrialized state capable of competing with the modernized states of the Western world, the USSR embarked on a mission of rapid industrialization, constructing in just a few years many dozens of factories, metallurgical complexes, and mining enterprises. To fund this radical modernization project, the Soviet state collectivized agriculture, which meant that the government abolished the private ownership of land and livestock. Peasants and farmers, who made up the overwhelming majority of the Ukrainian population, were coerced to join collective farms, where they pooled their equipment, resources, and land. Farmers who resisted—branded pejoratively as *kulaks*—became class enemies, and the state launched a relentless campaign against them, sending hundreds of thousands to the gulag or executing them.

Collectivization proved terribly bloody and generally unsuccessful. Many Ukrainian peasants resisted, and even on collective farms with compliant workers, production lagged, and the Soviet state failed to extract as much grain as it needed to support its industrialization projects. In the early 1930s, the state imposed strict grain requisition quotas on Ukrainian farmers. Often the quotas were set unrealistically high, leading to dangerous shortages in rural areas. People stashed away bags of grain to survive, but authorities searched houses and wagons, confiscating even small amounts, and people began to starve. In 1932 and 1933, throughout rural areas in Central and Eastern Ukraine, nearly four million people died of hunger. The event became known as the *holodomor*, or "death by hunger." Rare photos of the *holodomor* show emaciated corpses lying in the middle of a city street while others walk by. Stalin refused to acknowledge the famine and suppressed information about the scale of hunger and death; for decades afterward, the Soviet state denied its existence, and people were forbidden to speak of it.

Just a few years later, Stalin began a series of political repressions and mass persecutions later called the Great Terror. The Soviet secret police arrested, exiled, or executed millions of people whom Stalin perceived as internal threats to the Communist Party. People were encouraged to denounce one another to authorities, and a widespread atmosphere of fear and paranoia controlled Soviet social and political relations, the consequences of which altered the Soviet psyche for decades.

In 1939, just before Nazi Germany invaded Poland, the USSR and Germany signed a nonaggression pact, splitting up Poland in a deal that allowed the USSR to invade Western Ukraine, then ruled by Poland, and unite it with Soviet Ukraine. As the Nazis took western Poland, marking the beginning of the Second World War, Soviet authorities began a bloody invasion of the Western Ukraine regions of Galicia and Volhynia. Those regions had never belonged to the USSR, and they were home to a robust intellectual community that championed Ukrainian independence. The arriving

Soviet authorities began a massive Sovietization and Russification campaign in Western Ukraine. They appropriated land, collectivized farms, and brought in ethnic Russians to administer Soviet policy. Ukrainians resisted tooth and nail, and among many, an ardent, fiery hatred of Soviets and Russians took root, giving rise to an anti-Soviet partisan militia called the Ukrainian Insurgent Army.

Within two years, Hitler betrayed his agreement with Stalin and invaded Western Ukraine on his blitzkrieg to conquer the USSR, take the Caspian oil fields, and create lebensraum—living space—for the Aryan race. Timothy Snyder argues that central to the Nazis' ideology was a pursuit of fertile soil—"black earth"—which is abundant in Ukraine and has made Ukraine the breadbasket of the world for centuries. In Hitler's mind, the only way to rival Britain—the world's superpower at the time—was through achieving self-sufficiency by controlling enough resource-rich territories. In large part, this meant Ukraine. Many Ukrainians initially welcomed the Nazis, believing they could not be worse than the Soviets. Some collaborators were antisemites who sympathized with Nazi objectives, and some hoped that the Germans would liberate them from Soviet oppression. The fact that some Ukrainians embraced the Nazis in the 1940s and certain fringe groups of fascist Ukrainian ultranationalists fought against the Soviets for years led to Moscow's branding of pro-Ukrainian movements as being "Nazi" in nature. Decades later, picking up on this branding in his war against Ukraine, Putin consistently uses the term "neo-Nazi" to refer to anyone who is pro-Ukrainian, despite the fact that Ukraine's president, Volodymyr Zelenskyy, is Jewish.

In 1941, very soon after the Nazis established their own governance of Ukraine, it became clear that they were not sympathetic occupiers. In the Nazis' more than three-year rule, they proved inept at using Ukrainian land to their advantage and were unable to extract much Ukrainian grain, which led to even more famine. Millions of Soviet POWs starved in camps throughout Ukraine, and hundreds of thousands of city dwellers died of hunger. The Nazis carried out the Holocaust throughout Ukraine, emptying entire Jewish towns, shipping off hundreds of thousands of Jews to concentration camps or murdering them in mass exterminations, such as at Babyn Yar—a ravine outside Kyiv where tens of thousands of Jews were shot in just a few days, all laid together in one mass grave.

Following the Nazi failure to take Stalingrad and the stalling of the Nazi offensive in the north, the USSR went on the offensive and eventually retook Eastern and then Western Ukraine. In Ukraine between 1932 and 1945, mind-numbing numbers of people—millions upon millions—starved to death or were murdered at the hands of the Soviets and the Nazis. "There is no event of this scale in any other country in the world," writes Snyder. Reckoning with the atrocities of the 1930s and 1940s—many of which were downplayed or went unmentioned in the decades that followed—cultivated in Ukrainians a very specific trauma: a deep-seated fear of hunger, cold, conspiracy, and, above all else, war.

After the war, the USSR reestablished its control, including in Western Ukraine, which had previously been part of the USSR for only a matter of months. Still fighting fierce nationalist resistance, the Soviets shipped off to the gulag many of those who collaborated with the Nazis, squashed anyone who supported nationalist groups, further centralized control of the land and the economy, and sent in cargo loads of Russian language curriculums. Western Ukraine, which had been home to almost equal numbers of Ukrainians, Poles, and Jews in the decades before the Second World War, became increasingly Sovietized. The Jews of the region had almost all been killed. The Poles, too, had been massacred or driven out. By the early fifties, the nationalist project in Western Ukraine had largely been dismantled and in its stead, new Communist leaders—

brought in from Russia or Eastern Ukraine—established the predominance of the Communist Party, built up new Soviet institutions and schools, collectivized agriculture, and industrialized the land.

Stalin died in 1953, leading to a new Soviet era. As one prominent Ukrainian historian, Yaroslav Hrytsak, has written of Ukraine's post-Stalin trajectory:

> A unified and placated Ukraine was granted the role of a "younger brother" to Russians in the administration of the Soviet Union. Various results included the transfer of Crimea from the Russian Soviet republic to Soviet Ukraine. But the most important fact was probably this: during the last decades of the Soviet Union, the core of the ruling elite in Moscow was made up of the Dnipropetrovsk group, with Leonid Brezhnev as its top representative.

The Dnipropetrovsk clan to which Hrytsak referred was a mafia-like group of politicians, some of Ukrainian heritage, some of Russian, who emerged from Eastern Ukraine and exerted incredible power on the Soviet center. Leonid Brezhnev, who hailed from the group, led the Soviet Union for twenty years. (As Hrytsak later noted, this gave birth to a joke that the history of Russia is divided into three periods: pre-Petrine, Petrine, and "Dnipro-Petrine.")

Over time, most Ukrainians—especially in the eastern part of the country—became heavily Russified. Most city dwellers spoke Russian as a first language, and most people who worked in official state or Communist Party capacities exclusively spoke Russian. The Ukrainian language often prevailed in villages, where Russification policies did not reach as readily. In the "Thaw" of the late 1950s and 1960s, Nikita Khrushchev denounced Stalin's repressive policies and departure from true Communism, ushering in a time of relative liberalization. Ukrainian dissenters became more visible in this era, advocating for language freedoms and acknowledgment of Ukrainians' repression under Stalin. By the mid-1960s, however, Khrushchev had been ousted by conservative party apparatchiks, and Brezhnev—who had been raised in the mining towns of the Donbas—went on to rule the Soviet Union. Brezhnev's regime cracked down on Ukraine's nationalist activists, staging public arrests and sentencing many to decades of hard labor in the gulag.

When Gorbachev came to power in 1985 following the death of Brezhnev and his two immediate successors, he introduced perestroika (restructuring) and glasnost (openness), two campaigns intended to push the Soviet Union toward a more sustainable economic and cultural future. Nationalist movements emerged with new force; in Ukraine the cause attracted mass participation—not just from those who were passionately pro-Ukrainian all along but those who were ready to rid themselves of Soviet life and saw Ukrainian independence as the way out. For most Ukrainians in 1991— even those who spoke exclusively Russian and who believed the official narratives about Ukrainian and Russian shared identity— breaking ties with Moscow seemed intuitive.

The strength of Ukraine's independence movement proved decisive. Even after Lithuania declared independence in 1990—the first republic to do so—the USSR could have survived. But without Ukraine and its abundant natural and economic resources—to say nothing of its cultural influence—the USSR was not feasible. Moscow knew that if Ukrainians claimed their own nationhood, it would never retain control over smaller Soviet republics in Central Asia and the Caucasus. This proved true. When Ukraine's parliament voted overwhelmingly for independence in August 1991, Moscow's sphere of influence began to crumble: within one month, the governments of Moldova, Uzbekistan, Kyrgyzstan, Tajikistan, and Armenia followed suit.

By December 1991, the USSR was formally disbanded, leaving

in its wake fifteen new nations. The collapse of the Soviet Union taught many lessons, but for Moscow one of the primary takeaways was that Moscow's control over Ukraine solidified its control of the region at large—a truth that would inform its foreign policy for the next thirty years. Russian policymakers believed that keeping Ukraine in its sphere of influence—through political alliances, economic interdependence, and cultural propaganda—was essential to maintain their neocolonial influence in their own vast and multiethnic country and throughout the Caucasus, Central Asia, and Belarus. Essentially, without Ukraine, Russia could not be an empire.

In early 1992, Ukrainians adopted their new state flag. The striking blue and yellow horizons symbolized their identity as people from a frontier borderland marked by endless fields of wheat and sunflowers under a blue sky.

Vitaly was sixteen when these flags replaced the red hammer and sickle. His identity as a Ukrainian was still embryonic, as it was for most Ukrainians, but he knew somehow, deep down, that he was not Russian. As a first grader, he held sticks between his knees and pretended to ride horses like a Zaporizhian Cossack—it was not something anyone taught him to do, and he doesn't know where he learned it, but it reinforced a vague sense of apartness. He grew up speaking Russian, although he often spoke Ukrainian with his mom and grandparents.

Even as a teenage boy, with a limited understanding of politics, breaking with the Soviet Union was something he supported, especially following the nuclear disaster at Chernobyl in 1986, when he was eleven years old. He remembered busloads of evacuated people flooding his town—about sixty miles from the exploded reactor—in the middle of the night in late April. Many of them settled in Borodyanka, and he grew up understanding that something dark had occurred at Chernobyl—that his friends would never return home because the area was contaminated, it was all dead. As time went on, the environmental impact of the Chernobyl disaster became clearer, and he suspects that his body absorbed it, too, as millions did: by the time he was forty years old, most of his teeth had fallen out.

Naturally scrappy and prone to buck authority, Vitaly was made for 1990s Ukraine, where those with aggressive spirits figured out how to survive and make the new system work in their favor. He got married young, had two sons, then got divorced. He loved the boys, though he was not always present. Especially in the 1990s, when he scrimped and saved to get by every single day, he saw himself as engaged in a struggle, a kind of boxing match with life, a match that deep down he believed he'd win. In a theater in 2005, Vitaly saw the Russell Crowe and Renée Zellweger blockbuster *Cinderella Man*, about an obscure working-class boxer during the Great Depression who went on to become the world heavyweight champion. Vitaly left the theater deeply moved, walking out with his head held high. It's still his favorite movie.

During the difficult nineties, he served his mandatory time in the Ukrainian army, worked in construction as a welder, and for several years in a sawmill. But in the early 2000s, he wanted to try to work for himself, be his own man. He didn't have any money to start anything, so he began collecting trash to sell, scavenging through old buildings and junkyards, taking broken plastic from window frames, rusted-out elevator parts, stairway railings from abandoned buildings. He broke the garbage down into different piles—one for hard plastic, one for metal, one for softer plastic, like packaging and plastic bottles, and one for paper. There was a lot of paper, as people were throwing away Soviet books and manuals that had lost all relevance.

Over time, he was not just surviving but saving money. By late 2021, it was finally time for his coffee shop. He rented a modest commercial space on the roundabout entrance to Borodyanka from Kyiv, right next to his apartment building and courtyard. He budgeted and saved to get all the necessary appliances—a grill, a microwave, a refrigerator, and a small electric oven. Most of all, he coveted a professional-grade espresso machine like the ones he imagined baristas using in bustling New York cafés. Renting the machine would have been more fiscally responsible, but he allowed himself this one luxury after so many years of meticulous planning and saving. Although he was not much of a reader, Vitaly pored over the machine's instruction manual, meditating upon each of its features. He ordered frozen dough for baked goods from suppliers, "because what is a coffee shop without freshly baked croissants?" he insisted. His girlfriend sewed curtains and decorated the shop with fake flowers and coffee-themed wooden signs. He called the shop Coffee Break, and on February 1, 2022, they opened to the public, right on highway E373, the same highway that, a few weeks later, a long convoy of Russian tanks would travel on their way toward Kyiv.

YULIA

Chasiv Yar, Ukraine

BY THE TIME she was eleven years old in the late 1980s, Yulia had read every book in her local library. This was possible in part because she was bright and in part because her small town, Chasiv Yar, had few books. Chasiv Yar was a mining and manufacturing outpost, fifty miles from the important eastern city of Donetsk. The town had substantial natural deposits of clay with significant aluminum content and a high melting point. It was a valuable material, and Chasiv Yar's nearby factories used it to churn out refractory materials used to make furnaces, kilns, reactors, and molds. For decades, people from all over the USSR came to the area to find a job in heavy industry, but Yulia knew little of the mines and the clay; she came from a family of teachers who recited poetry and fairy tales and read books.

Chasiv Yar sat in the middle of Ukraine's Donets Basin—the Donbas—a fertile, undulating region rich in natural resources. The Donbas itself was on the "wild steppe"—a vast expanse of gently rolling grasslands. Over the centuries, the fertility and openness attracted many kinds of people fleeing persecution or upheaval. They settled on the agricultural frontier of the steppe, creating an ethnic and religious contact zone populated by Ukrainians, Jews, Greeks, Poles, German Mennonites, Russians, Serbs, and others.

It was here that the Cossacks ruled and the tsars most zealously pursued modernization, industrialization, and Russification. In the late nineteenth century, new railroads connecting the Donbas with Russia enabled greater migration, and foreign investors from Britain, Germany, France, and Belgium established industrial footholds. The region transformed—in one generation's lifetime—into a stark, fuming terrain dotted with factories, mines, and sludgy ponds where mining effluents settled, a metamorphosis that only intensified in the twentieth century.

With one of the world's largest deposits of coal and significant iron ore, refractory clay, and salt, the Donbas became the center of industrial production in the Russian Empire. Hundreds of thousands of migrating workers, many of them Russian, moved to the Donbas to pursue new futures for their families in mine shafts and steel mills. Over time, the area became the most Russified in Ukraine. Among these Russian immigrants were Yulia's grandparents, who left Kursk, Russia, soon after World War II, making a new home in Chasiv Yar to teach in the local schools. A few years later, they had a daughter—Yulia's mom—and by the early 1980s, their daughter had a daughter of her own.

The Soviet collapse was not kind to their region. In the transition from the planned economy to a market system, formerly state-owned enterprises were privatized at a scale never seen before in a modern economy. Since capital was owned by the state, there were no individuals who could bid directly for ownership of such large enterprises; there was not even enough money in the entire economy to pay the book value of the companies that were slated to be privatized. The metallurgical complex relied heavily on Russian natural gas, but after Ukrainian independence, the cost of importing the gas skyrocketed and the economic foundation of the region began to crack. Ukrainian mines depended on Russian timber for lumber used to prop up tunnel shafts; as the Soviet system collapsed, Russia curtailed its timber exports to Ukraine, making mines even more dangerous and less profitable. Workers' salaries exemplified the crisis: from 1990 to 1993, the average wage for a worker in the Donbas fell by eighty percent. Mines and factories closed, and many workers were left abandoned.

Economists in charge of planning the post-Soviet transition believed that the former Soviet economies should undergo a type of "shock therapy," with state enterprises transferred into private hands as quickly as possible, in tandem with a massive reduction in government economic regulation and the introduction of foreign trade and investment. In Eastern Ukraine, the privatization of the region's metallurgical enterprises, coal mines, and other industrial facilities was a complex process of auctions, tenders, and voucher systems in which employees and citizens were given coupons to purchase shares in the formerly state-owned enterprises. Distributing shares in each enterprise to common citizens seemed to make sense in moral terms, considering that citizens of socialism were always intended to be the actual owners of state assets and enterprises, while the state acted as the caretaker. The voucher programs would theoretically enable common people to deposit their shares in an investment company, which would monitor enterprises on behalf of shareholders. But as the scholars Kristen Ghodsee and Mitchell A. Orenstein demonstrate in their book on the post-Soviet economic transition, "one thing that this plan overlooked was that most people did not know what it meant or how to be shareholders nor did they want to be." It was no wonder. As the sociologist Simon Clarke wrote: "The Soviet enterprise is almost as different from the capitalist enterprise as was a feudal estate from a capitalist farm."

The shock therapy devastated the Donbas. As mines collapsed, so did much of the basic infrastructure on which society had rested for more than a century. Mines, in fact, were not just mines. They were cities and community frameworks providing resources and camaraderie to thousands of employees, as well as daycares, cafeterias, health clinics, and shopping markets.

In quick time, as catastrophic inflation left people hungry and destitute, most new citizen shareholders cashed in their shares, preferring a modest sum of cash to ownership in a failing metallurgical plant. When their shares came on the new market en masse, individuals who had occupied positions of power in former Soviet enterprises (oil and gas, mining and metallurgy, finance and banking, media, telecommunications, and real estate) bought up those shares quickly, amassing more than any individual was ever intended to have. Soon their acquired shares enabled them to establish ownership of the specific firms in which they had insider knowledge or control. As it turned out, the process of privatization did not end up spreading ownership of the state's assets to the common people; privatization concentrated ownership and wealth in just a handful of "investment companies" run by just a few people. Such people—all men—became powerful oligarchs, wielding influence on both the post-Soviet economy and the state.

As the sole owners of newly privatized Soviet industries, they catapulted into wealth and power, exercising unregulated, often corrupt control over the region with their unabated grip on not just the industrial complex itself but all the other arms of the economy that relied upon it, the people who worked in it, and the politicians who represented those people. When Ukraine created its first independent currency—the karbovanets—Russia refused to accept it, and it was very quickly unable to maintain its value against the Russian ruble. By 1994, the karbovanets traded fifty thousand to one US dollar, while just two thousand rubles traded for that same dollar. The lack of convertible currency led to widespread bartering, and under such a system, the oligarchs who controlled natural and physical resources brandished unencumbered power. Those years gave rise to the term "gangster capitalism," used to describe the post-Soviet market economy throughout the former Soviet Union. Oligarchs and their "investment companies" maintained control through organized crime, criminal networks, and connections with the recently demobilized former Soviet secret police.

As Ghodsee and Orenstein write: "The poor grew poorer and the rich became dizzyingly wealthy. Winners of privatization became billionaires—and losers were sent to the streets. Ukraine would never get back to its late Soviet GDP."

The dissolution of the USSR meant something different for people in Eastern Ukraine than it did for people in other parts of the country. The 1990s were hard for everyone, but the collapse of such a colossal industrial complex, the theft of state enterprises, the emergence of organized crime, and an explosion of inequality and corruption was especially traumatizing for Eastern Ukrainians. Many of them spoke nostalgically of the USSR, and the region overwhelmingly supported close ties with Russia, which they believed would provide economic stability.

As a ten-year-old girl, Yulia watched the fall of the USSR unfolding without understanding what exactly was going on. The end of the Soviet Union for many children in the Donbas was perceptible only in puzzling material terms: the appearance of Coca-Cola, an exciting proliferation of pornographic magazines, and new Ukrainian currency mixed with the old Soviet rubles. All the symbols that used to mean something—portraits of Lenin, Young Communist Pioneer pins and red ties, school history textbooks—were sold in grubby secondhand markets managed by older women whose pensions could no longer feed them. By 1995, 62 percent of Ukrainians made less than twenty-one U.S. dollars per month. Yulia's friends' fathers who still worked in the mines were on strike. They hadn't been paid in months and rarely ate meat, a classic metric for prosperity.

Yulia met Oleg when she was fifteen and he was twenty-two. The seven years between them did not stave off their romantic interest for long. From their first meeting, Oleg struck her as kind and stable, and she loved being around him. About as erudite as any young girl in 1990s Donbas could be, Yulia held her own in any conversation, and her understated, elegant smile suggested no pretension. She was smart and interesting, and with a heart-shaped face, blond hair, and striking, kind blue eyes, Yulia attracted plenty of attention. Oleg was handsome and gentle, though not bookish like Yulia. He was a woodworking instructor at a school for troubled teens.

Sometimes they went to the town's small club that showed movies during the daytime. On weekend evenings, the club transformed into a discotheque, but Yulia did not like the loud music or crowds, and went only a couple of times "for educational purposes," she told me—just to understand what it was. Mostly, they liked to walk. The areas around Chasiv Yar, untouched by industry, boasted abundant natural beauty: rivers and lakes where subterranean clay and chalk come to the surface, creating white shorelines. Overlooking the twisting rivers, green hills define the skyline, covered in tall grass, wildflowers, and shrubbery. Thirty minutes from Yulia's grandmother's house, through an oak grove, stood a small mountain made of chalk on which rare plants grew. As a kid, she climbed it to explore the crow's eye, oak anemone, wild irises, and peonies. Rocks revealed fossils of ancient mollusks and shells, artifacts that suggested life had existed there for much longer than the mines. For Yulia, it was paradise.

In the summertime, Yulia and Oleg packed sandwiches to eat

on the shore of a lake outside town before stripping down for a swim. They baked bread dough over an open flame and told stories. Sitting beneath a majestic oak tree, they watched the sky turn to fire as the sun went down. Walking back into town, they saw closed factories and shut-up mines with abandoned slag heaps, dilapidated relics of their former society that was beginning to crumble. So much of the world they grew up in seemed stuck in the past, and yet their future seemed as bright as anything they knew.

By the time Yulia turned eighteen, everyone knew they'd get married, and they did.

In the late 1990s, Oleg got a job as a woodworker in a local glass factory, and he and Yulia moved to the neighboring town of Konstantinivka, where they bought a small house in disrepair. She gave birth to their two daughters—Olya and Sonya—soon after they got married, one right after the other. Olya looked like Yulia, and Sonya like Oleg. Within a few years, by the early 2000s, Oleg was head of the wood shop, and with some financial freedom, they began renovating their ramshackle house. They replaced the shoddy indoor plumbing with new pipes, a septic system, and toilets, and Oleg hung new cabinets in the kitchen. One by one, they installed new windows, and in the living room Yulia pasted elegant patterned wallpaper that made the old walls look refined and new. Over time they added furniture—a couch, beds, chairs, a dining set. In 2004 they added a car, a Toyota Camry, of which Oleg took fastidious care. To go with the new car, Oleg carefully tiled a new driveway. "I can't say it's a castle," Yulia said, "but it's definitely a cozy house."

As Yulia and Oleg's relative prosperity suggests, the late 1990s and early 2000s saw a measure of economic recovery in the Donbas. For all the corruption, private ownership had helped revitalize some industries, and in the early 2000s, the Ukrainian government provided subsidies and state aid to boost production and modernize infrastructure. Nonetheless, many in Eastern Ukraine felt they had been abandoned by pro-Western politicians and activists in the tumultuous years following the Soviet collapse and feared going back to the uncertainty of the early nineties. Considering the region's historically strong trade ties and economic cooperation, maintaining close relations with Russia seemed, for many, the most economically responsible choice. Russia of course had a stronger influence on Eastern Ukraine than on other parts of the country—it had been heavily Russified for well over a hundred years, having been incorporated into the Soviet Union a full generation before Western Ukraine, and the sale of its industrial products made it reliant on Moscow as the center of imperial power. Not to be overlooked, the area was heavily populated by ethnic Russians who had moved to Ukraine in the previous century to work in factories and mines. Post-Soviet politics in Ukraine were split east to west, with Western Ukraine generally favoring democratic reforms and closer ties with Europe and the United States, and the east wanting closer ties with Russia.

Oleg felt the tensions directly. He was born and raised in Chasiv Yar, spoke Russian, and worked in factories, but his father, Ihor, was not local. Ihor had come from a small village in Western Ukraine. In the 1940s, as the USSR was reestablishing its control over Western Ukraine following the Nazis' retreat, Ihor fought in the Ukrainian Insurgent Army, the UPA, the partisan movement that engaged in guerrilla warfare against the Soviet Red Army. In the end, the Soviet army prevailed, and the UPA was disbanded in the late 1940s. For decades after defeating the Ukrainian nationalists, the Soviet secret police hunted and persecuted former members of the UPA. Ihor, fearing what the NKVD (later the KGB) might do if they found him, fled to the industrial fortress of Eastern Ukraine to build a new life. There he adopted the Russified name of Igor, started speaking

exclusively Russian, and adapted to the region, learning as much as
he could about repairing tractors, trucks, and excavators. He spent
his career working on those machines and using them to transport
gas to villages. After a couple of years he married a local girl from
Chasiv Yar named Elena. They moved in with Elena's mother, who
had some land and a small private house with a summer kitchen,
a primitive brick shed used for cooking in warm weather. In the
summer kitchen they made a new life. In the winters, they built
fires in an exposed hearth to keep warm. Within a year, they had a
daughter, Tatiana.

Survival was not easy in the summer kitchen with a young baby.
Elena often told the story of traveling to a small town, forty kilometers away, to claim free crackers that the local hospital was giving
to people with babies. They wrapped Tatiana tight and rode the
whole way on a rickety motorcycle, arriving in time to wait in line
for three hours until they finally received just one kilogram of plain
crackers. But at least it was something. At home, they soaked a few of
the crackers in water, then wrapped the mush in cheesecloth for the
baby to suck and chew on. Their impoverishment forestalled any desire for more kids until eighteen years later, when Elena became pregnant with Oleg in a late, surprise, high-risk pregnancy. She decided to
proceed with it, and Oleg was born healthy. Though they eventually
moved to a proper house, they stayed in Chasiv Yar—the town where
Oleg's mother was raised, and his grandmother before her.

The fact that Ihor was not from the Donbas was acutely felt in
their household. They all knew of his Western Ukrainian origins,
and at least by adulthood, Oleg was aware of his father's participation in the UPA. But they did not speak of it often. As late as the
1970s, KGB agents still occasionally approached Oleg's mother asking if she was sure that her husband did not have connections to
Western Ukrainian partisans. She always denied it.

Even though they spoke Russian at home, from the time he was a young boy, Oleg felt a vague sympathy for Western Ukrainians and the Ukrainian language, which his father occasionally spoke with him. Nonetheless, the family's affinity for Ukraine was not enough to keep Oleg's older sister, Tatiana, there in the late Soviet era, when Ukraine and Russia were considered, by many, indistinguishable. One of Oleg's first memories is of Tatiana getting married and moving away with her new husband, a local boy, to help construct the Baikal-Amur Mainline, a railway line traversing Eastern Siberia and the Russian Far East. In the mid-1970s, Communist Party leaders encouraged Soviet youth to join this effort, calling it "the construction project of the century." It paid good money, and for a young married couple from the rural Donbas with meager financial prospects, it seemed an attractive offer. They left to establish a new life on the other edge of the Soviet world. Even though Tatiana wrote home for the next fifteen years detailing the relatively good life their pay afforded them, Oleg knew he would never leave. The Donbas was his home, and by the time he and Yulia bought their own plot of land and began fixing up the house, their roots were firm.

The previous owners of Oleg and Yulia's house had planted fruit trees in the 1980s, and these continued to bear fruit: apples, peaches, plums, cherries, and apricots. Along the gazebo they built in the backyard grew vines of plump green grapes, which the girls plucked from above while they chased the family's chickens. To accommodate the chickens, whose number grew over time from four to sixteen, they designed and built coops. They let the rooster in a couple of times a year, but every other part of the year, Yulia expected beautiful deep brown eggs for her cooking. In their other aviary chambers they kept silver, golden, and red pheasants, and inside they had a gecko, an aquarium full of fish, and an American hairless terrier Yulia named Happy.

As the girls grew up, they relied on Oleg for wild fun and noisy games, while Yulia entertained with quiet crafts. Oleg let the girls bounce on his leg, or he'd wrap them in a blanket and swing them around the room while they laughed hysterically. Yulia had a calmer energy. Inspired by animals and nature, she liked to keep herself busy with creative activities. After her second daughter, Sonya, was born, she wanted to make a little money on the side and took up various artisan projects. Over the next few years, she became skilled in all the handicrafts she could afford to try out: embroidery, soap and candle making, homemade whistles, decoupage, stained glass, watercolor and acrylic and oil painting. She especially liked felting woolen toys. The felting process involved matting and compacting sheep wool, then wetting and agitating it to form a solid shape. Felting with sheep wool was meditative, and Yulia loved the contact with the pleasant natural fibers. She kept at it, at first making small brooches, mittens, and baby booties. But over time, she found that there was real money in wool felted houses for cats. Cat owners spared no expense for their felines' wool homes, and she sold them for a good profit. The homes ranged in size from one to two square feet, and her design was relatively simple—a small domed structure with an arched opening—but she embellished each one with detailed painted scenes and intricate designs sewn along the sides. Yulia developed a loyal clientele not only in Ukraine and Russia but as far afield as the United States, Australia, and Japan.

Every year Yulia and the girls planted something new in their garden, and in twenty years, their backyard had become a botanical oasis. In summer there grew a different berry on every bush— raspberries; black, red, and white currants; gooseberries—while in every corner of the yard grew aromatic herbs—mint, lemon balm, chamomile, thyme, clary sage. The abundant garden made for hard work. In the summer, they gathered and dried the apples and herbs, preserved the cherries, peaches, tomatoes, and apricots in jars, blended up raspberries and strawberries to freeze for fresh puree, and stockpiled their cellar with potatoes, carrots, garlic, and beets. In the winter, they drank fresh tea with dried apples and ate borsch that smelled like summer. Wherever even a small patch of earth was visible, Yulia planted flowers—spray and climbing roses, peonies, tulips, and daffodils.

In 2005, they bought a small juniper shrub from the Nikitsky Botanical Garden in Crimea, back when Ukrainians still vacationed there. By the eve of the war, after their girls had grown up but before the shelling and the missiles and the stench of gas and smoke took over the town, the juniper had grown six meters high, dense, full, and sturdy. Of all the lovely plants and shrubs in their garden, Yulia especially loved that juniper tree. It didn't bend or break in windy storms, and in the wintertime, sparrows and chickadees made their homes there. Watching them all year long, Yulia noted that inside the warm protection of the juniper tree, the birds were safe and happy, even in the ruthless cold. All through the winter they pecked the juniper berries, knowing that this tree would provide for them while they waited for spring.

TANIA

Mykil'ske, Ukraine

TANIA GREW UP in the south, at the meeting of the Dnipro River and its small tributary, the Inhulets. The village of Mykil'ske sat within the confluence of those two rivers, waterlocked on three sides. Tania had to cross the bridge to do anything outside her village—to get to the store, the open-air market, the universities, or to Kherson, the nearest major city.

Growing up in the 1970s and '80s in that tiny village, Tania knew few luxuries. Her mother worked as a cook at a kindergarten and made sixty rubles a month, a meager salary even by Soviet standards, which required that she keep a strict budget and prepare plain, straightforward food: in the winter, bread, pickled cabbage, bright-red beet borsch, and in the summertime, buckwheat and bowls of the fruit that grew near their house. Even though they lived close to the Black Sea, she never went there as a child. Her father, who worked as a truck driver, pulled in more money than her mom. But he squandered his earnings on alcohol and often exploded in angry fits when he was challenged. Her parents' marriage was not a happy one, and Tania doesn't remember much of her father in childhood beyond scandals and swearing and booze. She has only one positive memory of him in all those years: on her eleventh or twelfth birthday, in the middle of perestroika—when life seemed economically impossible—she recalls that he came in the front door, sober, holding a two-tiered cake.

Surrounded by the freshwater currents of the Inhulets and Dnipro, Tania spent her childhood summers studying and exploring the marshy lands along the rivers and the grassy slopes bordering the watercourse. The riverbanks—lined with bushes, river grass, reeds, cattails, and sedges—wound lazily around the village, creating a dozen marshy nooks within just a few minutes' walk from her house. The complex system of inlets, tiny islands, and marshlands offered nesting and feeding grounds for birds and amphibians. Late in the summer, one could hear frogs croak all night long. Across the river, flocks of white storks flew low to the water. Occasionally villagers could spot a heron, or, if they were lucky, a swan.

Eleven miles downstream was the city of Kherson, which often seemed to Tania like a completely different world—open and grand, with wide, tree-lined boulevards. Fashionable women strolled through manicured parks with shopping bags full of food. It was where everyone she knew went if they wanted to escape the village. The city was founded in the 1770s after Tsarina Catherine (known as Catherine the Great to Russians) conquered much of Southern Ukraine, annexing lands held by the Cossack state, the Crimean Khanate, and Ottoman Turkey. Kherson was built rapidly, in just a few years, by conscripted sailors, laborers, soldiers, prisoners, and serfs.

After Catherine disbanded the Zaporizhian Sich, the Ukrainian Cossack state that had ruled Central and Southern Ukraine for two hundred years, she granted supreme power over the area to one of her lovers, Grigori Potemkin. He oversaw the Russian colonization of the region, bringing in Russian nobility to settle the area, which was given a new name: Novorossiya—literally, New Russia. One historian of the region, Willard Sunderland, called the adoption of the name New Russia "the most powerful statement imaginable of Russia's national coming of age"—it was Russia's way of keeping up with its imperial competitors who'd created New Spain, New France, and New England in the conquered and colonized territories of North America. Southern Ukraine was proclaimed New Russia, and its inhabitants—Orthodox Slavs who seemed in some ways to resemble Russians but who spoke their own language and had their own customs, traditions, and stories—were called Little Russians. It's important to note, however, that many scholars debate whether "colonization" accurately describes the Russia-Ukraine relationship. After all, there was no racial difference between Russians and Ukrainians, and Russian and Soviet administrations generally perceived Ukraine as belonging to the imperial core, not as a colonial subject—an important distinction from other regions conquered by Russia, such as Armenia and Turkestan.

In time, Kherson became a vital Russian port, as well as a center for shipbuilding and commerce. It was still a smaller city, but not a forgotten coastal fortress; within a hundred years it was half the size of Kyiv and a quarter the size of St. Petersburg, and acquired the accoutrements of a significant entrepôt: docks and factories, workshops and institutes, railways and churches. Potemkin demanded, a few years after its construction, that one of the first cathedrals in the area, the Cathedral of St. Catherine, be remodeled to resemble his Tauride Palace in St. Petersburg. Perhaps with a green dome on the horizon, he could make himself feel more at home in this New Russia, a wild wetland a thousand miles away from the seat of imperial power. After his death, Potemkin's remains were eventually buried in a tomb at that cathedral.

As a teenager, Tania wanted desperately to get out of the village, move to Kherson, study medicine, become a nurse. Unfortunately, even though she was a good student in high school, she was not admitted to nursing school, missing out on the required grade by one point. Her mother decided Tania would enroll in the technical shipbuilding school instead, in the specialty of "ship automation." And so it was decided: she spent four years studying the automation systems of commercial and military ships, Kherson's founding legacy. She lived in Kherson in a rented apartment, returning home, over two bridges, to Mykil'ske on weekends.

Walking along Kherson's paved river boardwalk, Tania liked the feeling that she was part of something bigger than a provincial waterlocked village. Kherson had attractive shops and parks and well-developed public transit. The city had been built up with fountains and boulevards, and some people there could afford to eat from decorated glass plates atop tablecloths at sidewalk cafés along the river. The city promised a different future. But for all the appeal of Kherson's modernity, it was plainly quite fragile: the farther south you went, past the art museum, past the Hydropark, the more you saw how the river broke up the land, how the water flow slowed and the city gave way to channeled wetlands, small streams and ponds dissecting tiny islands skirted with lily pads, trees bending into the water, and walls of tall river grass. In any basic rowboat—nothing sophisticated, nothing like the ships Tania had studied all those years at shipbuilding technical school—one could drift through the Dnipro's delta, just a few miles downstream from Kherson, wandering through a floating canyon of grass so tranquil it was as though it had never been touched by conquerors.

After graduating from the shipbuilding academy in the mid-1990s, Tania went to work as a laboratory assistant at a technical school in Kherson. Within a few months, she met Viktor, a thirty-year-old veterinarian from a small village about seventy-five miles to the northeast. He came to Kherson to work on a large farm operation, handling breeding, nutrition, and the diseases of cows and pigs. He moved into a single rented bedroom in the apartment of an old woman, and his neighbors happened to be Tania's best friend and her husband. When Tania and Viktor met on September 29, 1995, Tania was drawn to him. He was educated, older, and stable—serious, with a good job. Most important for Tania, he did not drink or smoke. In November, Viktor invited Tania to go to his village to meet his parents. When they returned to Kherson, they filed an application to wed and were married by the end of December.

They were poor—everyone was in the 1990s—and Tania's grandmother made room for them in her small house outside Kherson, in the same village in which Tania had grown up. They had no indoor running water, and they heated the house with a primitive iron stove. A year later, they had a daughter, Viktoria—Vika, for short—and decided they needed more space. Soon after Vika turned one, Viktor and Tania bought an unfinished house, a concrete box with four walls and a roof, on the other side of the village. While Viktor worked long hours at the farm—which was failing and required him to labor overtime, often overnight—Tania, her mother, and her brother turned the house into a construction site. Stone by stone, they built it, with their own hands. Tania was a hard worker; and she didn't mind the manual labor. She was precise, organized, tidy, and disciplined. Tania's grandmother, born in 1926, nannied Vika for two years while the building went on.

By the time the house was finished, the farm enterprise that Viktor worked for had gone bankrupt, and Tania and Viktor were left with a small child and without an income. Strategizing, they decided to combine forces and try their hand at pig farming. They purchased two piglets from the failed farm, as well as one ton of feed grain, and after building a small pigsty, they mated the two pigs and the sow became pregnant.

In time, they purchased eighteen acres of land just outside the village and began planting vegetables and strawberries, which they sold at the market. They worked without breaks, sunup to sundown, often in the middle of the night if a pig was in labor. They never took a day off—the pigs always needed to be fed and cared for. But managing the farm was satisfying, and in time, they could see their hard work paying off. After a couple of years, they had a herd of thirty pigs—large, productive sows, healthy piglets that grew into fat pigs for slaughtering. Viktor handled the slaughtering in a different barn, where he would separate the pork meat into its various cuts: the ham, the shoulder, ribs, hock, and back fat. The back fat, which came in white strips, the best of them "six fingers thick," is known as *salo*, and is one of the most desirable and expensive items in Ukrainian cuisine. It is calorie dense, salty, smoky lard, often spread on black rye bread with fresh garlic or ground pepper, or eaten as an indulgent, stand-alone dish, usually washed down with a shot of vodka.

Tania handled the births. Never having lived on a farm, she trained on the job with Victor's help. She learned to identify good, strong sows, the ones with robust backsides and shoulders, longer, wider bodies—in which they could carry more piglets—healthy feet, and filled-out nipple lines that could easily feed large litters. Tania learned to detect when a sow was in heat—with a characteristic restlessness, a red and swollen vulva, and perked, twitching ears. Once the sow was in heat, Tania let the boar into the sow's sty, watched to make sure he mounted the sow, and ensured that they successfully mated. Over the next four months, Tania watched the sow grow, becoming larger and rounder. In the middle of the night, when Tania knew a sow was soon to begin farrowing, she went out to tend to her. At that stage, the enormous pig—three hundred pounds or so—was desperately running around the sty, carrying straw in her mouth to build a bed on which to birth. On her homemade bed of straw, the sow began laboring, and with a pile of twenty clean towels, Tania crouched near her. Out would come spotted pink piglets, covered in blood and mucus and a furry layer of hair. Tania helped guide piglets out of the birth canal, her hands bloody, the piglets squealing. Picking up a new piglet by the feet, Tania wrapped her in a towel, cleaned her off, and placed her in a hay-lined box with a heat lamp. In the sow's winding two-pronged uterus, piglet fetuses are stacked one by one, up to fourteen of them. One at a time, the piglets are born, and in a feat no human mother can fathom, a sow nurses the birthed piglets—eight or ten at a time—while she continues birthing the rest of her litter.

In time, Tania, Viktor, and Vika prospered. They were good examples of working people whom market capitalism had, in time, advantaged. Their parents had been collective farm workers, truck drivers, and kindergarten cooks. Now their effort on their farm allowed them to rise through the poverty of the '90s, and eventually be able to live well. By the time Vika went to school at six and a half years old, they had outfitted their house with appliances—a refrigerator, a new stove, a washing machine. They had a car, and in the summertime, they could afford to vacation by the sea as a family.

Though the region had felt less stable since Crimea's annexation in 2014, their produce and pork remained in high demand. In the mid-2000s, Vika was a foreign exchange student in Texas, and later she went to a university in Poland. She learned to speak Polish and English fluently, in addition to Ukrainian and Russian, both of which they spoke at home. In Poland, Vika met and fell in love with an American man, whom she eventually married before starting an MBA program in Boston in 2021. Watching Vika excel in her studies—wearing nice clothes, driving a new car, working hard at her job—Tania swelled with pride. She felt she never got a shot to study just what she wanted—she had stayed home, in that tiny village, bringing piglets into the world, raising them on ground feed, growing strawberries in the summertime, selling everything at a provincial market. On the basis of that hard work, her daughter was living out Tania's dreams.

On the morning of February 24, 2022, Tania's neighbor woke them up, pounding on the door. Her son had called. Thirty miles away, Kakhovka was being bombed. Tania ran outside. She looked into the sky. There was smoke near the airport. Her heart thudded. The event that everyone had been talking about was happening. She and Viktor stood as though paralyzed; they could hardly get words out, even to each other. From the vantage point of their home, perched above the two rivers, they could hear and see everything— explosions, smoke, roaring aircraft. Russian equipment hummed so loudly it was audible two kilometers away, and Russian helicopters flew low, scattering land mines in the fields where Tania, Viktor, and their neighbors planted vegetables, strawberries, and watermelon. Watching from outside her house as the mines dropped onto their dirt, she felt violated.

Vika called in hysterics, begging them to leave. She suggested that she and her husband could depart Boston that day, meet Tania and Viktor in Georgia or Turkey; Tania and Viktor could drive down through Crimea, then up through Russia, and take a flight out. Vika said she'd pay for everything and meet them there. They could live with her in Boston.

But how could they leave? This was their home, the only place Tania had ever known. And what about the animals? The pigs they bred from scratch, which Tania, with her own hands, guided into the world. The thought of leaving the pigs—of driving away while she knew they were terrified, squealing and crying and running frantically in their sty—no—she could not. Within a couple of hours, shells flew over their house. The next day, tanks arrived, and several men—Russian soldiers—set up roadblocks and dug shallow trenches to control who came in and who left, establishing a checkpoint at the entrance to the village.

Within two days, more Russian soldiers came. They were everywhere, and they occupied the empty houses of those who'd fled
with their young children in the first hours of the invasion. Some
stole and plundered, pocketing jewelry, sending home appliances
and clothing. And some terrorized: in the first day, soldiers who occupied the village identified two young brothers who supported the
Ukrainian government, took away their phones, put bags on their
heads and wrapped the bags with tape, threw them into a basement,
held them for several days, and beat them, making the brothers into
examples of what would happen to anyone else who dared to resist.
Locals shuttered their windows, locked their doors, and did not go
outside. Many more tried to leave, standing for days at dangerous
checkpoints, risking interrogation, violent intimidation, or worse
to get away.

Still, Tania and Viktor decided to stay. Their village, their land,
their animals—was there a life for them outside of that? Even if
there was, what would become of all they had worked for and built
if they left it behind? Thousands of Ukrainians left the country.
Thousands of others joined the military, made Molotov cocktails,
and stood in lines for weapons. Tania and Viktor resolved to begin
their own resistance, the kind of quiet dissent that one might easily
dismiss as just living but is not: in the face of cruelty, they would continue to care for living things—soil and earth, trees, rivers, plants,
and pigs.

VITALY

Borodyanka, Ukraine

THOUGH RUMORS OF war were on everyone's lips, in late February, just before Russia's invasion, Vitaly stayed focused on his coffee shop. Walking into the shop every morning around six, he began by turning on the oven to bake the croissants. Next, he brewed the coffee. People would start wanting their coffee by six thirty or seven, and by eight o'clock there might be a line. The first weeks of business went well. He had chosen a nice location without competition nearby and got good foot and car traffic.

When the rumors proved true, on the twenty-fourth, Vitaly tried to keep calm. He ordered refills of cups and lids and stocked up on coffee beans that he bought from a wholesale supplier. Business was slow. People were scared, and although Borodyanka had so far been quiet, many people were already fleeing, standing in days-long lines at the Polish border or hiding in basement shelters. He had no interest in leaving. On the twenty-fifth, as Russian troops swiftly approached Borodyanka, Vitaly had no customers, so he did a full back-flush of the espresso machine, scrubbing out the coffee grounds with a brush and flushing the machine with detergent. On the twenty-sixth, he washed the floors and organized the freezer.

On the twenty-seventh, Russian tanks rolled into Borodyanka. At one of the recycling centers where Vitaly sold materials before the war, people started making Molotov cocktails, and he closed up shop to help in the effort. He poured gasoline into old bottles and placed strips of cloth inside them to serve as wicks. Ukrainian media began sharing infographics on how to throw the homemade incendiary devices onto enemy vehicles, aiming for windows, wheels, and the driver. For two days, trying to stay calm, he joined any effort to protect the town, and even when a Russian tank drove into the windows of the store across the street from his coffee shop—with no other purpose than to destroy it—he continued brewing tea to distribute to people freezing in basement shelters.

On March 1, as Vitaly made coffee in his shop, he heard the distinct rumble of planes flying overhead. He ran out the door and into a potato cellar underneath a building across the street from his own, where his mother and brother and sister-in-law and their four-year-old son had taken shelter. The basement under their apartment building was too full, so Vitaly and his family had found a different space in the neighboring building's damp cellar. Despite bringing mattresses and blankets, they sleeplessly huddled together, letting the four-year-old boy watch cartoons on their phone while tanks puttered by.

There was a peephole onto the street from the cellar. Within two minutes of hearing buzzing overhead, Vitaly watched through the hole as a plane dropped a small package. It fell as though in slow motion onto his apartment complex across the street. Before he could realize what was happening, his face was slammed into the wall and his head began throbbing. The ground shook, and the only thing audible was the tumbling of concrete and glass and the clanging of steel and iron collapsing. For a few seconds, it seemed there was no air, as though everyone in the world had inhaled when the bomb dropped and had yet to exhale. Vitaly raised himself to the peephole and saw chunks of the burning building falling to the ground. As he watched in shock, it took a few seconds for Vitaly to realize that there were people inside—and not strangers. It was his apartment building. His best friend, Serhiy, was there with his wife and parents. So were his son's best friend and his mother—all the people he saw all the time in his courtyard.

Knowing there might be another explosion to follow, Vitaly screamed that everyone had to get out of the cellar and into the empty field across the street where a bomb would be unlikely to drop. They wrapped his nephew in a blanket and ran to the field, where they crouched in frozen ditches to wait out the air raid. After thirty minutes, Russian helicopters appeared overhead. Believing they wouldn't be able to hide from the helicopters in the ditch, they decided to run again. But where would they go? They needed to get to an area without Russian troops, but many of the surrounding villages to the southeast, in the direction of Kyiv, were already occupied. Vitaly called Natalka in New York City. "We are under fire here," he said, trying to remain as calm as possible. Natalka called her brother, Artem, the blond kid from the courtyard, whom Vitaly had let hang around when he and Natalka were teenagers. Artem had purchased a small house on the northwest outskirts of Borodyanka a few years earlier, and Natalka arranged with Artem for Vitaly and his family to shelter there.

Although the journey to Artem's was only a couple of kilometers, Vitaly swears it took half his life. He and his brother, sister-in-law, nephew, and elderly mother needed to get across a large highway down which a convoy of tanks was rumbling closer to Kyiv. To get to Artem's, they had to cross the street as fast as they could between the passing tanks. Vitaly's brother would lead the way and Vitaly would go last. After a tank went by, their mother, Tamara, in her seventies and with poor knees, lunged into the street. The others did the same. The four-year-old child bounced on his father's hip and burrowed his face in his shoulder, covered in a blanket. Machine-gun rounds started being fired from the tanks, but they did not look around or stop. Reaching the other side of the highway, Vitaly yelled to keep running, and they ran for another thirty minutes until they reached Artem's neighborhood. Later, Tamara recounted: "I don't know how I ran like I did. God moved my legs. An angel carried me."

There were many people gathered at Artem's, which was in one of the last unoccupied areas of the town. Artem's hard work in college had paid off, and he made decent money as an agricultural engineer. As buildings in the center of Borodyanka were destroyed, he invited close friends to his house for shelter while they made plans to evacuate. If they intended to go to the western part of the country, they needed only to make it seven kilometers farther to Zahal'tsi, the closest village to the west, where evacuation vehicles waited.

As Vitaly sheltered at Artem's, a paramilitary group of ethnic Chechens called Kadyrovtsy arrived in Borodyanka. Their name refers to their founder, Ramzan Kadyrov, the Chechen leader who'd aligned his country closely with Moscow following well over a decade of brutal war with Russia. Chechen leaders built strong paramilitary mercenary forces that Moscow often called upon to do its military bidding; before Ukraine, Kadyrovtsy had been most recently seen in Syria. Vitaly's ex-girlfriend, Svitlana, had been staying with her mother in the countryside outside Borodyanka with her two teen-age sons when Kadyrovtsy arrived and occupied their village. Pan-icking, Svitlana called Vitaly after he was already at Artem's. He had lived with the boys for several years and felt a fatherly respon-sibility for them. He agreed to help get the boys out of the village, because teenage boys were likely to fare poorly under a Kadyrovtsy occupation.

Vitaly arranged to meet the boys in a field halfway between Borodyanka and the village. He slipped out of Artem's house, ran back to his destroyed apartment building, found his bicycle—mostly intact—inside the rubble, and started riding as fast as he could. The streets were full of smoke. Everything was burning. His bicycle wheels crunched over shards of shattered glass. Abandoned cars and shops lined the road. After hiding in basements for days without food and water, desperate people had looted abandoned grocery stores to feed their families. One old woman told me of the Borodyanka basement she sheltered in, where a hundred people crammed into a space meant for thirty, crouching low and eating tiny individually wrapped chocolates that someone had found in what remained of the bulk candy section inside a demolished store.

As Vitaly pedaled down the street he saw a car with a man behind the wheel and pedaled faster toward it, hoping the driver would offer a ride. As Vitaly approached he saw a shattered window, two bullet holes through the driver's temple, and blood still dripping down the man's chin. There was likely a sniper nearby. His heart racing, Vitaly pushed forward as fast as he could, knowing that if the sniper was still around, he had almost certainly seen Vitaly. Sensing his inability to control his fate, Vitaly focused on the mundane rhythms of breathing and pedaling.

When he crossed the main street, he spotted Kadyrovtsy two hundred feet away in an armored car. They sped toward him, and he jumped off his bike and ran into a blown-up shop. Lying between piles of rubble on the floor behind the checkout counter, he closed his eyes and prayed that the soldiers would not get out of the car and search for him. After listening to his breath for half an hour, he stood up, went back outside, grabbed his bike, and continued to the field to meet the boys.

When he got there, he hid under a cluster of trees. Within a few minutes the boys appeared. They arrived with two women who had come with them to find food to carry back to their own village several kilometers away. Vitaly and the boys accompanied the women to Borodyanka to help them collect some food in the looted grocery stores there. Before parting ways, Vitaly gave the women his bike, and they went back to the occupied countryside to feed their families. Vitaly then took the boys to Artem's.

One of the boys carried a live cat in his backpack and the other carried a dumbbell, hoping it would prove valuable in any hand-to-hand combat. As they worked their way back to Artem's house along the same path Vitaly had taken out of the city, the younger of the boys happened upon the same murdered man sitting in the car's driver seat. Months later, Vitaly wrote: "The boy still talks about that man."

Back at Artem's, they made plans to leave the region. Vitaly and his family would go west to the city of Kolomiya. Artem and his family would go still farther west to Lviv. After a day preparing for the journey, they put on backpacks and set off on foot to Zahal'tsi. Along the road they passed burned-out cars and buses with bullet holes piercing the metal and glass. In the distance, black smoke billowed from an oil depot on fire. They heard tanks battling a few kilometers away. The younger of the boys Vitaly rescued carried his cat in his arms, and the cat did not meow once.

As they walked away, Vitaly glanced over his shoulder. His building did not fill the skyline as it had his entire life. He saw some version of it—mangled, crumbling, the smoke and ash. His chest burned and he choked on the smoky air. He looked over his shoulder again. The coffee shop was gone, too, crushed in the collapse. All those buildings his father spent his whole career constructing had been destroyed in minutes. The kindergarten where Vitaly learned to write his name was gone. The kitchen where his father sat when he came home to show off his new military uniform had disintegrated somewhere under a pile of bricks. The courtyard where he learned to play soccer and first fell in love was no more.

Could the world continue to exist without that place? And even if it did—who was he in it?

MARIA

Mariupol, Ukraine

ON THE TWENTY-FOURTH of February, Maria awoke at home
in Mariupol—first to the sounds of thunder in the distance, then
a phone call. It was her mother, on the other side of town, calling
from the Soviet-era apartment over on the Left Bank where Maria
had grown up with her father, mother, grandmother, and two older
sisters. It was a busy household of girls—all with strong personali-
ties, big feelings and opinions, and very few reservations about ex-
pressing them.

They were poor—her father was disabled and received a meager
pension, and her mother worked as a seamstress—but Maria was
proud, and she refused to let herself act poor. Determined to make
her own way in the world, Maria proved to be both remarkably enterprising and loyal. In elementary school, Maria's parents gave her
extra change to pay for breakfast, but sensing how tirelessly they
worked for almost nothing, Maria saved the money to buy gifts for
them. When her schoolteacher complained that Maria was not eat-

ing enough, Maria did not change course, even when her teacher began feeding Maria individually with a spoon.

Maria was the youngest sister, and as such, she developed a special kind of fieriness that kept her upright, refusing to be bulldozed. She was her sisters' fearless shadow, even when her sisters lamented that she was always on their tail. She watched her sisters carefully—what kind of clothes they wore, the music they listened to, how they did their makeup, how they flirted with boys. When Maria was ten years old, her oldest sister began dating the man she would end up marrying. The way he carried himself, his character, and his relationship with her sister left a lasting impression on Maria. She considered him the ideal man.

As a teenager, Maria's middle sister took great care of her appearance, working out, manicuring her nails, becoming an expert in beauty. Maria took note and learned all the tricks her sister mastered. With long light brown hair, slim legs, and a pretty face, Maria made an impression, as did her older sisters. Although she fought with them at home, if she heard a bad word about them, she'd create hell for whoever said it.

They lived across the river from the center of town, just beyond Azovstal, the giant steel manufacturing monolith that dominated Mariupol's skyline. The neighborhood was built up in the 1930s to house the workers who came to work at Azovstal and the city's other major steel plant, both towering icons of Soviet industrialization. Over time, the Left Bank became a densely populated residential area marked by sleepy private houses on dirt roads and blocks of working-class apartment buildings.

No one who lived on the Left Bank had much money, and Maria spent her whole childhood there—she was twelve years old before she ever left Mariupol's city limits. Between her father's pension and a seamstress's salary, there was hardly any money to travel to the center of town, let alone beyond. Her sisters grew up collecting empty bottles to sell to buy bread. "I remember, in the 2000s, I always dreamed of winning twenty thousand [hryvnia (several thousand dollars)] in the lottery," she said. It was the absolute limit of her imagination. "Once, my sister joked with me, she said, 'Masha, we won the lottery!' And I was like, Wow! Cool! We're rich! And when she said she was joking I was so offended. I had a friend whose dad worked in the police, and she always had a lot of toys, they ate food with walnuts. That is, she had absolutely everything. But I had nothing."

When Maria's oldest sister, Sveta, was fifteen years old, she got into a technical school on a scholarship, and soon after, she began making a little money. Sveta would buy candies for Maria—just for fun, just so that Maria could try everything that they had never had. Later Sveta got a scholarship for university studies and then started her own business. Sveta was now making real money, and as Maria grew up, her eldest sister clothed her entirely.

Not until 2010 did Maria take an hour and a half drive to Donetsk, the nearest major city, to watch a professional soccer game with Sveta and Sveta's new husband. Mostly Maria stayed in Mariupol, on the Left Bank, with its dynastic steelworking families and neatly tended garden plots. She complained that the city was boring and run-down. She declared as a teenager that she hated it, but what did she have to compare it to? She knew only Mariupol, but she knew it nearly inside out—all the parks and beaches, where to find trouble and where to avoid it.

Their apartment was nothing fancy. Everything in it was old, but it was all clean, thanks to Maria's grandmother Vera, who maintained the household with military precision. Maria always credited Vera for her stubbornness, scrappiness, and tireless spunk. Maria knew they were quite similar: at their worst, impetuous and demanding; at their best, enterprising, indefatigable, and loyal.

Vera had been eight years old when World War II began and German soldiers assaulted Mariupol with tanks and planes. Maria grew up hearing all of Vera's stories—how the Nazis had bombed Mariupol relentlessly, how they all hid in the basement, how Nazis came to live in the house above them, how even in her old age, Vera sometimes thought she heard the rumble of German planes. Food had been scarce, but a German soldier who took pity on the children crowded into the basement slipped them a package of butter, which they ate in greasy chunks with their fingers. From then on, Maria said, until the day she died, Vera couldn't eat butter—it made her physically sick.

Grandmother Vera grew up in the 1940s and '50s taking care of her younger brother and sister. After Vera's father was killed in action in northwestern Russia in 1943, Vera's mother became sick. In their ravaged Mariupol, slow to rebuild after the war, eleven-year-old Vera became a provider. She took care of her mother. She took her siblings to the beach, bathed them, and in the wintertime stuffed rags into the drafty crevices of their window frames. She made sure grease did not build up on the stove, took care to scrub mildew and calcification off the sink and spout, and constantly swept corners and underneath furniture. She worked compulsively to take care of other people, a trait that intensified when she got married and had her own children and grandchildren.

Vera liked order, but mostly she did not like to look tired or weak, and Maria, who grew up watching Vera decline from old age to decrepitude, said: "She was stronger than any man I've ever met." Vera could be difficult, she would rail against people when she felt let down or disappointed, and she almost never said "I love you." But inside, Maria knew that Vera was sensitive and ruled by love, wearing out her life making sure others were taken care of.

When Maria went to college, she met a boy named Leonid and immediately fancied him. He was quiet but self-assured, tall and sporty, and shied away from attention. He liked her, too. She played it cool for a few weeks, feigning indifference. But Leonid was undeterred by her brush-offs, and eventually they started seeing each other. He loved that she was opinionated and smart. Her sassiness was sexy when it was not infuriating, and Leonid complemented her well—he was mild and easygoing, gentle and principled.

Theirs was a sincere teenage love, punctuated with carefree adventure and occasional angry breakups. They lived on opposite sides of Mariupol, separated by an hour-long bus ride. Between 2017 and 2019, they met nearly every day to walk, spending hours strolling up and down the boardwalk, the manicured green space outside the drama theater, the sandy coastline, the potholed asphalt in residential areas, the mall, the city garden. He was steady and helped her feel steady, even if he rarely challenged her in disagreement. They walked outside for a year like that, even in the winter when it was so cold that their phones wouldn't work. Like her grandmother, Maria was quick to laugh and quick to anger—and she felt too nervous to commit and scared she'd be abandoned. She struggled to say "I love you," even when Leonid said it freely. Leonid was typically willing to accommodate Maria's wishes and demands, but after two years he felt hurt that she would not reciprocate his words of affection, and they broke up.

A few months later, Vera died suddenly of a brain hemorrhage. Her death shocked the family, especially Maria, who felt guilty that she had not spent much time with Vera in the weeks prior, leaving her at home to clean and sit alone.

The night of Vera's death, the only thing Maria wanted was to call Leonid—he would know what to say, he would know how to comfort her in her anguish. But calling Leonid required yielding her pride. One thought, however, motivated her: Vera had met Leonid only once, but she had seen something principled, dependable, and generous in him—and she had let Maria know that she believed Leonid to be "a very good boy." So Maria called, on the night of Vera's death, to say "I love you" to Leonid for the first time.

In time, they got married and had a son, David. They worked hard to make themselves financially secure, eventually moving from a tiny studio apartment into a one-bedroom. From 2018 to 2021, Maria worked almost around the clock at a pizza shop; Leonid joined the National Guard, then began managing gyms. They saved enough money to buy new kitchen appliances and iPhones, and the month before the war, they bought an impressive new TV, which Leonid had dreamed of for a long time.

On February 24, 2022, Leonid was in their apartment when he answered a phone call from Maria's mom. He had been watching television, and the news Maria's mom brought—that the war had begun and buildings in the neighborhood were under fire—did not come as a surprise to him. No one wanted to believe it, but to Leonid, the signs of impending invasion were clear. Although he had been just a rank-and-file cadet in the National Guard, and although it was early in the morning of the twenty-fourth and lines of communication were still weak, Leonid had a gut feeling about what was going on.

Leonid and Maria had been in high school back in 2014, eight years before, which was when one could say the war really started. At the end of 2013, Ukrainian president Viktor Yanukovych had refused to sign an association agreement with the European Union, spurring uprisings throughout the country. The agreement had been in the works for years. It was perceived as one of the most important steps Ukraine could take toward joining the rest of Europe. Although the country's relations with Europe had polarized Ukrainians since the collapse of the Soviet Union, by the early 2000s, most Ukrainians, especially young ones, wanted closer ties. They saw the relatively wealthy Poland as a painful reminder of what post-Soviet life could have looked like, and the EU agreement represented the dream of catching up. The agreement would commit Ukraine to economic and judicial reforms in exchange for political support, financial aid, and preferential access to EU markets. The Ukrainian parliament overwhelmingly approved finalizing the EU agreement before President Yanukovych—a politician with close ties to Russian elites—bent to pressure from the Kremlin by reversing course and refusing to sign.

After so many years of corruption and economic instability, this was the last straw for many Ukrainians. More than a million gathered—in the central square in Kyiv and other squares through-out the country—to protest. The demonstrations gained traction and attention, and soon garnered a name: the Revolution of Dig-nity. In January and February 2014, violent protesters clashed with police, leaving more than one hundred dead and a thousand in-jured. Fearing for his safety, Yanukovych fled to Russia, and parlia-ment terminated his government. It was a watershed moment when Ukrainian civil society took to the streets to resist the doings of the pro-Russian state. In a talk he gave at the Harvard Ukrainian Research Institute in September 2023, Yevhen Hlibovytsky, a Ukrai-nian public intellectual, argued that 1991 was Ukraine's Declara-tion of Independence, but 2014 was when Ukrainians truly asserted their independence from Russia.

Vladimir Putin did not take it well. Throughout the 2000s, he'd demonstrated a clear pattern of retaliating against former Soviet states that rebuffed inclusion inside Moscow's sphere of influence. For example, ten years earlier, he'd arranged for the poisoning of the Ukrainian pro-Western presidential candidate Viktor Yush-chenko on Yushchenko's campaign trail in 2004. Yushchenko had established himself as a highly popular politician who intended to break ties with Russia and align Ukraine with Western democra-cies. His opponent at the time was Yanukovych, an obvious puppet of Moscow who favored close ties with Putin. That September, Rus-sian agents administered to Yushchenko dioxin that was so pure and potent, he should have died quickly. But he didn't, and he kept

campaigning, and when the election was called in favor of his opponent, Yushchenko—deathly ill—went to the main square in Kyiv
and called upon all Ukrainians to join him until the election results were withdrawn. Many hundreds of thousands went and their
movement became known as the Orange Revolution. Yushchenko
won a new vote and established a government that favored relations
with the West. That year, 2004, was a pivotal moment for Ukraine's
fledgling democracy. Politics became highly competitive, and the
government began exercising less control of the media and election outcomes. As the political scientists Oxana Shevel and Maria
Popova have argued, it was in 2004 that Ukraine made the transition from a competitive authoritarian regime to a burgeoning, dysfunctional democracy—but a democracy nonetheless.

Putin was furious over Yushchenko's win. In the years after the
Orange Revolution, Russia raised natural gas prices, a move that
significantly damaged Ukraine's economy, which heavily depended
on Russian gas imports. For Russia, the Orange Revolution was also
a critical juncture. The Putin regime interpreted the Orange Revolution and Yushchenko's election as a development caused only in
part by domestic dynamics. The Kremlin also saw what happened
in Ukraine as evidence of a broader Western plot against Russia. In
essence, Putin believed, Ukraine was being stolen away from Russia's sphere by the West, and he began consolidating his autocratic
regime. In the years that followed, Putin developed his theories of
the "Russian World," and worked to tether Ukraine to Russia by
casting Russian identity in an imperial mold. He did this not just in
Ukraine: another example of Putin's willingness to intervene when
a neighboring nation pursued closer relations with the West was
in Georgia in 2008. Amid rumbles about the possibility of Georgia becoming a member of NATO, Putin backed local secessionist
movements that plunged Georgia into war, setting back its hope to
pursue a European future.

Two thousand fourteen would also be a pivotal year. Within a week of Ukraine's Revolution of Dignity, as President Yanukovych fled the country, pro-Russian protests sprang up in Crimea, and Russians in unmarked military uniforms (called by the media "little green men") appeared, carrying weapons. In less than a day, the protests disbanded as the little green men raised Russian flags over the newly conquered Crimean airport, ferry terminal, and government buildings. Russians and pro-Russian separatists appointed a new prime minister and set a date for a "vote" on Crimea's secession from Ukraine. In a move that shocked the world, Russia swiftly and silently annexed the peninsula.

Once again, as in 2004, Russia blamed the West for Ukraine's revolution. The protests, Yanukovych retreat, and prevailing pro-European attitudes were all, according to Russia, a coup organized by the West against Russia. Russia has demonstrated again and again an inability to accept domestic political developments within Ukraine—chosen by Ukrainians—that shift Ukraine away from Russia. Putin annexed Crimea to send a strong signal to Ukraine and the West about the consequences of interfering in what Russia perceived to be its domain. The West, and the United States in particular, responded weakly, slapping sanctions on Russia but generally permitting Putin's dramatic violation of international law.

In early March, smaller pro-Russia protests began in major Eastern Ukrainian cities. There were attacks on government buildings, and buses with Russian license plates packed with armed men appeared in the area's two largest cities, Luhansk and Donetsk. Pro-Russian protesters took over significant government buildings in Kharkiv as well as Luhansk and Donetsk. Russia shipped in weapons to arm the Ukrainians involved in the protests, and clashes erupted between the separatist militants and local police and the Ukrainian military.

In April, Russian-backed separatists tried to take Mariupol.

They shelled the city, and during the shelling Maria's grandmother Vera took Maria to their basement to wait it out. To repel the separatists, a Ukrainian militia group known as the Azov Brigade sprang up. It was an ultranationalist volunteer paramilitary militia with members who espoused antisemitic and racist ideologies and wore fascist symbols such as the Wolfsangel, the Black Sun, and the swastika. The Azov Brigade's primary financier was Ihor Kolomoysky, a powerful Jewish oligarch from Dnipro who made his fortune in the banking and finance sector. The second-richest man in Ukraine, his Jewishness did not bear on his funding the brigade, a reflection of a broader political situation in which identity politics generally takes a back seat to political jockeying. The Azov fighters prevailed against Russian and separatist forces in the summer of 2014, securing Mariupol under Ukrainian control.

As the 2014 fighting subsided, Russian-backed separatists occupied the cities of Luhansk and Donetsk and all the areas farther east toward Russia, while Kyiv retained control of the western portions of the Luhansk and Donetsk regions, including Mariupol. What Russia continually failed to see, as the political scientists Shevel and Popova have demonstrated, was that the more Russia pulled Ukraine eastward, the more Ukrainians looked West. After Crimea was annexed, Ukraine lost the most pro-Russian population in the country, and in subsequent elections, more nationalist deputies were able to win the majority, pushing through legislation that even Yushchenko had been unable to enact a decade earlier. More people began to say, in official surveys, that "Ukrainian is their native language." Shevel and Popova clarify that whether they speak Ukrainian in daily life is a different thing—but increasingly, people in Ukraine began to identify as native Ukrainians, a major shift from the late 1990s and early 2000s.

It's difficult to overstate how substantially Ukraine and Russia diverged between 2014 and 2022, a shift that was imperceptible to many in the international community, leading to shock at Russia's brutal invasion. Beginning in 2014, Ukraine became increasingly economically integrated with Europe through new visa-free travel to the EU. Ukraine pushed through vast comprehensive reforms of the state administration and the judiciary. A vibrant civil society sector cooperated with the EU's monitoring missions, and both civil society and the EU pressed the Ukrainian government to make concrete reforms. When Volodymyr Zelenskyy—a deeply flawed politician whom many perceived as laughably unqualified for his post—took office in 2019, he nonetheless took hard stands against Ukrainian oligarchs and severely limited their political power. All the while, Russia under Putin was becoming more autocratic and repressive.

In the years that followed 2014, the Ukrainian government focused on building up its army, especially in areas proximate to Russian occupied territories, and Leonid was one of its recruits. The National Guard of Ukraine absorbed the Azov Brigade in late 2014, and the group shed its far-right ideologies. In fact, within just a couple of years, Jewish Ukrainians joined the Brigade. Nonetheless, the ultranationalist Azov fighters of 2014, who quelled Russia's attempt to take Mariupol, contributed to Russia's branding of Ukraine's government as neo-Nazi. Like other young recruits in Mariupol's divisions of the Ukrainian National Guard, Leonid knew that taking over Mariupol in 2022 was unfinished business for Russian soldiers.

On the morning of February 24, 2022, Leonid sensed that this time the fighting would play out differently. Mariupol was a key strategic city that Russian forces were hell-bent on taking quickly. Situated thirty miles from Russia, Mariupol offered a land corridor between Crimea and the Donbas. But Mariupol was also symbolically important as the home of the Azov Brigade, despised by Russian military leaders. Leonid believed in Ukraine and its ability to withstand Russia's attacks, but the bombing of the city's Left Bank, where Maria had grown up and where her parents were still living, portended violence on a scale not seen in Ukraine since World War II, and hearing the explosions shake the city, Leonid began to harden.

Even those who hours earlier had claimed they would never leave Ukraine were shaken by the sounds of those first explosions early in the morning on February 24. The booms registered not only in the ear but in the flesh. The explosions shook the earth so powerfully that you could feel them in your heart, an actual shake, as though every organ sloshed around with each thunderous blast. Thousands of people in Mariupol and across Ukraine dropped everything and ran to cars and buses on the streets to get out, hoping to find safety as quickly as possible. After hearing those explosions, they would abandon everything, if only they could avoid hearing them again.

That morning, the twenty-five-year-old Leonid told Maria that he would do his duty by joining the resistance. Maria refused to listen. When he said it again later, she demanded that he not go. If he left, she said, leaving her and their one-year-old son, David, to fend for themselves, she would consider it the ultimate betrayal. Leonid was a proud, doting dad, taking David with him like a sidekick around town, teaching him new tricks every day, showing him off to all his friends. Surely he would not leave David.

Over the first few days of the full-scale invasion, Leonid's undeviating will to join the resistance infuriated Maria. She was used to getting her way in their relationship. Opinionated and assertive when angry, Maria burned hot. For days, Mariupol was shelled and bombed relentlessly. Missiles fell indiscriminately, and explosions rocked the city, tall buildings swaying in the shock waves. Despite the Ukrainian army's efforts, by the beginning of March, the city was surrounded on all sides.

Soon it was hard to find cell service, and soon after that, the natural gas, water, and electricity supplies were shut off throughout the city. Inside grocery shops that had been shaken by explosions or shock waves, glass covered the floor and shelves lay on their sides, with produce and packaged food strewn in the aisles. In moments of relative quiet, people scavenged in the stores for whatever they could find and returned home, where they would wait out the next round of explosions while feeding their children looted juice and canned beans.

As the days went on, Maria, Leonid, and Maria's family tried to prepare themselves for the worst. They gathered water and whatever nonperishable food they could find. Leonid broke an old Soviet padlock on a basement door in their apartment building and discovered a small concrete space they'd never seen or even taken note of. He began cleaning it out, hauling out broken furniture, old jars, and crates and sweeping it meticulously and washing the walls with a cloth drenched in bleach to kill any mold. From their apartment upstairs, he and Maria brought down their mattress, blankets, and toys. "We need to move down here right now," he said resolutely, "and you need to leave the city when I go to fight."

Sitting in the basement shelter that first night in early March, Maria and Leonid and David were bewildered and terrified, hardly able to speak. Maria had been in a place like this only once before, with her grandmother in 2014, and sitting there, Maria kept thinking about the days just before the war began. David had been sick. On the twenty-third, Maria had taken him to the doctor for an antibiotic. Leonid had had the afternoon off work, and they all went to the appointment together, picked up David's prescription, and decided to spend the evening strolling slowly back home. They wove through the city, stopping at a local grocery chain to pick up their favorite pizza. Eating as they walked, their baby in tow, Maria had felt happy.

She and Leonid must have been among the last residents of

the city to take such a stroll; it was late February and chilly—most people were at home, getting children ready for bed, washing the dinner dishes, flipping on the television, falling asleep. Looking back on that night, Maria saw this as a gift from the universe—not just that she had felt happy in that moment but that she had recognized that she was happy. Maria thought maybe this feeling had come from her grandmother, a woman who herself had survived war as a child, and who now had returned to place a seraphic hand on Maria's head to warn her, to protect her against all that would begin in just a few hours.

ANNA

Starobilsk, Ukraine

IN STAROBILSK, LESS than forty miles from the Russian border, eighteen-year-old Anna was not a natural fit for the police academy she attended. She'd been there only a year. Anna was fair and sensitive, with a quiet, stubborn disposition. Living together with two hundred other students in communal barracks, subjected to spontaneous drills and checks, Anna never felt at ease. Every morning they exercised on a field, running a few kilometers and lining up in formation for calisthenics and aerobics. Every cadet ate breakfast, lunch, and dinner at the canteen, filing in line, placing borsch, chicken cutlets, and cabbage salad on their trays, then eating in silence with their backs straight. They rotated helping in the canteen with cooking, cleaning, preparing vegetables, and setting tables. During the day, they studied from eight in the morning to four in the afternoon. Their commanders and faculty were strict, yelling harsh reprimands for mistakes and sloppiness or just because. Cadets had little free time for relaxation, but some students relished the structure and strenuousness of it all. Anna hated it.

She'd chosen to pursue a career as a police officer because it offered a certain stability. When Anna was nine years old, her family's financial prospects collapsed with the economy of her home city, Luhansk, which was overtaken by separatists in 2014. Her dad was a mechanic by trade, her mom an accountant, but after the war began and Luhansk was captured, her dad joined the Ukrainian military, and her mom's employment, in displacement, was never secure. Graduating from the police academy was a reliable path to steady employment, and Anna was decently smart and disciplined. Her parents discouraged her from applying, suggesting that it would be challenging and she wouldn't enjoy her time there. But Anna's mind was made up: if she got in, did well, and graduated with good marks, she could rely on regular employment and a decent salary.

In 2021, when she was admitted to the Luhansk State University of Internal Affairs—the best police academy in Eastern Ukraine, which had been relocated since 2014 to Starobilsk—her parents showed no emotion or approval, but later, she found out that her dad had been bragging to everyone he knew, and Anna, who wanted her parents' approval more than anything, swelled with pride.

Mild mannered and soft spoken, Anna did not like conflict, nor was she motivated by competition or humiliation as tougher kids at the university seemed to be. Anna seemed sensitive and fragile, though a stubborn strength was present, too, especially in her relationship with her parents, whom she often fought with or dismissed. She appreciated those who saw both sides of her, the delicacy and the durability. When she was a kid, her dad and her grandmother were those people.

When Anna was growing up, her grandmother took her for weeks at a time during the summer to their dacha—a small summer home in the countryside—where they'd work in the garden, collect bugs and flowers, build mud houses, and climb trees. In town, during the school year, her grandma picked Anna up from school and took her to dance classes and shops. Her grandma was gentle, didn't like to scold Anna, and was nonconfrontational, sometimes to a fault. She had once adopted a stray dog in the street and cared for it for many years.

Her grandma was plump, with a short bob dyed dark brown every month by the hairdresser. When Anna was a small child, her grandma would pet her head and face, sing her songs, make her food. Her grandma didn't have much money—she worked as a teacher and speech therapist—so she didn't spoil Anna with gifts, but she doted on her, listening attentively, delighting in Anna's jokes, praising her good grades and resourcefulness, whispering loving words into Anna's ear at bedtime. Anna remembered, "As a child, I knew she loved me so much. I was always with her."

Anna's dad, though he could be stern and occasionally snapped at her if she behaved poorly, was similarly doting. Pampering Anna and her mother with gifts, he was warm and attentive. Anna remembers watching him arrange surprises for her mother, observing how they'd kiss and hold hands. In the summertime in Luhansk, they often grilled kebabs together over an open-flame grill in the park. He marinated the meat in a small plastic bucket, and they stabbed metal spears through pieces of chicken and pork and sometimes beef before roasting them over coals. As a family, they went to the beach in Crimea almost every summer, and on vacation her father would buy her ice cream several times a day. Anna remembered how on one holiday, he whispered that he had a surprise, climbed onto the roof of a small shed and pulled Anna up by her arms, hoisting her onto his shoulders so that together they could watch in wonder as fireworks exploded above them.

But in 2014, he changed. When the war began, school was canceled, explosions drove everyone into a frenzy, and her dad was angry. Nine-year-old Anna didn't understand what was going on, and no one explained it clearly. Her father left for a few days at a time, then came back, then left again. He was an ordinary mechanic before the war, but when their city was overtaken and the economy in the region plummeted, he stopped going to the mechanic shop. Many men were left unemployed, with no choice but to either move to another city or pick a side and fight on a military wage.

She couldn't even remember for certain when he left the first time; there was no fanfare, no big send-off.

Her mother told her offhandedly after he'd already left that he'd gone to fight. For what exactly, Anna wasn't sure at the time. Even when he came home, they didn't talk about what he had been doing, though she came to know later that he had been engaged in serious fighting for the Ukrainian army.

Reserved and matter-of-fact, even as they underwent major upheaval, Anna's mother tried hard to create a sense of stability in complete chaos. But this often meant they simply did not talk about what was going on.

"Mom just said that 'they're shooting, we have to leave.'"

Perhaps her mother thought that if there were no dramatic conversations, Anna would not notice that their world was falling apart, that neighbors were fleeing and fighting. Maybe if they did not talk much, Anna would not absorb the stress of war and displacement, maybe she would not worry constantly about whether she was safe, about whether she had a future. Conversations about the new war were often underdeveloped and curt.

"The word 'war' never left my parents' lips, even when shells flew nearby," Anna recalled. "I didn't even realize that these were explosions. Only when I saw the equipment and the guys in uniform, I realized that military operations were taking place." Nobody wanted to say the word "war" out loud. Everyone around knew about war through the World War II–era stories of their grandparents. People always said "we can endure anything except war," and they thought the attitude was shared by Ukrainians and Russians alike.

At nine years old, Anna learned to follow her mother's lead, approaching their situation matter-of-factly and not asking many questions. One morning in the early summer of 2014, Anna woke up when a rocket flew into the house across the street. Her father wasn't home; he was stationed in Starobilsk. But Anna's mother called him immediately—frantic, one of the first times Anna had seen her unhinged—and her father said he would send a colleague immediately to get them. Only later did Anna realize this was an evacuation team and not her dad's buddy coming to do him a quick favor while he was busy with something else.

Her mother packed quickly and conservatively. There was no time or space for anything large. They would not bring furniture, rugs, not their television, none of their decorations, no heirloom trinkets, no kitchenware. All the stuff they'd accumulated over her lifetime, they would leave behind. They took just their pet rat, some food, and warm clothes for the fall, "because mom didn't know how long we were leaving for," Anna said.

Her mother told her immediately that they could take no toys—no bike, no stuffed animals, no art supplies, no dolls. They left behind everything, including her grandmother, who refused to leave after living in Luhansk for seventy years.

Her father's colleague dropped Anna and her mom off in a village under Ukrainian control outside Luhansk. Anna pestered her mom for weeks, asking when they'd be going home. But the answer was always elusive: *I don't know. Soon, we hope. Maybe in a couple of months.*

They never went home. Anna and her mother hopped from village to village that whole summer of 2014, until finally, in the fall, they settled in Sievierodonetsk, a city that had been under separatist control until late July, when it was retaken by the Ukrainian army. Her mother, who was trained as an accountant, struggled to find a new job, and they learned to make do with very little, surviving on humanitarian aid, her father's small military salary, and whatever money her mother picked up from her occasional work as a cleaning lady or at the post office. There was no money for new toys, so Anna collected magnets from inside cracker snack bags—cartoon boys and girls surfing, riding skateboards, or breakdancing—and played make-believe with them.

Most of her classmates stayed behind in Luhansk, and later they wrote on the social networking site VKontakte that Anna was a *khohol*, a derogatory Russian term for Ukrainians that refers to the traditional hairstyle of Cossacks. Anna did not make friends easily; integrating into the new school was especially challenging for internally displaced kids, who were often branded with harsh stigmas—poor, homeless, dependent on aid. They changed apartments regularly in the first several years, and it was four years before she had a close friend, a girl in their apartment complex with whom she played in their courtyard.

Although they didn't talk openly about what was going on, for years Anna wondered: Why had they left Luhansk, especially when so many stayed? She regularly kept in touch with her grandmother, who still lived in Luhansk and at her dacha in the occupied village outside the city. Her grandmother spent most of her summers there working in the garden, growing cucumbers, tomatoes, squash, potatoes, berries, and a bit of corn. She watched only Russian TV now. Life for her grandmother often seemed peaceful enough, but when Anna asked her to come visit them in Sievierodonetsk, she always said no; she was scared to go too far. Some people traveled back and forth over the new borders separating occupied Ukraine from the rest of the country, but it was often dangerous. Even when periodic cease-fires were negotiated in the following years, leading to occasional periods of relative calm, the situation was fragile. At least her grandmother cried when she said she couldn't come, and that meant something to Anna.

Over time, Anna started to make some sense of what had happened. Her friends in Sievierodonetsk talked about being "for Ukraine" or "for the Russian world." In school, teachers explained some of the events—the EU association agreement, the revolution, the busloads of Russian *touristy* who showed up in Luhansk a few days after Yanukovych fled and brought weapons with them. They came in vans with Russian plates and took over city buildings, forming coalitions with the relatively small, radicalized group of local separatists who had proved too weak to fight Ukraine on their own.

Many in Luhansk scoffed angrily at news about Ukraine's "civil war," as though there had been a robust locally sustained movement calling for secession in the lead-up to Ukraine's revolution. The majority of Ukrainians in Luhansk were not pro-Russian in the sense that they claimed to *be* Russian or wanted to join Russia; they were pro-Russian in the sense that they supported trading with Russia, maintaining economic ties, and speaking Russian. After the collapse of the USSR, throughout the 1990s and early 2000s, Eastern Ukrainians experienced profound disillusionment in the promises of Western institutions and governments. Under Communism, they had been promised that their hard work would earn them material blessings, but it didn't, and later they were promised that capitalism would dramatically raise their standard of living, that they'd be able to consume, travel, and modernize, but throughout the 1990s, things only got worse. In addition to their cultural affinities, relations with Russia seemed, to many, to offer the only economic and political stability they could find.

In 2012, under Yanukovych's government, the Ukrainian parliament implemented a new law granting the Russian language regional status, which enabled its use (along with other minority languages, such as Hungarian and Romanian) in courts and schools. The law proved extremely controversial. Its supporters claimed that it made life easier for Russian-speaking Ukrainians, while its critics argued that it would exacerbate polarization between Western and Eastern Ukraine and eventually marginalize the Ukrainian language. The day after Yanukovych fled his presidential office, the parliament in Kyiv voted to overturn the law. In Eastern

Ukraine, many Russian speakers perceived the vote as a betrayal. Most people in Luhansk and Donetsk fell into this category, and the tensions were palpable, though only a small portion were radicalized enough to fight for secession.

Ukrainian separatists rallied hard in Luhansk and Donetsk in the spring of 2014, and their movement gained traction. But like their sibling separatist movements in other Eastern and Southern Ukrainian cities such as Odesa, Dnipro, and Kharkiv, they would not have survived on their own without Russian aid. There simply was not enough support, financially or politically. However, when Russia armed separatists with sophisticated weapons, bused in soldiers, and replaced local separatist leaders with Kremlin-picked Russian citizens who were sent to the Donbas to take charge, the situation in the east transformed from a civil conflict into a localized war of Russian aggression.

That first summer, Anna's father was one among many in the region who fought back. With major cities in the Donbas firmly under separatist control, the Ukrainian resistance tried to reclaim nearby towns, with limited success. Over the course of the summer, the Russian-staffed and -supported separatist movement imprisoned and tortured or killed many of them. The Ukrainian army, which at the time was underfunded and underdeveloped, could not beat the Russian-backed separatists, and it was able to reclaim only some of the territories that the separatists controlled.

The war destroyed any semblance of stability in the region. Mines ceased operations and then flooded, most industrial plants and factories closed, and by the fall of 2014—just a few months into the war—a million and a half Ukrainians had fled the area, leading businesses and shops to close. Universities and many schools in the occupied regions relocated to Ukrainian territory. The pro-Russian forces used revenue from the region's natural resources primarily to pay for militiamen, and Russia sent humanitarian aid such as food and clothing, which was primarily "sold off on tables in 'everything but the kitchen sink' bazaars, where it [went] for ridiculously low prices to those who still [had] the means to buy anything at all—even at such reduced prices," wrote a local Donetsk journalist, Stanislav Aseyev, who stayed in the area and watched it all play out.

Many supporters of Ukraine were forced to move. Those unwilling or unable to, usually the elderly, disabled, or the plain old stubborn, could often find employment only by working for the new regime. The new separatist republics' military was made up mainly of people who'd lost their jobs in the upheaval or were what Aseyev calls "local riffraff," with severe addictions or criminal backgrounds. But many who stayed were more or less respectable people who bought into the extremism or at least were no longer interested in combating it.

When I spoke with a head engineer at one of the biggest metallurgical plants in Luhansk—a highly educated man in his sixties who was known among his friends and family as a rigorous, nuanced thinker—he had succumbed to apathy. Since the fall of the USSR, he had supported an independent Ukraine, but, fearing economic instability if he left the relatively well-paid metallurgical job he'd held for nearly forty years, he decided it was better to stay in 2014. He'd seen thousands of the plant's employees laid off; many had moved away to other parts of Ukraine, some now worked for the Luhansk People's Republic and its military, others were dead. When I asked him why he was still there, he shrugged and couldn't really answer: "Nothing's actually true in politics, you know," he said, consoling himself. He added, however, that he had kept his Ukrainian passport.

When it came to Ukraine and Russia, the Donbas had long been marked by a distinctive ambivalence. In a region where most people were of Russian ancestry or heavily Russified, the ideal of a pan-Slavic nation of Ukrainians, Russians, and Belarussians coexisting in a primordial community was deeply attractive. Though the war tarnished or destroyed this ideal for many, it became all the more imperative to those who followed Russian media outlets and rationalized the conflict as protecting their mythical community that was under attack. The Ukrainian historian Yevheniy Monastyrskiy, a native of Luhansk, wrote in 2023: "For the past nine years, Luhansk has been like a close relative who was brainwashed into a cult and is now unable to communicate."

Within a year, the cultural and geographic landscape of the Donbas was obliterated. A brand-new modern airport—the recent pride of the Donetsk region—was destroyed in a long, gruesome battle. Children were taught to carry guns. Stores and restaurants were heaped with sandbags.

Displaced from home, Anna's father changed. He saw many of his hometown friends take up weapons and fight on the Russian side. He became hardened against them. After their move to Sievierodonetsk, Anna's relationship with him grew increasingly strained and difficult. He became strict and demanding, and scolded her harshly for poor grades.

Occasionally Anna still thought about the Luhansk of her childhood, before the war, before everything became confusing. She recalled her trips to the museum with her class, dance and art lessons, playing in the park with her grandma. Some scenes recurred without warning, rushing her across time and space to the quiet dirt road where she and the brawling neighbor boys ran amok, picking tulips from people's yards, splashing in puddles after rainstorms, coming home filthy every night. Then she remembered Timur and Denys, the neighbor boys. What had become of them? The week before the full-scale invasion, Russia had begun forcibly mobilizing tens of thousands of locals in the separatist-held regions. Timur and Denys—were they fighting somewhere? And if so, on which side? Were they even alive?

In the first hours of the war, Anna was awakened by a loud explosion that shook the barracks. Soon after, a siren blared and students were ordered to gather on the parade ground immediately, their usual place of formation.

"You can hear what's happening," one of the faculty members said matter-of-factly. "The air raid alarms, the explosions. Yes, it's all what it sounds like. Pack your things, everyone is going home."

Their cadet formations, usually orderly and synchronized, erupted into chaos. Anna rushed back to the barracks to gather her things. As she did, two more powerful explosions quaked in the near distance. She had not heard these sounds since she was evacuating Luhansk eight years earlier and passing long columns of Ukrainian army men and equipment.

Back then, she recalled, "these guys were full of enthusiasm," she said. "They were smiling, they assured us that the war would end very soon, and we had believed them." Now students, faculty, and administrative staff were to get out as quickly as possible. There were limited buses, which were filled on a first-come, first-served basis, with students fending for themselves to get to safety. Despite the evacuation plan, the school—renowned for its order—devolved into mayhem. Some prepared to enlist in the army, young men and women alike, and everyone called their families.

Anna brought only what she could fit in a small backpack before running to the bus. Later, she learned that the two explosions she'd heard while packing had destroyed the small airport in Starobilsk. Later that day, Russian tanks and infantry assaulted the town and many like it throughout the region. One of the university's evacuation buses drove northwest and got stuck in a traffic jam on a road blocked off by burning cars and trucks.

Once home, Anna and her parents packed their car with a few valuables and began to drive to Dnipro, the largest major city to the west, where they had relatives. Her parents were quiet yet agitated. Conversation on the drive was strained. Fleeing war in search of safety was something they all knew well, as was the silence of Anna's mother when confronted with loss.

Anna sensed that her mother's mind was spinning, but what was she thinking about? Her parents were tired and angry. The family spent a few hours of the night sleeping fitfully in their car on the side of the road, not knowing what would come next and afraid to talk about it. Perhaps they would stay in Dnipro together to wait out the worst of it? Or maybe they'd all go to Western Ukraine to find shelter?

After a few days in Dnipro, Anna's parents put her on a train going farther west. When her parents unloaded her stuff and hugged Anna, she could tell her mother was in emotional pain—agony, even. But there was no conversation. She was to get to the relative safety of Western Ukraine, secure a place to stay, get a job. Anna sensed that her father would go to the front and continue his military service, but as she left, Anna could tell somehow from her mother's subtle cues that she did not intend to stay in Dnipro either. Later, just as she arrived at a shelter in the west, Anna learned that both of her parents had turned back to Sievierodonetsk to fight. They were both joining the army, and they would not be meeting her in Western Ukraine for a long time, if ever.

In Western Ukraine, she was to begin a new life. She knew something about how to start from scratch; she had seen her mother do it eight years earlier. Anna mustered all the courage and grit she had—she was young, she could piece together a life for herself, she could move forward and try not to look back.

POLINA

Lviv, Ukraine

IN THE BACK of a car in LA on February 24, 2022, Polina sat in a Zoom meeting when messages started rolling in on her phone. "I'm so sorry, Polina." "We are thinking of you and your family." "Let me know if you ever need to talk." Confused, she flicked each of them away and tried to remain focused on her call. Like most people, she had been following the Russian troop buildup along the borders for weeks, and a month earlier, she'd returned home to Kyiv to celebrate her grandfather's seventy-fifth birthday. The war was all the buzz there, but still, most people seemed to brush it off as rumors, and Kyiv felt as it always had, like an old friend—familiar, relaxed, nurturing.

The summer before the full-scale invasion began, Polina and her husband, John, an American, lived in Kyiv while Polina worked high up in operations at BEVZA, one of the most prominent Ukrainian high-fashion designers. Polina is understated and fashionable, quiet, restrained, and very modest.

Born in the 1990s, she watched Kyiv's transformation from a dingy, poor post-Soviet metropolis to an occasionally upscale city with a special kind of gritty cool that led admirers to call it "the new Berlin." As in any city, the outskirts were shoddy, but central Kyiv reflected a broadening moneyed class, boasting designer boutiques, contemporary art galleries, a chic restaurant scene, and a fleet of Euro-edgy bars. She and John, a young, smart guy she met in 2016, epitomized this kind of cool, and they fit right in among downtown Kyiv's stylish stratum.

John first came to Ukraine as a missionary for the Church of Jesus Christ of Latter-day Saints. He'd been in Western Ukraine for two years, from 2013 to 2015, and he'd watched the series of mass protests that unfolded across the country after Yanukovych refused to sign the EU association agreement. The events made an impression on John—he remembers empty stores and ATMs, watching police forces patrol the streets and line up outside government buildings, observing a crowd of young men compete in a push-up competition to earn a seat on a bus to Kyiv's protests. As a missionary, he was unaware of the nuances of those events, and he wanted to return to Ukraine to make some sense of what he had seen a few years earlier and document their aftermath. In 2016 he went back on a student research grant to spend the summer traveling throughout the country, with a brief stop in Kyiv before going home.

Like John, Polina was also a member of the Church of Jesus Christ of Latter-day Saints—a Mormon—and had grown up attending church every week with her parents and siblings. Polina's parents joined the church in the early 1990s, when missionaries from many different faiths flooded the former Soviet republics, preaching religion in what had been overtly atheist lands for nearly a century. Religious observance had dropped markedly over the course of the twentieth century, but the 1990s saw a spike in fervor throughout the area and especially in Ukraine. People wanted religion, and a new spirituality formed a major part of the post-Soviet zeitgeist. Many returned to the local faiths of their grandmothers—Eastern Orthodoxy or Ukrainian Greek Catholicism—and many experimented with far-flung religious traditions like Buddhism and Hare Krishna.

Protestant missionaries came to Kyiv, and Baptist and Pentecostal preachers, as well as young suit-and-tie missionaries from the Church of Jesus Christ, were successful in bringing many kinds of people into their congregations. Polina's parents were among them. Her mom, Sveta, then young and single, was one of the first to be baptized into the church in Ukraine. Sveta ended up serving a mission of her own, just two years after joining, and was assigned to Moscow. A few years later, she met another young convert to the faith, Ihor, whom she'd eventually marry. Ihor had inherited a nascent belief in God from his grandmother, with whom he spent time in her village when he was a young boy. "My grandmother always had a routine," he said. "Every evening before going to bed, she put on a nightgown, combed her long braids with a comb, knelt before an icon of the image of God in the corner of the house and prayed." Like many Ukrainian grandmas, she regaled him with preaching of the heaven of the righteous and the hell of the sinners.

When the USSR collapsed, Ihor was serving in the Soviet navy, stationed in Liepaja, Latvia. The news of the Soviet Union's death didn't mean much to him. He didn't really care about it—or anything else, beyond physical survival. Later, when he returned home to Kyiv in the spring of 1992, it was clear to him that things were changing, but he was an immature twentysomething guy, and focused his attentions on getting by day to day and finding dates.

When he met young missionaries in the early 1990s, he was transfixed by their message of faith. He recalled later that "it seemed that I had always known it, but as if in a dream I had forgotten. It seemed that I woke up and returned to the real Ihor." His parents were adamantly against his conversion to what they perceived to be an American cult, but later he reconciled with them, and they were pleased to find that his new faith had, in fact, helped Ihor to steer clear of alcoholism and other troubles that plagued young men of his generation in the 1990s.

Sveta and Ihor married, had four kids, and raised them all in the church. They found meaning in their new faith, and the growing church community provided not just a space for spiritual discussion but friendship and belonging. By 2010, when the church built a large temple in Kyiv, it had about ten thousand members throughout the country.

Polina grew up in a very different Ukraine from the country her parents knew as children. She was born in independence, with no memories of the USSR, raised a member of a small Christian church, and lived in increasing affluence. Ihor made relatively good money working for the church, managing a distribution center and organizing youth education classes and summer camps. In the mid-2000s, her parents bought land and built a relatively nice house outside Kyiv. She and her friends got phones as young teens, then they got smartphones, then eventually iPhones.

In 2004 Polina, who was seven years old, went with her dad to Independence Square to protest in the Orange Revolution. The revolution unearthed deep feelings of national identity in Ihor, as it did for millions of Ukrainians. After 2004, Ukrainian society became more amenable to a nationalizing agenda. For example, more people began demanding that the *holodomor*—the man-made famine of the early 1930s—should be framed as a genocide. In general, many Ukrainians wanted to assert themselves as a nation distinct from Russia. Ihor and Sveta began speaking Ukrainian at home with their kids, the language they had learned from their grandmothers and known since childhood but had not used as a first language in adulthood.

"Many things that had been in a state of lethargic sleep for a long time—" Ihor said, "traditions, culture, songs, language—also came to life and began to be restored in people's lives, like a genetic code."

"Looking back," he went on, "I realize how naive we were to think that putting on an orange scarf and participating in a demonstration would lead to a bright future. Later, when Yanukovych was elected in 2010, there was a sense of defeat and decline. It seemed that everything was lost. But there were enough people in Ukraine with historical memory who would never have come to terms with the course of the country at that time."

For Polina and her friends, notions of Ukrainian independence and nationhood, democracy, and civil responsibility felt intuitive. They were an entirely new generation. In the summer of 2016, a mutual friend introduced Polina and John. They spent one whole day walking around Kyiv—through parks and across bridges, along the Dnipro river beaches, and past golden-domed churches. John was set to fly home two days later, but he liked Polina's angular, pretty face, dark brown hair, and self-assured style. More than anything, she struck him as intuitive and wise, despite being young; she was attuned to frequencies that he missed: "She feels things, dreams things, her bones hurt when the weather is soon to change," he said. Coming from a family with ten kids, raised by thoughtful parents, John was scrappy and hardworking, sensitive, and creative. When John called his dad to ask advice on whether he should stay in Kyiv to get to know Polina better, his dad told him to eat his plane ticket and follow his heart.

John stayed the rest of that summer, and two years later, they were married. By early 2022, they had moved to LA, where John scored a job with a creative design studio called PlayLab and Polina was working on launching a fashion line of her own. The studio consulted and designed for clients like Louis Vuitton, Nike, and

Post Malone; for him it was the dream job. There was little else like it in design, and he and Polina staked their future on a move to LA.

As Polina sat in the back of the car in LA and the messages rolling in on her phone started to refer to Ukraine, she knew the war had begun. She flipped to the news, and as she scrolled through the headlines and watched newscasts about the invasion and footage of missiles flying into civilian infrastructure, her heart pounded. A new, foreign adrenaline washed over her body, and she trembled. Once home, she and John tried calling her parents, siblings, and grandpa, none of whom could be reached.

They stayed up through the night watching images from Kyiv, waiting for every new video that surfaced: bombed buildings, traffic jams, political commentary, Zelenskyy speeches, tanks rolling in the streets. Most believed that Kyiv would fall within a couple of days. Russian planes would land at the Hostomel airport just outside the city, the capital's elites would be killed, and then Russian troops would march through Independence Square, symbolizing the futility of the fight for independence.

During the next four days and nights, Polina hardly slept or ate, instead alternating between refreshing the news and messaging people at home. Though physically safe, she felt as though she herself was under attack. A new kind of worry took over her body. She vacillated between sound problem-solving—calling and messaging everyone she knew, locating bomb shelters in Kyiv, sending directions to her friends—and doubling over, nauseous, crying. When she dozed off for just a moment, she awoke with a start, her heart crashing into her stomach, racing and pounding without respite, anxious to get back to the news and see if Kyiv was still standing.

She tried to think clearly—to not fear the worst—and once she was able to contact her parents, her mom calmed her down, reassured her that everything would be okay. The world around seemed to move in slow motion. When she and John stepped out of their apartment to attend a pro-Ukraine rally in LA, it seemed that they existed in two realities, one in which the world was actually coming to an end, and one in which people strolled outside with their families, complained about traffic, laughed, and took selfies.

Like many people, within hours they were scheming what to do. For the first seventy-two hours, they brainstormed how to raise money, helped arrange evacuations, posted constantly on social media, and went to rallies in Southern California. But still they felt their efforts were paltry. They tried to get creative; maybe they had some specific skills that would be useful? John decided to design a T-shirt to raise donation money. "I was so out of it at that time, I stopped designing completely for a few weeks," he said, but a close friend and talented designer worked up the design after John came up with a concept. The T-shirt was screen-printed with a simple single-word design: SVOBODA—"freedom" in Ukrainian. Several hundred were sold in a few days, and they donated all the proceeds to relief efforts.

But they couldn't shake the feeling that they needed to do something more. Over and over again, John watched the viral video of Ukrainian men and women lining up to enlist in the army—accountants, pastors, IT workers. He watched them saying goodbye to their families, standing in lines, taking up arms for the first time. "They don't need a new logo," John thought. "They don't need me, with my design skills, helping to brand their defense. They need manpower, and I have that." He had been reading of people from around the world making their way to Ukraine to join the army's International Legion and fight alongside the Ukrainians. He considered the idea for a few hours, tried pushing it out of his mind several times, only to feel it float back.

Eventually, on Saturday, he floated the notion with Polina, and she didn't reject it; in fact, her first thought was "I will go, too." They began to discuss that scenario hypothetically, and as they said the words out loud—*go back to Ukraine*—they felt a spike of energy, as though they had struck something that they knew deep down was a true path forward. The rest of Saturday, they strategized. In one scenario, he could join the International Legion of the Ukrainian Armed Forces, and she could join as a frontline medical assistant or work in humanitarian aid. Stories of retired American servicemen joining up were already in the news. They didn't know exactly how it would play out—and there wasn't much readily available information on how to do any of this—but by Sunday night, they decided to leave.

They called close friends and family that night. John's parents, who had a good track record of trusting him to do what he thought was right, respected their decision. Others weren't so supportive— one of John's friends was caught off guard and oscillated between being patronizing and alarmed—"I know you're feeling really upset about this, man . . . but you should under no circumstances go to Ukraine." And yet, another friend, one of John's former mission companions in Ukraine, flew to LA that very night to help them pack and fill their bags with emergency first aid. By Monday they decided to stop telling people they were going unless they absolutely had to.

On Sunday night, they purchased tickets to Warsaw for Wednesday. In two days they gave away most of their stuff, packed up everything else, canceled their lease, quit their jobs, and bought body armor and combat boots. Their suitcases were at total capacity, filled with over-the-counter medication, first aid supplies, and power banks for phones, so John wore his combat boots and body armor on the plane to Poland. From there, they would find a way to make it across the border, the same one Ukrainians crossed en masse, fleeing in the other direction.

The train station in Warsaw was unlike anything they'd ever seen— crowded, chaotic, lined with people camping out with nowhere to go. Finding information on how to get to Ukraine proved more difficult than they imagined; in that first week of the war, there were no scheduled trains going into Ukraine, and most buses and cars had to be arranged privately. They discovered that their best chance of getting a train to Western Ukraine was in Przemysl, a small Polish city seven kilometers west of the border. Hundreds of thousands of Ukrainians were transferring there on their way to other cities in Poland and Central Europe. At the station, they were told, they could hop on one of the trains emptied of refugees returning to Ukraine for another load.

The Przemysl train station was a special kind of hell. Sleeping refugees, piles of luggage, and endless lines and crowds occupied nearly every square foot of the place. It was an old and modest station, serving a small city of sixty thousand people, that had never experienced even a fraction of the traffic it saw in the first two weeks of Ukraine's full-scale war. Paper and cardboard signs, awkwardly handwritten in Ukrainian Cyrillic letters, hung everywhere, covering every wall and pillar, indicating where housing was available: *Up to three people in France, call this number,* or *For work and housing in Dusseldorf, email Jorg.*

The people at the depot had traveled long distances with no place to stay or shower, and the smell coalesced into a mixture of bodily odors, urine, coffee, and the salty aroma of kielbasa on open-faced sandwiches. Lacking ventilation, the air was oppressively muggy, and the few windows were covered in steam. People slept on the floor hugging their backpacks to their chests, and teenagers sat cross-legged, their backs slouched and faces blue in the light of a cell phone. Middle Eastern and African students who had been studying in Ukraine huddled to figure out next steps. One of the station's rooms was set up for women with children coming from Ukraine. A shrieking rumble blared from its doors. Children fell to the floor in tantrums or jumped hyperactively, laughing, coping. Adult women openly wept.

Polish locals lined up to help, handing out water bottles, juice, crackers, fruit, toys, toothpaste, toothbrushes, soap, hand wipes. Others distributed food on cheap disposable plates, which buckled in half with the weight. Piles of donated clothing, shoes, and coats sat outside the station; arriving Ukrainians could riffle through them and take what they needed.

During their short layover in Warsaw, John and Polina had done as much research as they could. Given how desperate Ukraine seemed for military recruits, they were surprised how challenging it was to join the International Legion, which was looking only for people with combat experience.

This wouldn't work for them. They were designers and had never handled firearms. They would need to pivot, but in which direction, they didn't know. When the next train from Ukraine arrived, they planned to hop on, regardless of where in Ukraine it was headed.

No one really knew when trains to Ukraine came and left. The cars were operating in emergency conditions—leaving as quickly as they could, moving through the day and night, crowded far past capacity. John and Polina located a track where a train had just departed for Ukraine. Assuming it would be back eventually, they heaved their four suitcases over the tracks, to get to the platform. They stood in the cold, waiting, occasionally taking a sprinting break to go to the bathroom or buy some crackers. Finally, after about four hours, a train pulled up. People were packed in so tightly that they fell out onto the platform when the doors opened.

John watched as old men and women stepped gingerly down onto the platform, carrying plastic bags filled with clothes and documents. One mom with young children stepped off the train. Aid workers threw them toothpaste, soap, toys, crackers, and water bottles. She accepted it all, dazed, struggling to carry everything. Her young son tugged on her sleeve repeatedly, pestering: "Mom where are we going?" She was silent. "Mom—where are we going?"

"*Ne znaiu*," she finally said—*I don't know.*

Several major news organizations were on the scene to document the plight of the refugees. Seeing John and Polina standing in line for a return to Ukraine, they pushed their microphones forward: "Why are you going back?" "Are you going to fight in the International Legion?" "Are you crazy?"

In Ukraine, reports had started coming in—many real, some fake—about people getting shot randomly in the forests of Western Ukraine as they moved to safety. Missiles fell on civilian buildings every day, and the Russian offensive progressed so rapidly in Northern, Southern, and Eastern Ukraine that, standing on the platform, John and Polina started to wonder whether they had made a serious mistake. "If we hop on this train, are we sitting ducks?" This wasn't joining the Peace Corps. This was war.

Their hearts had not stopped pounding in days, and as the train emptied and a few other people returning to Ukraine hopped aboard, they looked at each other and climbed in. On the train, there were no tickets, no payment, no schedule, nothing—they didn't even really know where in Ukraine they were headed, but they assumed it was to Lviv. There were no posted destinations or stops; John and Polina just got on the train and sat down.

Nearly every train in Ukraine was being deployed to evacuate people, and this one was a Soviet-era model, full of old wooden benches. It had been running back and forth between Poland and Ukraine for days, stopping just long enough to be refueled. The train car looked as though it had been transporting livestock. Trash, bottles, dirt, and urine covered the floor. Bathrooms didn't work, and people had been packed so closely together that some feared they would suffocate. With no access to toilets, children and older people had peed on themselves on the journey, an additional humiliation. Lights did not work either. The conductor played no announcements as the train pulled from the station; it simply began crawling away.

It was dusk. John and Polina were among the few in the train car. As they moved closer to Ukraine through the night, the sky blackened. Looking out, John and Polina could see the windows of passing trains moving the other direction, toward Przemysl. The windows were all fogged up. Bodies pressed against them. People stood with their cheeks to the window, some with their eyes closed, trying to sleep, some with their eyes wide open.

When John and Polina arrived in Lviv, the time was near curfew, and they ran—past the crowds of people lined up to catch the next trains, past the many thousands congregated outside the station, past the barrels burning bonfires to keep people warm, past churches and grocery stores and bread stands, past the buildings erected by Ukrainians and Poles and Jews over the last centuries, through the parks that had switched hands back and forth between Nazis and Soviets—the whole time pulling their suitcases behind them, their heads throbbing, their lungs burning, the suitcase wheels popping off one by one on the cobblestones until they were forced to lug the bags without wheels, pulling them up the stairs to the small, crowded student apartment where they had arranged to stay that night. When they arrived, the three twenty-year-olds who lived there greeted them with dinner. Sitting around that table with strangers in a war zone, eating simple student food at eleven at night—past curfew, when every soul in that city was sequestered behind whatever four walls they could find—Polina's heart stopped racing for the first time since she rode home in the car in LA and the war began.

Volodymyr—1989

IN 1987, VOLODYMYR Shovkoshitny was ready for a change.

Trained as a geophysicist, Volodymyr spent nine years, from 1978 to 1987, working at the Chernobyl nuclear power plant, eighty-five miles from Kyiv. He became a geophysicist because of his older brother, Viktor, whom he idolized and who had left their small village in Central Ukraine to attend the Geological and Exploration Technical College in Kyiv when Volodymyr was thirteen years old.

"I had no questions about who I should be," he said. "I clearly knew that I would be like Viktor." Three years later, Volodymyr attended the same college, and after that—just like Viktor—he worked with scientific crews in remote regions throughout the Soviet Union looking for precious natural resources.

In the Caucasus, they searched for tungsten and molybdenum, metals the USSR used to manufacture tanks and armor, and in the Russian Far East, he surveyed for uranium to manufacture nuclear weapons. But they found none of that. Instead, when panning in a river one day in the North Caucasus, Volodymyr found a real diamond. He looked around, careful that no one saw, and slipped it in his pocket. Later he polished it and gave it to his wife, Halyna, who kept it as a symbol not just of her husband's love but of his spirited intuition. He was the kind of man who could look into a stream, see a dull, opaque stone—rough and uneven—and know it was a diamond.

In the mid-1970s, Viktor became a dosimeter—someone who helped to measure exposure to radiation—at the construction of the Chernobyl nuclear power plant, and because Viktor went, so, too, did Volodymyr. Starting as an operator, then a senior operator, then an engineer, Volodymyr rose through the plant's ranks through the early eighties.

He developed an expertise in the RBMK1000—a common type of graphite-moderated nuclear power reactor designed and built in the Soviet Union. This specific reactor had an inherent safety flaw: it was unstable at low power levels, making it susceptible to sudden power surges. Volodymyr spent years working with the system. He knew it by heart—every button and function, the modes, the valves, the tubes. He worked at the power plant while he completed a doctoral degree, and he wrote his dissertation on all the possible technical failings of the reactor and how to prevent them.

Volodymyr was cheeky and good-humored, and when he went to Moscow to defend his dissertation, he began his presentation in verse. When the examiners asked what the hell he was doing, he responded that "nuclear energy, at the very least, deserves iambic pentameter." It was April 24, 1986, exactly two days before so many of the failings he wrote about came to pass.

On the morning of April 26, after successfully defending his dissertation, he returned to Pripyat, the town where all the plant's workers lived. As his train pulled in, helicopters flew overhead and armored personnel carriers and tanks drove through the streets. Someone from the plant met him at the station, along with Volodymyr's wife. "There's been some sort of accident," the man told Volodymyr.

Volodymyr rushed home with his wife to their children. On their way, a fire engine sped by, spraying down the streets with white foam solution. He knew immediately that this was some sort of decontaminator, and they picked up their pace. Along the way they saw neighborhood children running barefoot through the white foam solution. It was late April and starting to warm, and the white foam was an entertaining new attraction.

Volodymyr screamed at them to get out of the foam. "It's not safe! Get out!"

A patrolman came up to him: "Hey, what're you doing yelling at these kids?"

"You are fools!" he responded. "You see that the children are running barefoot, and this is radioactive water. Why don't you kick them out?"

The patrolman shook his head, bewildered. He didn't know what was going on. "I'm not an atomic scientist," he said to Volodymyr, "I am just here to make sure this white foam gets sprayed everywhere."

The centralized structure of the Soviet Union prohibited Ukrainian authorities from determining how best to handle the disaster without seeking Moscow's input and approval, so an evacuation order was not arranged for another thirty-six hours. In that time, the state distributed iodine pills to try to salvage people's thyroids while children continued playing in the radioactive foam.

With every hour, as the magnitude of the catastrophe became clearer, Volodymyr felt a sickening sense of responsibility. Though he bore none, he understood better than anyone else the mechanisms that had caused the explosion and meltdown, and he volunteered to help. For eighteen months, Volodymyr worked at the destroyed Chernobyl plant, in charge of its liquidation. He managed teams working to haul the radioactive waste—contaminated debris, molten metal sheets, nuclear waste sludge—into storage facilities that he helped build; he also oversaw a group of several thousand liquidators who for months hosed down streets, cut down trees, and barreled up contaminated soil and grime.

Within a few months, a concrete sarcophagus was erected over the exploded reactor to limit contamination from spreading farther, and several months later, in the fall of 1987, specialists from other Soviet nuclear plants were brought in and put in charge. It was time for Volodymyr to leave, and he gave his notice, tired, disillusioned, and full of radionuclides.

It was the middle of perestroika, the era of dramatic political and economic change that preceded the Soviet collapse. Championed by the last leader of the USSR, Mikhail Gorbachev, perestroika was a radical reform campaign that its most ardent supporters believed would reinvigorate the Soviet Union. Gorbachev's government permitted greater latitude for the media, eased repressive policing, introduced limited economic freedoms, established some democratic election processes, and promoted younger, reform-minded Communist cadres. As the rigid, authoritarian Soviet Union of decades past dissolved, many praised Gorbachev for bringing the USSR out of the dark ages, while many others despised him for destroying any semblance of stability left in Soviet society.

Even though no one knew they were living in the final years of the USSR, everyone felt that in perestroika, things were different. Something had ruptured. People talked about the past in a new way, uttering words that would've gotten them arrested a decade earlier: purges, corruption, and even *holodomor*—the artificial famine created by Stalin's collectivization policies in which more than four million Ukrainians had starved to death in the 1930s. In perestroika, Ukrainians started talking about themselves in a new way, and the Ukrainian national movement that had largely been forced underground in the previous thirty years reared its head. Rukh, the People's Movement of Ukraine—an organization that emerged in the late eighties and advocated for Ukraine's political independence from the USSR and promoted Ukrainian culture and language—gained attention and members.

Freed from his cleanup work at Chernobyl, Volodymyr felt the spirit of this moment of change, and he decided to spend a year pursuing writing, a career he had been interested in from childhood. Becoming a great writer was a dream for many young Soviets. Literature was held in particular reverence by the Bolsheviks and founders of the Soviet state, who were themselves intellectuals who believed in the power of literature to shape human consciousness. Stalin famously wrote that writers are "engineers of human souls." Given how the state partnered with writers to produce ideology, it's no wonder that writers were, depending on what they wrote, either exalted as celebrities or killed, imprisoned, or exiled.

Volodymyr wanted to help society, but he was tired of engineering, and especially following the Chernobyl disaster, he wanted to do something he believed in. So in the fall of 1987, he entered the Gorky Moscow Literary Institute—a prestigious Soviet institution that produced some of the best Soviet writers.

With Gorbachev's reforms in full effect, Moscow was at a moment of radical transition. Discussions of nationalism were becoming more common, and they interested Volodymyr. He knew the idea from hearing it denounced in school or alluded to in hushed conversations in his adolescence when someone mentioned their uncle who was a nationalist, and he knew it was dangerous business, even during perestroika. But in 1988 Moscow, it wasn't just Ukrainians who were talking about their repressed past, it was people from many national backgrounds: Lithuanians, Georgians, Kazakhs, even Russians, among others. For some, nationalist mobilization felt annoying, even embarrassing, undergirded by a sense that the expression of grievances was petty or unnecessary and counterproductive to Soviet society writ large. For others, the mobilization in the late 1980s felt like an awakening, giving language and voice to beliefs and loyalties that had been left unarticulated.

Though he was born and raised in a Ukrainian village, Volodymyr was trained and socialized as a classic late Soviet man. For generations his family had lived in his village. In the eighteenth century, when Ukrainian peasants were made into serfs in the Russian Empire, his ancestors—the grandparents of his grandfather— did not take to serfdom well. They went to court, rebelled, and were evicted from their home. Eventually they moved to infertile land, pulled peat from the swamp, and made it fertile. Their new village began to be called Natyagaylivka, from the Ukrainian word meaning "to pull out." In the early 1960s, Volodymyr spent summer evenings sitting on a stool thumbing corn kernels from their cobs, knocking sunflower seeds from their flower heads with a paddle, and listening as his father regaled him with stories about where they came from, their ancestors, the Cossacks, how the Soviets collectivized their land, took the grain, starved the villages, how people fled and new people moved in, how the land changed and the people living on it did too.

Volodymyr heard his first word of Russian on the radio when he was five years old. Later, when there was a television in their village, he heard Russian on TV, broadcast from the Soviet television stations in Kyiv and Moscow. Sometime after World War II, three women from Russia appeared in their village. One of them, a war widow, had remarried a Ukrainian man and would live the rest of her life there. Her eldest son, Valery, was Volodymyr's classmate and first friend. Volodymyr spent lots of time at their house and in the neighborhood, catching frogs and climbing walls. It always struck Volodymyr as strange that his friend's mom, Auntie Anya, never learned Ukrainian, and never tried. "She had the same number of legs and the same number of arms, but she did not speak the same way we did, she did not understand us or anything about us, our customs, our songs."

When Volodymyr went away to study at the Kyiv Geological Exploration Technical College as a teenager, all the coursework was in Russian. He studied exclusively in Ukrainian in his village school, and adjusting to math, physics, and chemistry in Russian made him homesick. Once, he was riding on a trolleybus and tapped the young man in front of him to hand his ticket to the conductor. "*Bud' laska*," he said, meaning "Please" in Ukrainian. The young man turned and looked him up and down with a grimace: "*zhlob*," the young man said, disgusted—a pejorative term meaning backward, stupid, illiterate, uncultured.

Not all Ukrainians supported speaking Ukrainian—it seemed to many a village language, one that lacked refinement and culture. Ukrainian-speaking parents in the village were often pleased that their children were educated in Russian because it would serve them better in a professional career. Ukrainian, such parents came to believe over time, would only handicap them in their studies, or worse, have them branded as backward or nationalist.

"Why am I a *zhlob*?" Volodymyr protested.

"Speak humanly," the young man responded.

"You are wrong," Volodymyr said, then followed the young man as he got off at his stop. When he called Volodymyr a *zhlob* again, Volodymyr started beating him, swinging his fists angrily and socking him in the face and jaw and stomach. Volodymyr didn't knock him down in just one blow—he was just fifteen years old, after all—but with a series of punches he pushed the man over and hopped back on the same trolleybus before the doors closed.

In his thirties in Moscow in the late 1980s, Volodymyr could fit in easily if he wanted—a luxury that many national minorities, including Muslim and Armenian migrants, did not have. He spoke clean Russian, without a pronounced regional accent, and looked and sounded, and therefore could pass as, Russian. But he was increasingly uncomfortable with that designation. His time in Moscow deepened his awareness that Ukrainians were often "othered," and this bothered him fundamentally. He only rarely heard the term "Ukrainian" to describe who he was; usually, Ukrainians were called

the ethnic slur *khoholy*. As the Soviet periphery and Ukraine in particular became more restive in its final years, anti-Ukrainian attitudes grew in Moscow, where for many, Ukrainian nationalism was
annoying at best, infuriating at worst. He and his Ukrainian friends
used to joke with one another: "If you want to become a Ukrainian nationalist, go and live in Moscow." He started to think more
critically about home—about where he was from, how he'd grown
up, the language he felt compelled to speak but often did not. He
thought about Chernobyl, how the Ukrainians couldn't make the
decision to evacuate the town on their own, and about those kids
playing in the contaminated foamy water, the way their feet blis-
tered and the skin sloughed off.

As a student at the literature institute, he took classes in film
writing and directing. In 1988, just two years after the disaster, he
started making a film about his experience at Chernobyl. He called
the film *Threshold*. It was the first documentary anyone had made
about the accident. He interviewed people who'd survived the catastrophe, showed unpublished footage from Pripyat on the day of the
meltdown and the days immediately following, and explored how locals were kept in the dark about what was happening. The film pre-
miered in Leningrad in late 1988 at the Union of Cinematographers
of the USSR and in the first "Message to Man" International Film
Festival. Almost immediately afterward, the tape was confiscated.
In January 1989, the film—deemed illegal for its disclosures about
radiation doses, how people were exposed directly to radiation during and after the accident, and the number of military personnel
involved in the clearing of the accident—was banned throughout
the Soviet Union. A few months later, the film was released with
very limited circulation in the USSR but still prohibited from being
shown in Ukraine, where the issue of Chernobyl was emotionally
charged and politics were volatile.

But *Threshold* put Volodymyr on the map. A few months later, he received a call from a famous director, Borys Savchenko, at the Dovzhenko Studio in Kyiv, one of the most prestigious film studios in Ukraine. Savchenko invited Volodymyr to visit. When Volodymyr arrived, Savchenko said: "Listen, we have some people who want to make a film about Vasyl Stus. Do you want to make it?" Volodymyr was only vaguely familiar with Stus, a Ukrainian poet and dissident who had been killed in a gulag in Perm, Russia, in 1985. He had read of Stus in a Kyiv newspaper sometime after his death. Now, in 1989, four years after his death, Stus's wife and son, Dmytro, were trying to organize his reburial—along with those of two other Ukrainian writers and human rights activists who had died in the same prison, Oleksiy Tykhyi and Yuriy Lytvyn—in Ukraine.

Stus had been a prisoner in Perm-36, a forced labor colony sixty miles northeast of Perm. Originally built in 1946 as a timber production camp, by 1972 Perm-36 had been converted into a prison for people charged with political crimes—prominent dissidents, those who opposed the Communist government, writers of anti-communist literature, advocates for human rights, and other kinds of dissidents. With such a high concentration of political prisoners, it was the only camp of its kind in the Soviet Union, and the prison administrators separated its prisoners into isolated cells, subjecting them often to solitary confinement, hunger, disease, and torture. In the wake of Gorbachev's reforms, the Soviet state closed the camp in 1987, two years after Stus's death, and with news of the camp's closure, Dmytro Stus set to work on having his father's body returned to Ukraine.

Dmytro would manage the reburial in Ukraine; what Volodymyr would need to handle were the logistics in Perm: the exhumation, the coffins, the film crew that would come along. Dmytro was then in his twenties and had corresponded with his imprisoned father for much of his life. Those letters affected Dmytro deeply, and when his father died, he took responsibility for his father's memory and physical remains.

Of course, trying to rebury Stus was absolutely crazy. Although it was the middle of perestroika, the Ukrainian general secretary—the president of the Ukrainian Soviet Socialist Republic—was Volodymyr Shcherbytsky, a dogmatic conservative leader who fiercely opposed Gorbachev's reforms. Nationalists had not fared well during his tenure. He repressed dissidents harshly; it had been under Shcherbytsky's rule that Stus was arrested twice, imprisoned for many years, and eventually died. Shcherbytsky's time in office was marked by intensified Russification and cultural stagnation, and trying to rebury Stus in Shcherbytsky's Ukraine was asking for trouble.

As he considered the offer, Volodymyr borrowed a foreign edition of Stus's poetry book, titled *Palimpsests*, from Dmytro. The volume's publication had been completely prohibited in the USSR, but Dmytro possessed a rare copy. Stus had written the poems in the collection—nearly four hundred—throughout the 1970s, while imprisoned, and the collection was published in New York months after Stus's death.

Volodymyr liked the title. A palimpsest is a manuscript, usually on parchment, with an older text erased but still visible beneath a newer one. Reading the poetry in its original Ukrainian, Volodymyr was impressed by the language, the flickering images, the pulsation of new ideas.

"Ever since I was young, I have noticed that nothing happens in my life by chance," Volodymyr wrote. "Events happen that I was ready for, that I had been working toward all along. It was the same this time."

This was just the kind of change Volodymyr was ready for. He studied Stus's lines carefully before he went to sleep each night. They caught at his throat. One poem began, "How good that I am not afraid of death, and I do not ask if my cross is heavy." Stus wrote it on January 20, 1972. At that time, Volodymyr was in the Far East looking for minerals, and Stus was in the pretrial cell at the Kyiv

KGB detention center, eight days after his first arrest. Stus revised the poem four years later at a Leningrad prisoners' hospital after he survived a brutal operation in which he had two-thirds of his stomach removed, and he ended the poem with a credo, which Volodymyr read over and over again in the dark in his Kyiv apartment:

"My people, I will return to you, and in death I will turn to life."

Years later, reflecting on his experience in 1989, Volodymyr said: "That's exactly what happened."

PART 2

THE
FIRST SPRING

MARIA

Mariupol, Ukraine

BY THE END of February, Leonid had begun taking food and supplies to the Ukrainian soldiers at the front lines of Mariupol's defense. He talked about them constantly—he called them "his guys"—and he worried about them, regaling Maria with how their positions were changing and they weren't getting the help they needed. He bought carton upon carton of cigarettes and as many jugs of water as he could find, then drove through the shelling to deliver them. He was eager to help, and even as the barrages intensified and Maria said she didn't want him to go anymore, he still went several more times.

On March 1, Maria and Leonid decided that staying in their apartment for any length of time during the daylight hours was no longer an option. They would shelter in the basement. For the time being, they would still sleep in the apartment—mainly for comfort—but if things got even worse, they'd begin sleeping in the cellar, too. Explosions, shelling, and shock waves were so frequent that darting from the basement to do anything—grab an item from the apartment, get some fresh air, cook food—risked sudden death. Maria's older sister, her husband, and their toddler son had also joined Leonid, Maria, and David by the beginning of March, and they stayed in the cellar for twelve hours at a time, trying to keep everyone warm and fed and entertain the two babies. In their court-yard, Leonid broke down the crates and old furniture they found in the basement to build a fire. He melted snow to boil and cooked soup and dried pasta.

On March 3, Leonid began preparing his military clothes. He had received some ribbons from those he visited on the front lines—ribbons that suggested a specific group or unit—and she saw him sew them on the chest of his uniform. He was enlisting, and she was watching it happen. Before the full-scale invasion, young men in Ukraine were required to serve twelve to eighteen months in the army, but as Russia invaded, Ukraine did away with that policy. The state instead implemented new conscription practices, allow-ing the government to summon for service any able-bodied man between the ages of twenty-seven and sixty, including those without former military experience. Later, Ukraine would lower this age to twenty-five years. Men would often receive a summons to report to a recruitment center, after which they would be medically examined and sent off for a short stint in training. Early on, many men and women volunteered without a summons, a surge that sustained the army in the first months of the war.

Leonid had completed his compulsory military service in the previous years. Though he was not summoned, seeing the situation deteriorate so rapidly in his hometown compelled him to rejoin the ranks.

On March 5, Leonid drove across town to wish his mother a happy birthday. It confused Maria that he'd risked exposure dur-ing an air raid simply to see her, but he insisted on going there in person.

Early the next morning, Leonid gently woke Maria. "We need to say goodbye," he whispered. Still groggy, she shrugged him off. "Maria, it's time to say goodbye," he insisted. He had already been out that morning on a reconnaissance mission. She didn't understand. "What are you talking about?" She yawned.

"Let's say goodbye. I need to go."

She pushed her eyes open, and he looked at her with a seriousness that scared her. He did not look away.

"No, no, Leonid," she whispered. She would have to talk sense into him, beg him to stay. "No, Lyonya," she said, using his familiar shortened name. "You can't leave me," she pleaded, "David, our life. What goes on there is not for you. Let's leave together, we can try to get out through the humanitarian corridor, we can go as a family."

He cast his eyes down. "I have to go, Maria." Watching him carefully, she knew he was serious—she had never seen him this resolute, as though his face had turned to stone, as though nothing she did, no threats, no pleading, no weeping, could keep him there. He tried to embrace her, and she stiffened, flaring with anger and grief. He turned to walk out into the stairwell.

"I was in a stupor, I just lay there, stuck. I didn't understand," Maria said.

Her parents then told her to go chase after him, talk to him. Following him into the stairwell, Maria caught up with him. Leonid was upset. He twitched with agitation and emotion.

"Maybe you'll at least hug me?" he said, and she did, and the pain sliced through them. Before he could change his mind or she could say anything, he turned and jogged down the stairwell.

Telling me the story several months later, her voice wavered with emotion: "I truly did not think he would go. But I watched him leave."

The next day, Leonid's father came to check on them and bring some food.

"Where's Leonid?" he asked.

Maria realized that Leonid had not told anyone else, not even his parents when he'd gone to see them.

"Where is Leonid?" her father-in-law asked again.

"He went to fight," Maria said.

With Leonid gone, Maria knew she would need to fortify herself. Despite her stubbornness and resilience, she had come to rely on him in their relationship. Without him, Maria knew she could not expect anyone to help her anymore.

By the time Leonid left, her parents and sister, along with her sister's husband and young son, were staying with her in the same basement. Their basement was large, and to get to the part of it where they could sit down, where they had built a small encampment, they had to walk through dark tunnels, feeling their way along the cold stone walls. Her mother did not hear well and her father did not walk well, and Maria's days quickly evolved into the singular pursuit of food, water, and heat. *I will do everything now*, she told herself constantly, like a mantra. *I can do everything now. I will be the strong one.* Later that day Leonid's colleague came and brought Maria a letter from Leonid. It was a short note, but he wrote that everything was okay with him, he was safe and healthy, he was thinking about them, he loved them. She knew he felt guilty for leaving, she could hear it in his note. If he would just come back, she thought, they could have a long talk and sort it all out. But with every passing day, he didn't. She got very little concrete information from him—only an occasional check-in to say that he was okay and he loved them—and she was furious.

Though they never took off their coats or shoes in case they had to run, the children screamed constantly from cold. Maria and her family tried occupying them in the basement by playing games, telling stories, and rocking them to sleep. But explosions roared outside relentlessly, frightening and waking the children. They could not let the kids watch TV or play on tablets or phones because any battery life they had on their devices was a precious commodity reserved exclusively for communication.

They became dirty quickly, and there was no water to wash themselves. Maria crawled out of the basement a couple of times a day to make a fire in the courtyard and prepare soup with potatoes and canned fish. They also boiled pasta and fried it with tomatoes and onions. Sick to their stomachs with anxiety and constantly cold, Maria and her sister couldn't bring themselves to eat much. They were both breastfeeding and started to lose their milk supply, which further distressed the children, who batted at their breasts begging for milk that was not coming.

Every day was the same: they were awakened by the sounds of shelling, a distinct metallic whir followed by concussive blasts at impact, then a couple of hours of silence. They waited every moment for it to begin again, wondering if the shelling would be closer this time. When the bombing began once more, she'd go so rigid that the edges of all her body's muscles would ache. Taking a deep breath, she'd run to David, pick him up, hold him close, sing him songs, and rock him gently, a meditative motion she did as much for her own comfort as for his.

Periodically, at her own risk, she took David to the apartment to run around for ten minutes or so. "It drove me crazy that I was sitting there in the basement," she said. "It was so dark, my eyes couldn't see at all when I came out into the light."

When a bar of service appeared on her phone, she'd receive a handful of messages—from her sister in Kharkiv, from friends who had already evacuated, from Leonid. He would not say where he was fighting, but she knew he was in the city. Witnessing the daily carnage, he urged her and the family to leave Mariupol as soon as they could.

After he left on March 6, Leonid came back in person three times: once on March 8 to wish her a happy International Women's Day—

a major holiday in former Soviet countries—then on March 11, and
finally on March 13. Each time it was, as Maria writes, "for literally
one minute," except the last visit, when he was able to stay for five.
He met her outside the basement, hugged her, and ran quickly to
the cellar to see David, swooping in, picking David up, and hugging
him tight, trying to make him laugh. The last time Leonid came,
he ran to the basement, where David was sleeping, and laid his face
near his son's for a moment.

What kind of conversation can two people have in one minute?
She told him that she had been making a fire in the courtyard, what
they were eating, if they'd had any news from her sister. He told
her to leave the city immediately, as soon as they could arrange an
evacuation vehicle. He'd meet them wherever they went as soon as
it was over. As he shifted to leave, they hugged, and she looked away
so that she didn't fall apart and cling to his clothes, begging him to
stay like a woman possessed. Then he ran off.

"I didn't know what he had become," she wrote later. "I didn't
understand at all. I didn't understand the essence of the disaster."

Because the city was constantly, indiscriminately shelled, leaving
it posed enormous risk. People who tried to escape were killed every
day, hit by shells or shrapnel or snipers. At checkpoints, Russian soldiers often forced evacuees to undress and examined their tattoos.
They confiscated phones and searched texts, emails, and photos for
any indication of Ukrainian patriotism. Maria was twenty-three years
old, and small. She worried that at a checkpoint she would have
no capacity to defend herself against rape, assault, or abduction,
especially because she would travel with her parents, both of whom
were in poor health and could do little to protect her. They decided
they'd wait a few more days to see if things calmed down. "How
long could this unending bombardment possibly continue?" she
wondered. But Leonid insisted that they must get out—that things
would never return to normal, that there was no life left to be had

in Mariupol. By then the police force in Mariupol had collapsed, and the next day, the Mariupol Drama Theater was bombed. A thousand civilians had sheltered underneath the building and several hundred were killed.

By mid-March, corpses littered the street like newspapers, victims of violence, hunger, or untreated infections. People were scared to look too closely. What if you recognized them? Eventually the Russian troops occupying certain parts of the city began collecting the bodies in trucks and depositing them in the city square.

Maria occasionally returned to the apartment to retrieve toys or secure the windows and doors, trying to keep it pristine. She still held out hope that eventually they'd return to that apartment and resume their life. From there, she caught broader views of the city. "I had a view from the window, I saw absolutely everything," she wrote. "The whole city was burning." She could see, in the distance, one of the large steel factories in town, Azovstal, glowing. Smoke rose in a continuous black cloud over the horizon. At night, the sky glowed pink, and buildings crackled in flames or smoldered, collapsing piece by piece.

By the nineteenth of March, Maria decided they needed to leave. They had no more candles or matches. "We were just walking by inertia, in the darkness. I was trying to feel my way to the doors to get out of the basement." She and her sister gathered their possessions in the apartment, letting the children get a better sleep in the beds a final time before departing in the morning. Through the middle of the night, Maria and her sister pumped breast milk for the journey to ensure that they would not need to lift their shirts and could calm the babies with bottles in a pinch. As they pumped in silence, they heard a whistle and planes roaring overhead. Somewhere near them an air assault was underway, and when the bomb dropped, they felt their building sway, the furniture sliding across the floor.

For most an evacuation ride was extremely difficult to secure. Though drivers came with their cars and buses from throughout Ukraine to help in the effort, the route was dangerous, and drivers began charging high prices—several hundred dollars—for rides just beyond the city limits. Maria and Leonid's car had been damaged by a shell, so it was not reliable, but Leonid's father agreed to take them. Only part of their group—Maria, David, and Maria's dad—could fit on the first trip; the others, Maria's sister, nephew, brother-in-law, and mom, would need to wait until Leonid's father got back and was ready for another trip. It would be, they hoped, just a day or two. With a white ribbon tied to the car to indicate they were civilians, they inched through the city toward the checkpoint. They lived on the outskirts, and it was a short drive to the edge of the city. "As we pulled out onto the main street, I saw that every house was burned down. There were tanks lying around on the roads, buses overturned, people were digging graves at every step— every step, wherever there was a free spot." Their city was gone, replaced with ghosts. She went on: "Where there had been trees, or in the fields, where there used to be just gardens, now bodies are just lying there. And people walk, people walk on them."

They crossed through fifteen checkpoints to leave the city. Russian soldiers rifled through her bags, patted her body, looked at her son. They made men strip naked and stole food and belongings. After hours of waiting, Maria's party crossed the city limits into a village on their way to Zaporizhzhya, the closest major city under Ukrainian control, 120 miles away. She had never been to Zaporizhzhya. In fact, she had never been much of anywhere at all. Except for a few short trips to neighboring cities and one to Kyiv, she'd spent her whole life in the city behind her, just like her parents, just like her grandmother Vera before her.

"She is nearby," Maria said, "I know this for certain."

YULIA

Konstantinivka to Dnipro, Ukraine

AT HOME IN Konstantinivka, Yulia spent the first six weeks of the war trying to remain calm, working on her felting projects, and trying every day to get their oldest daughter, Olya, out of Kharkiv. Occasional explosions rocked the small town, but thankfully there had been no troops. But in Kharkiv, where Olya studied and lived with her boyfriend, Sasha, relentless bombardments were unleashed on the first day of the war. The battle for Kharkiv—a key strategic city near Ukraine's northeastern border with Russia—began in Olya's neighborhood, northern Saltivka. Under brutal, constant fire, Olya and Sasha spent nearly the entire month in an old Soviet bunker built in the basement of a factory after World War II. It was constructed to protect against a nuclear explosion and was meant to accommodate one shift of the plant's workers, about fifty people. Residents in her neighborhood packed themselves tightly in, and around two hundred people crowded together in the dark, damp shelter for days on end. Each morning, if there was cell service,

Yulia called Olya to see if she and Sasha were still alive. Bombs and missiles exploded almost without ceasing, and within a month, northern Saltivka was almost completely wiped from the earth—nearly every building had been flattened, and what had been a sleepy, densely populated suburb turned into a charcoaled ghost town.

When Olya and Sasha managed to escape to an evacuation point, they headed in the direction of Konstantinivka. Although the town was in the heart of the Donbas—not far from occupied Donetsk—at that point it was much safer and calmer than Kharkiv. In Konstantinivka, shops and pharmacies still operated, and gas, electricity, and water pipelines and other infrastructure had not been destroyed.

As days passed, the front lines crept toward Konstantinivka, and they all decided Sasha should go west to stay with relatives. Despite the danger, Yulia, Oleg, and the girls would stay. After all, it was their home, the location of their well-established life, their animals, garden, and land. Where would they go?

When they dropped Sasha off at the nearest train station, in Kramatorsk, thirty minutes from their home, there were at least two thousand people, mostly women with children and older people. Everyone was stressed and anxious: the surrounding towns and villages were constantly subjected to violent shelling, and families were split up at the station so women could take their children to safety in the West while their husbands stayed behind.

Volunteers tried to organize the queues, but the station was far past capacity, and people stood in large crowds awaiting evacuation trains that would take them to safety.

Nonetheless, winter was beginning to ease, and the sun shone brightly. People sitting on benches leaned their heads back for a moment to take in the new, healing warmth. A group of kids played tag while their moms tried to figure out their next steps, and vol-

unteers treated people to hot tea near a tent with phone chargers.
Yulia approached the volunteer tent to ask where the line for their
train was, telling Olya to go get Sasha and gather their things.

Standing in line to talk with a volunteer, Yulia took in a deep
breath to calm her nerves; the station's environment felt desperate,
but the air felt good. She was not wearing a heavy coat for the first
time in weeks. As soon as they confirmed that Sasha was safely on
the train, they could go home and begin preparing their gardens
for spring. Earlier that week she planted blueberries and a new va-
riety of currant in a small corner of the yard. The soil had always
been restorative for Yulia, and as she watched Olya walk away, she
planned what they might do in the garden that afternoon. Perhaps
they'd find some relief there, she thought, just before hearing the
hiss of a sinister, cold whistle above her head.

Frozen, confused, for just a split second, Yulia realized that the
sound was an approaching projectile. She scanned for a place to
take cover and darted to a nearby stand of pine trees, crouching in
a dirt bed beneath their limbs. Then came a powerful explosion,
like the sound of a whip multiplied by a hundred thousand, and
she was thrown by the shock wave into a bench where two elderly
women were sitting. One of them was wounded in the head, and
her blood splattered onto Yulia's face. They managed to look briefly
into each other's eyes, horrified. Yulia tried to crawl away, covering
her head with her hands, but realized there was a problem with
her legs. She had just pushed herself up with her hands when there
was another explosion on the other side of the station, where her
family was.

Yulia said the two explosions were followed by dead silence,
though she likely lost her hearing in the aftermath. Raising her
head a little, she saw that the people standing and sitting opposite
her were covered in blood. Then a terrible howling began. Everyone who had been standing near the volunteer tent offering free

tea was dead. Yulia pushed herself to a sitting position to look at her legs. On the ground next to her were her broken bones and yellow marrow mixed with muscle and blood. She said it looked like kasha—porridge. She tried to yell for someone to give her a scarf or something with which to gather the fragments of her legs and stanch the bleeding. A pool of blood formed beneath her. But she was in shock and could hardly open her mouth. Even had she gotten out a scream, it would have been difficult to hear her above the wailing of wounded people all around her and those frantically searching for their loved ones. Remembering that sound, she said, was worse than remembering the pain.

For an interminable ten seconds, Yulia stared at her legs, desperately considering what she should do. That something was very wrong was obvious, but her mind buzzed with another potential tragedy: Were Oleg, Olya, and Sasha alive?

Finally, she said out loud the only thing that was self-evident: "Legs—my legs."

Realizing there was no one to help, she decided she should first try to make a tourniquet and apply it where her legs were hemorrhaging. After that she would think further. Her tight jeans held in some pieces of her legs, but what wasn't contained by the jeans was now entirely detached from her body, covered in pine needles and dirt on the earth around her. She took off her sweater and pulled it tightly around her right leg, which was the most damaged. To slow the bleeding on the left leg, she removed her belt and tightened it around the wound. As she worked, she noticed that the middle finger of her left hand had also been torn off and hung only by the skin.

She could barely hear the phone in her pocket ringing. It was Olya. They were all alive and desperate to find Yulia.

"I am almost exactly where you left me," Yulia said, glimpsing Olya's pink jacket in the distance and waving her arms to catch Olya's attention.

As Olya approached, her eyes opened wide as they focused on the pool of blood that Yulia lay in. Olya began shrieking and sobbing, but Yulia interrupted, knowing they could not spare a single moment to succumb to their emotions. Olya understood and gathered herself before rushing to find Oleg and Sasha.

When they arrived, they slid Oleg's jacket under Yulia to lift her up. Oleg, Olya, Sasha, and a nearby policeman dragged Yulia to their car, put her in the back seat, and sped to the nearest hospital. The windows and mirror on the passenger side were broken and dangling, occasionally shedding shards of glass onto the passengers.

On the car ride to the hospital, Yulia was overwhelmed not by her pain but by her thirst. Later she learned that the volume of blood she'd lost—and was losing—triggered the hormone system that regulates blood pressure and electrolyte balance, resulting in her central nervous system responding with a profound craving for water.

"I wanted to drink so unbearably," she said, "as if I would die of thirst and not of my wounds."

When they arrived at the hospital, the corridors were filled with the wounded. Sixty people were killed at the Kramatorsk railway station, and more than a hundred injured. They lined the hallways, and many lay in the middle of the floor, directly on the tiles.

Frantic nurses and doctors stepped around bodies to get more bandages and towels. A trembling nurse tried to register Yulia by writing her data with a permanent marker on Yulia's shoulder, but she kept making mistakes and crossing out what she had written. Yulia's mouth was so dry from blood loss that she could not clearly pronounce her last name. Yulia asked for water, just a sip to moisten her mouth, knowing they probably would not give it to her because she would soon receive anesthesia and they would not want her to vomit. She begged for anesthesia, but there was still someone else ahead of her to be seen by the anesthesiologist—a child, a young girl. She died while Yulia waited.

Yulia could still move the toes of her left foot, and though she was barely conscious, she knew that she was the only one who could advocate for that leg. Before getting anesthesia, she told the nurses and doctors near her that she could move the toes, that there was still hope for that leg, and asked them to try to save it if they could. While Yulia was in the operating room, Oleg helped to unload other wounded people from the ambulances. Many were already dead.

Yulia lost enough blood that the anesthesiologist thought that that might kill her. During the operation, doctors gave Yulia a blood transfusion and worked to try to manage her injuries. Facing hallways of wailing patients, the small crew of surgeons did away with specialization; the attending surgeon performed whatever surgery was needed, even if she had only read about it in a book. They focused their efforts on stopping bleeding, sewing up what could be patched, and cutting off what was hopeless. For more specialized work, Yulia would need to go to a larger hospital with more resources. Out of surgery, nurses made sure she was clean and bandaged well. They gave her opioids to manage the pain. After several hours of observation, the small hospital in Kramatorsk arranged for her immediate transfer to Dnipro, a major city five hours to the west with a large hospital. There a team of doctors waited for Yulia.

What might take some time to sink in for Oleg and the girls was already clear to Yulia: everything was different now. They would not be going home together for a long while. Yulia asked Oleg to please return first to Konstantinivka before meeting her in Dnipro. He would secure their house, make sure the animals were okay, take the dog, talk with the neighbors, and ensure that they could care for the garden and birds. They needed to collect the girls' schoolbooks, some clothing, and all their toiletries. But this was not a vacation: Oleg was to board up the windows, turn off the water, lock all the doors with padlocks, remove everything valuable, and retrieve their important documents, in case, God forbid, some unfriendly soldier tried to make their home his own. Yulia had one other request: could Oleg please bring one of the flowerpots filled with their soil.

POLINA

Lviv, Ukraine

WAKING UP IN Lviv on their first day back in Ukraine, Polina and John slipped on their clothes, stepped outside, and set off to find something to do. The city was familiar to them. They had both lived in Lviv at different times and could navigate to all the well-known spots—the old town with its cobblestone streets and colorful main square, the opera house, the universities, and several large, tree-lined parks. Ukrainians are very proud of Lviv, and rightly so: the city is quaint and charming and unequivocally the least Soviet-looking major city in Ukraine, with a robust café culture, labyrinthine paths lined with Habsburg architecture, and a pervading air of intellectualism.

Walking through the center of town, they passed a group of middle-aged men sandbagging the monument to King Danylo, the king of Kyivan Rus' during the Mongol invasion in the mid-thirteenth century. The bronze monument shows Danylo riding on a horse midstride, his arms outstretched, finger pointing. The whole monument was vulnerable to an attack on the city center, but especially the horse's slender legs and tail as well as Danylo's head and reaching arm. The men around the statue heaved sacks of sand onto its base, filling the space between the horse's legs and between Danylo's stomach and the horse's neck, and then building out a sandbag barrier kept in place by wooden beams.

Lviv was alive with volunteerism. In a week, the city transformed into one of Ukraine's major centers for displaced people coming from Eastern and Southern Ukraine, with several hundred thousand people making their way there on their journey to somewhere else in Europe, and several hundred thousand hunkering down to live out the rest of the war. The city was crowded. It was difficult to find lodging, especially for those with little money, and it was even more difficult to find work. Every conceivable space in the city was being transformed: all schools, churches, gymnasiums, local businesses, yoga and dance studios, auditoriums, museums. Any free indoor space was liable to become someone's bed, even if there was no bedding to put on it; old women slept in their coats with their purses as pillows.

A week earlier, Polina and John had watched the war play out on their cell phones in LA. Now they walked through Lviv, having given up their jobs and most of their possessions, looking for something to do. Aid organizations were everywhere, and Polina and John approached different organizations asking if they could help, but they were surprised to be repeatedly turned away. The city was overwhelmed by displaced people, but it was also overwhelmed by volunteers. After a couple of days, they decided to go see what was going on at their church. They had been to a dozen churches and organizations in the previous few days asking to help but hadn't thought of going to their own. They assumed that if anyone had their ducks in a row, it was probably members of the Church of Jesus Christ of Latter-day Saints, who had made themselves expert in disaster response and relief aid. "I remember so clearly when the wildfires happened in 2009 in California," John said, "there were hundreds of people the next day who came to help, literally working to find people's lost wedding rings and solving problems. It was so organized that I assumed for some reason that that was happening here, but it wasn't."

When they showed up, a member of the church congregation came to the door. Lviv had a local LDS congregation, a few hundred members, most of whom were Ukrainian, with only a handful of American members and missionaries. "Are you guys refugees, do you need help?" he asked.

"Actually, we're here to help, if you need it," Polina said.

"Oh, we need it," he said. They stepped inside. The place was crawling with people. It was a mess. "We need soap, we need towels, we need blankets, we need pillows, we need sheets, we need teakettles, we need dried pasta, we need pasta sauce, we need oatmeal, we need baby food." He kept listing things, almost without taking a breath. "We need help."

The building was relatively new, constructed in the early 2000s, and had all the components of a standard meetinghouse. On the side of the large chapel where the main Sunday sacrament meeting took place were classrooms, restrooms, and what church members call a "cultural hall": an all-purpose room with a basketball hoop, used for potlucks and talent shows and sports. Off to the foyer's side was a tiny kitchen with a flat-top two-burner electric stove, a small refrigerator, a metal sink the size of a serving bowl, and a two-person table.

All through late February, people showed up at the church's front steps from the train station or bus station, bags in hand, making their third or fourth or fifth stop in search of a place to stay. They wanted to spend the night. But the local church struggled to know how the building should be used and who should be in charge. Whereas many Protestant congregations make decisions for themselves, the Church of Jesus Christ of Latter-day Saints operates according to a specific hierarchy in which local congregations have local leaders but they are overseen by regional leaders, and those regional leaders are overseen by still other leaders, all the way back to church headquarters in Salt Lake City, Utah. Many of the Lviv leaders—laypeople who had been assigned their roles only temporarily, as is customary in the church—had fled with their families in the first days of the war.

The bureaucratic chain of command had been disrupted, and congregations struggled to adjust and make decisions. The stakes were so high and the pace of the war so swift that thinking about how to staff and organize the church building was something that members just couldn't take on. But the building—centrally located, with so much available space—was already full of displaced people trying to get by in Lviv for a few nights before traveling on to Poland, and it was chaos. The fridge was full of people's random bottles of milk and sandwiches from the train. People competed to use the two burners to make fifteen different dinners, and others staked out corners of the church where they set up private encampments.

Polina and John were struck by how hard it was to keep systems running in wartime. Without someone to organize the space and establish rules and protocols, those who showed up would continue to feel that they needed to fend for themselves. Instead of providing a peaceful, orderly shelter, the building would remain a microcosm of conflict.

"We can help here," John thought. They knew the area, they knew how to plan meals, make beds, get groceries. At first Polina and John thought they'd just provide groceries. But after they made the first meal, they decided they'd come back the next day to make breakfast. While they were there, they planned dinner, too, and then breakfast again. The local members of the congregation who had been trying to run the shelter were relieved to have some help and to pass off many responsibilities—they had their own homes and displaced relatives to worry about. Polina and John made some rules, established quiet times, figured out a system for how to share the fridge, assigned sleeping areas to maximize efficiency. Soon they were going back every day to prepare breakfast, lunch, and dinner, and within a few days, they knew they wouldn't stop.

At first Polina and John and the small church team housed thirty people, then fifty, then seventy-five. To expand their operation, they needed specific tools—a washing machine to launder bedding after people left, a food storage system, a set of pots and pans, and dozens of mattresses so that everyone had a designated spot. They set up beds in the classrooms, the cultural hall, and the chapel and made sure each sleeping station had clean sheets, a comforter, and a pillow. In the kitchen, which John described as "one of the worst I've ever been in," they had to work in small, alternating teams to prepare and serve three meals a day for seventy-five people. The stove had two burners, but only one worked well, and to bring a large pot of water to boil for spaghetti could take an hour.

At the store, they could usually buy just enough for one day, because ingredients for three meals of seventy-five portions were a huge haul for two people who had to carry the bags full of potatoes, carrots, eggs, and rice. Back from the store, they prepped dinner in the afternoon and into the evening, served it, cleaned it up, then got ready a cold breakfast of yogurt, open-faced sandwiches with cheese and meat, and fruit. In the morning, they assigned someone to set out the breakfast while they went shopping again for food or other necessities—usually a four- or five-hour affair—before they came back to prepare lunch and do the whole thing again.

Their menus were simple. With the city so overpopulated,

shelves emptied quickly, and they had to work with what they could find. They tried to cook only familiar Ukrainian comfort food. In a new environment far from home, in a foreign church building, the refugees wanted what they had eaten as children, the kind of food their grandmothers prepared: buckwheat, potatoes, ground meat cutlets, soup, cabbage salad, and tea with simple cookies.

Polina and John worked with a small team: within a week, Polina's family had left Kyiv and joined them. They had found other housing in Lviv, but every day, her parents, two brothers, and teenage sister came to the building to prep food and wash sheets. Polina's hairdresser from Kyiv also joined with his girlfriend.

To fund their efforts, John and Polina tried to raise money from friends and family in the United States. News of their efforts spread by word of mouth, and people in the United States, who were anxious to help Ukraine in those first weeks, sent donations through Venmo and PayPal. Polina began a Telegram group to keep people updated on how the money was spent, sending daily updates—in Ukrainian, Russian, and English—on the activities in the shelter. On March 24, she wrote:

> Hello everyone! We had a very busy day today. We prepared breakfast, for dinner we cooked chicken broth and buckwheat with meat. Everyone was full! Also, today we ordered 30 bedding sets that we can use for those who stay with us. We have a lot of new people who are staying with us, 18 of them came from Mariupol. We also managed to buy medicine that will go to Kyiv for elderly people who stayed there. Thank you for this support! Because of you we can help those people. Today we spent: 25 631 UAH-872$.

They put flyers up in the train station: "If you need a place to stay in Lviv, come to this address and call Polina." Soon Polina was getting calls at all hours of the day, and not just from people in the train station in Lviv. Pictures of the flyer circulated around Ukraine, and people in Eastern Ukraine who had not yet left home would call to ask if the shelter had space for a few more.

Some people would call Polina just to talk. Once, she got a call at seven in the morning, just as she was waking up, from an old woman in Mykolaiv, a town in Eastern Ukraine that had been under near-constant shelling since the beginning of the war.

"Hello, is this Polina?"

"Yes, hello, this is Polina."

"Hi, this is Tatiana. I am in Mykolaiv. How are you?"

"I'm okay, thank you, how are you? Do you need a place to stay?"

"Yes, perhaps, but I mostly just called to talk." And she told Polina her whole life story, how she came to live in Mykolaiv, her children, her grandchildren, her former husband, her house, why she was reluctant to leave but felt she needed to.

Polina asked: "So do you need a place to stay? When are you coming?"

And Tatiana responded: "Oh, I'm still figuring it out, but I don't think I'm going to come." A week or so later, the same woman would call again to check on Polina: "I'm so worried about you," she would whisper into the phone from her house in Mykolaiv, not far from the shelling. "Are you guys okay over there?"

The church shelter functioned as a stopover point. When someone arrived at the church's door, Polina or John or one of their team met them. They told them the rules of the place: No one can store personal food in the church refrigerator—that is for food preparation only. Keep your space tidy. No loud music. Wait until everybody has dished up food before getting seconds. Help with cleaning duties. Do not fight or argue with other people. All languages are allowed.

Most people in the shelter came from Eastern and Southern

Ukraine, and each carried themself differently, coping in a myriad of ways. Some told stories about seeing bodies, about watching buildings fall onto people, about walking many kilometers, from village to village, escaping their city. Some did not talk, just sat on their mattresses and rocked, looking at the floor. Some would come to the serving table, get their food, go to a corner, and eat as if they had never had a meal in their life. Others cried constantly, their eyes red and swollen for days. Some chatted frivolously, made new friends, and played games in the almost endless free time; others spoke of nothing but the war. Some focused all their energy on finding a route to Europe and a place to stay once there; some couldn't even think about it.

Because the borders were not open for men between the ages of eighteen and sixty, many women came alone with their children. On occasion, whole families arrived at the shelter before they split up, the mother and kids going across the border to somewhere else in Europe, the father returning to join the military after he saw them off.

One mother, a kindergarten teacher, stayed at the church with her two young boys, and she would repeat scripts with her children throughout the day: "Papa is not here, Papa is fighting. He is protecting us. People are protecting us and all the other people in Ukraine, and everything will be okay." She led the other children in games in the church's children room, teaching them songs to be brave and rhymes to help them when they felt scared. She taught everyone to repeat what she told her sons, and they said it like a mantra: "People are protecting us and all the other people in Ukraine, and everything will be okay."

When there was an air raid, a car with a megaphone drove through the streets saying "Air alarm! Air alarm! Take shelter." Then air raid sirens—installed around the city after World War II— sounded.

"It's an analog sound, it's something you're not used to hearing anymore," John said. It winds up from a low pitch to a higher, ringing in a blare, then descends again. "It feels like you've heard these sounds before, but only in movies, and it's weird to realize that they still have these speakers up from World War II. When you hear the sound, it really shakes you, especially the first time you hear it. It's hard to explain how truly scary it is. But then, somehow, a week later, you hear the same thing and you're just like, okay, all right, it's fine."

Polina and John made a rule that air raid alarms were to be respected. In the first weeks of the war, people became used to the alarms and started to disregard them, but John and Polina felt a responsibility to everyone in the shelter, and they implemented a mandate that everyone would go to the basement for every air raid.

"That was a commitment that we kept," John said, "and I don't know of anyone who was doing that, because it is so much effort and it really sucks." Responding to the alarms with children was a particular feat, especially children who were sensitive to overstimulation. Sometimes they would be down in the cellar for hours, people's phones dying, kids sleeping on the floor. If they were close to a mealtime, they'd serve food down there.

The costs of keeping the shelter running added up quickly, even though they prepared relatively simple food and the whole team donated all their time. Most donations they received from people—even a generous gift of a thousand dollars—would last only a couple of days. When donation funds ran short, they spent their own money, just to keep the system moving and to make sure there were always three meals a day.

As the weather warmed and winter turned to spring, they found themselves accustomed to the shelter rhythms. Food prep, shopping, washing linens, welcoming new people, bidding farewell to those leaving for the next part of their journey through the war.

One afternoon, Polina watched as a young dad spun his baby daughter around in the foyer. He was there with his wife and kids, wanting to get them settled before he reported to his army summons. The baby cooed, and he held her next to his face, kissing her nose and rubbing his forehead against her cheeks. He was saying goodbye.

VITALY

Kolomiya, Ukraine

VITALY AND HIS family arrived in Kolomiya in Western Ukraine on March 8, with just their backpacks, his stepson's cat, and the last remaining cash from the short-lived coffee shop. He'd seen the Russian army advance south from Belarus and western Russia and, in a swift land grab, occupy Borodyanka and other Kyiv suburbs within days. But the Russians never made it to Kyiv, despite advancing within miles of the capital's downtown. In the first two weeks of the full-scale invasion, Kyiv's northern neighborhoods were shelled, and the mayor claimed that nearly two million people—half of Kyiv's population—had fled. Those who stayed made Molotov cocktails and hid out in basements and in subway stations, which had been designed and constructed primarily during the Cold War and were to serve as shelters in case of nuclear war. The government banned the sale of alcohol in the city and handed out nearly eighteen thousand guns to residents of neighborhoods proximate to advancing troops.

Vitaly's friend Artem and his family, with whom they'd sheltered before fleeing town, left for Lviv, and within a few weeks, Artem's wife and son went farther west to Germany. By mid-March, Artem was summoned to join the Ukrainian Armed Forces. "He could not forgive his ruined Borodyanka," Vitaly said. Artem did not refuse the summons, saying that after he had seen what he had seen, he would go. He trained for a few weeks and was sent to the front lines in Eastern Ukraine.

In Kolomiya, Vitaly wandered around the city like an orphaned child. "I just started walking. I had so much nervous energy, I had to move, but I had nowhere to go," he said. The shelter was full of hundreds of people like him, people who fled their homes and lost everything. Everyone had a horrible story to tell. Everyone was disturbed. In the shelter his grief compounded, so he tried to keep busy to keep despair from taking firm hold of his mind and heart. He helped with shelter responsibilities, unloading food and supplies from the back of trucks and helping to organize them.

But his nervous energy did him no favors when there wasn't a job to do. Lying on a sleeping bag on the floor, his mind drifted to the image of his apartment building under a plume of smoke. Without warning, screams would fill his head. He tried shaking his head to get the sounds to stop, or he'd jump up and down in place as though he were an Etch A Sketch with scary pictures on it, and if shaken enough, the screen would reset to blank. At night, when he tried to go to sleep, he promised himself he would rebuild the coffee shop, and, drifting off, he dreamed of the types of appliances he would buy, the food he would serve, the things he would say to people who came into the shop . . .

On March 22, the Ukrainian army launched a counteroffensive in the Kyiv region, pushing the Russians from the city's outskirts and retaking towns and villages throughout the region. The counteroffensive shed new light on the horrors of the occupation. By early April, images of the atrocities in Bucha, Borodyanka, and Ir-pin flooded international media—mass graves filled with mutilated bodies and corpses lining the street. Many of the victims had been tied up and shot at close range. But Vitaly was undeterred: by April 3, he was on his way back home, as though pulled by a mag-netic force.

When he arrived in Borodyanka and walked through the streets for the first time since running away, he hardly breathed. His chest felt tight and pulled against him. It was as though his heart was try-ing to push through his ribs to see it all for itself. When he was able to cry, after many hours, he howled like an animal. "My heart ached," he said. He was not invoking a cliché—his heart *literally* ached, and he began visiting a pharmacy for medication to manage his cardiac palpitations and pain.

The whole area was mined, so he walked cautiously, and he stayed in the apartment of some friends who'd fled in the first days of the war. If their apartment was still standing, they said, he was welcome to stay in it. When he arrived, the windows were shattered, but everything else was relatively intact: the damage came from blast waves. Within an hour, Vitaly swept up glass and debris and threw out furniture and hung plastic over the holes in the windows. He began working without breaks, almost compulsively.

The morning after arriving in Borodyanka, he went to the site of his apartment building and started digging in the rubble with his hands. He threw bricks and small pieces of concrete into piles, trying to sort debris by muscle memory from his recycling days. He didn't really know what he was doing, but he had to dig. His urge to dig was desperate and almost ungovernable. He carried chunks of concrete, pieces of wood, and sheets of metal to piles near the street. He tore through mounds of bricks. His father had laid these bricks fifty years earlier. Vitaly wanted to touch them all. This place was al-most as familiar to him as his own body—and he to it. "Every single cat and dog knows me here," he wrote. As he dug, he went as deep as he could without the use of an excavator. For days he went back, waking in the morning after a chilly, uncomfortable sleep, slipping on his shoes and, without eating, making his way back.

Sorting through the rubble was a way of sorting through his own mind. Within a few days, he came across a mangled but familiar object—the coffee machine for which he had saved his money for so many years, covered in dirt, chipped, and almost unrecognizable. As he dug, he found objects more or less intact and felt a vague thrill at seeing something that had survived, a feeling followed by a wash of anguish when he imagined those objects sitting peacefully inside a warm apartment two months earlier. He found an Orthodox icon. Later, when one of Vitaly's sons from his marriage in the mid-1990s came to town and joined in the digging, the son located more of their icons, which had hung in Vitaly's brother's room. Holding the dirty objects in his hands, Vitaly wanted to keep at it. Maybe he could prove to himself that the past was not a matter of memories alone.

In the evening he would draw. He sat at the desk in the apartment, and on some scratch paper he'd sketch Borodyanka, the way things used to look, so he wouldn't forget. He was skilled with the pencil—his sketches were nuanced and detailed. When he was growing up, drawing had been a way to cope in school—when he was bored out of his mind, he filled every homework page with doodles. When I asked him if he ever took drawing lessons, he responded cheekily that he had learned to draw in school, but not because the school was trying to teach him. He drew mythical scenes of cottages in the forest or birds in the sky, but sometimes he also drew from real life, and especially, since the war began, he drew to memorialize. At night, he'd lean his cell phone flashlight against the wall and draw everything he could remember.

Drifting back in memory, he pictured the apartment when he

was nine or ten years old and the parties his parents used to throw, how his mom would bake all sorts of cakes and pies, his dad would tell jokes, his uncle would play the accordion, and everyone sang melancholy ballads around the kitchen table. When they got a TV, his dad and uncle sat and watched Dynamo Kyiv, the capital's professional soccer team. His dad was a crazy Dynamo Kyiv fan and followed all the seasons and games, the players, the trades, up until the day he died of cancer in 2018. His relationship with Vitaly was often difficult, and now, years after his death, Vitaly sketched the apartment where they had lived together for so many years and wondered why fathers and sons struggled to understand one another.

When I asked Vitaly to send me photos of himself and his family when he was a child, his response was quick: "I can't," he said. "They all burned."

MARIA

Zaporizhzhya to Ternopil, Ukraine

AFTER TRAVELING SUCCESSFULLY through fifteen Russian block posts on their way to Zaporizhzhya, Maria, David, and her father sheltered in a small Russian-held village twenty kilometers outside Mariupol. The village had only two roads, thirty houses total, and Maria had never heard of it. It had fallen to Russian forces in the first hours of the war and for a month, the residents of the village had watched and listened from a near distance as Mariupol was systematically destroyed. Every day people fleeing Mariupol came through, and villagers offered an extra room, or bed, or couch. Maria, David, and her father slept on a narrow bed—all three of them together—in the house of an old woman. It was uncomfortable, but it was warm and quiet. There were no explosions the whole night.

The next day, Maria's father-in-law, Leonid's dad, drove Maria's mother, sister, nephew, and brother-in-law out of the village and they made their way to the house of another woman, who took them in and fed them a simple meal. Supply chains had been destroyed, and tiny villages such as this suffered extreme conditions; the stores were empty, and people ate whatever was available—in this case, eggs and milk. Getting beyond the village and into Ukrainian territory proved difficult. Leonid's father was nearly out of fuel, and he worried that if he took them to Ukrainian-held Zaporizhzhya he would never make it back home to his wife. He left Maria and her family in the village and set off back to Mariupol.

An evacuation vehicle took them into Zaporizhzhya a few days later, and as they entered Ukrainian territory, full cell service bars appeared on Maria's phone. She stared at them for a long time. She hadn't seen this in weeks, and it startled her how quickly they appeared, as though occupation brought with it an invisible force field that cut people off from others. Suddenly reintegrated into the world—with unfettered access to cell data, messaging, and media—she was only more aware of how unimaginable the scene in Mariupol was for anyone who had not been there to see it with their own eyes.

They didn't know what to expect as they entered Ukrainian territory. In Mariupol, propaganda ran wild claiming that Ukraine was already fully under the control of Russia and that if residents of Mariupol tried to leave, they would be met with more extreme conditions elsewhere. Only when she achieved sporadic contact with people outside Mariupol—her oldest sister or other friends who had left—did she ascertain that those reports were untrue. "For weeks, everyone was running around shouting that they had surrendered Ukraine, that there is no Ukraine. That is, we were driving into the unknown."

As they approached the city, there was a large gathering of cars and crowds of people. They stopped in a Toyota sales lot just off one of the main roads entering the city. "I didn't understand that there would be people waiting there for us," Maria said. "When we drove up, people ran toward us, they immediately ran to us, carried our bags because we had little children. *Here*, they told us, this and that,

go eat and get what you need." The volunteers took them to a kindergarten, where they sat and were fed and clothed. People brought
them coats, blankets, and bottles of water.

Maria could hardly speak—she could barely form words to
respond to them, just nodding and staring and occasionally saying *spasibo*—"thank you" in Russian. The women wrapped a blanket around her shoulders and opened a bottle of water for her,
placing it in her hands. Only then did she realize how thirsty
she was, and she gulped the water down so quickly that it spilled
down her cheeks and neck. A man brought plates of hot food,
and Maria sat with David, feeding him with a plastic fork as he
devoured it.

"We truly didn't expect that we would be fed," Maria said. After
a month in Mariupol, they assumed that everyone in Ukraine had
succumbed to a dystopian fend-for-yourself mentality.

Just a hundred miles northwest of Mariupol, where bodies lay
decomposing in the streets, brigades of women organized hundreds of hot meals for evacuees. Dozens of people were risking their
lives every day making trips back and forth between Mariupol and
Zaporizhzhya, evacuating as many people as they could. Maria had
seen the worst of humanity in Mariupol, and just over an hour's
drive away, she saw the best.

Their kindness touched Maria, and yet, even though she had
narrowly escaped from one of the most dangerous centers of the
war, even though she was alone with her toddler son, accepting help
felt unnatural for her. She hadn't practiced what to say, how to respond graciously. She may have looked ungrateful, but she was in
shock and was unprepared, and the feeling humbled her.

And she still burned with anger that Leonid had abandoned
her. As she rifled through piles of free clothes and ate her free food,
she thought: "I couldn't believe he would do this to us, and especially to our child; our baby is sixteen months old."

Over the next several days, they drove from Zaporizhzhya to Uman, and from Uman to Ternopil in Western Ukraine, where they found temporary housing. Every few days she received a text message from Leonid, and sometimes they would have short conversations—how are you, where are you, how's David, are you healthy? His service was unpredictable, and Maria lived with her phone in her hands, waiting. Any ring or vibration from her phone sent a visceral shock through her hand and up her spine. It could be Leonid. He might have news. She held out some hope that he would escape or be transferred somewhere out of Mariupol. He never told her exactly what was going on or where he was. She assumed this was an issue of protocol—it was dangerous to reveal the happenings on the battlefield over text message. At night she compulsively reanalyzed every single message she had received from him. But he revealed very little. "He always just said that he was fine, everything will be fine. Deep in his soul he believed that everything would be fine," Maria said.

News from the front in Mariupol did not look reassuring. Surrounded, with Russian troops advancing, Mariupol was predicted to fall soon. In April, Maria learned that Leonid was fighting with his unit in Azovstal, the enormous steel plant on the Left Bank of Mariupol that she had passed almost every day of her life. It dominated the skyline, and many of her friends' parents worked there.

As an elementary school student, Maria toured the plant, and as she and her classmates walked through it, the cathedral-like halls towering above them, she was impressed with its complexity and powerful machinery, the conveyor belts, glowing furnaces, and molten metal poured into molds. It felt like a separate world, a fortress.

The plant specialized in the production of various steel products—slabs, billets, hot-rolled coils, cold-rolled coils, and wire rods—which emerged from its blast furnaces, converters, casting machines, and rolling mills. Arranged in a series of open halls, loading docks, and offices, and connected by a complex system of tunnels and bunkers, it was originally built during the First Five-Year Plan in the early 1930s, modeled after a steel plant in Gary, Indiana. After the plant was nearly destroyed during the Second World War, Soviet leaders rebuilt it, that time even stronger, reinforcing it to be capable of ostensibly withstanding a nuclear attack. It was one of the largest and most productive factories in the Soviet Union, an industrial monolith in which multiple generations worked their entire lives.

In 1991, after Ukraine became independent, Azovstal was privatized, along with other large state assets, and eventually bought up by the Ukrainian business conglomerate Systems Capital Management, a holding company owned entirely by Rinat Akhmetov, the richest man in Ukraine. The son of a coal miner turned self-made billionaire, Akhmetov is known across Ukraine as the King of the Donbas.

In April, as Russian troops took over the city, Ukrainian soldiers retreated into Azovstal, using the plant as a fortress. By early May, it was the last stronghold of their resistance: the plant's enormous, winding campus made locating the fighters difficult. More than two thousand soldiers and several hundred women, children, and elderly people remained inside the steel plant, hundreds of them wounded. The soldiers came from several military and law enforcement units, including the Azov regiment, which had been incorporated into the National Guard years earlier, a marine brigade from Ukraine's naval forces, and the 12th Brigade of the National Guard, in which Leonid served.

By the end of April, most of Mariupol had been destroyed, but the soldiers refused to surrender. On April 21, Vladimir Putin ordered Russian troops to blockade the plant and prevent the delivery of supplies, starving out those inside and ensuring they ran out of ammunition. Russian forces bombed the plant almost unceasingly: on the night of April 27, more than fifty strikes blasted the factory. Such an intense offensive against Azovstal might suggest the battle had not yet been won. But it was effectively over: Russian ground forces in Mariupol had the plant completely surrounded, and troops were being pulled out to reinforce the major Russian offensive taking place elsewhere in the Donbas. But by refusing to surrender, the Ukrainian fighters in Azovstal, including Leonid, stalled the Russian army for much longer than the Russians anticipated, giving other Ukrainian forces more time to prepare their defenses.

By early May, Russian soldiers were inside the factory. According to some Ukrainian sources, this was thanks to a Ukrainian electrician who had worked in the plant for many years and gave them information about the underground tunnel network.

By May 7, the Ukrainian government had managed to evacuate all the remaining women, children, and elderly left inside Azovstal. Zelenskyy publicly gave the soldiers who had been fighting for Mariupol's defense instructions to surrender. "Ukraine needs Ukrainian heroes to be alive. It's our principle," he said.

Maria and Leonid were able to communicate only sporadically. Electrical and phone lines were down, but if anyone in the plant happened to find a bar of service, they would write as many messages as they could to the family members of the soldiers around them. For weeks, Maria had received text messages at all hours of the day and night from unknown numbers: "It's me, Lonya, I'm okay for now. I love you very much."

By May 20, Azovstal was fully under Russian control. Thirty-one years after the relatively calm collapse of the Soviet Union, the famed industrial site had become a bombed-out and dilapidated graveyard for Russian and Ukrainian corpses. As the plant approached its one hundredth birthday, Russia announced that it would be razed to the ground.

Just before Leonid went silent, he sent one last message off to Maria, referring to the Russians: "They are taking us out of Azovstal."

Maria read the words as soon as they came in. She didn't know when he had typed them—maybe just a split second earlier, maybe a while before, depending on the cell signal. He had time for only seven words, and Maria replied as fast as she could, trembling as she shot off messages to him in quick succession—

"Hello, I am here"

"I love you, I am here"

"Are you there still?"

"I love you. I will always love you"

"We are waiting for you"

"I am here"

But there was no response. The phone likely buzzed in a pile of other phones somewhere in a bag in the factory or on the floor of a tank. By the end of the day, she understood that no more messages would be coming for a while.

"And then I didn't know anything about him," Maria said.

Volodymyr—1989

EVEN TODAY, IT'S hard for Western observers to grasp the pervasiveness of bureaucracy in the Soviet era. The USSR was run by bureaucrats who believed, above all, in the supremacy of two things: rubber stamps and forms. Rank-and-file Soviet bureaucrats oversaw permissions for both important matters (which grocery stores would receive shipments of meat, for example) and the seemingly trivial (how many pencils to send to a specific institution). Not only were pencils numbered and carefully accounted for, but an employee at the institution requesting pencils would need to fill out extensive paperwork to receive said pencils. There must be signatures from multiple supervisors, and the form would move through layers of offices before finally being stamped. The bureaucrat who signed off on these decisions was often surrounded by an army of doormen, secretaries, and assistants who told incoming petitioners that they had come to the wrong office, or argued that the petitioner didn't have the forms necessary even to speak with the bureaucrat in charge, or insisted that the bureaucrat was far too busy to meet with anyone else this month. To accomplish even the most mundane of tasks required extraordinary persistence and nearly superhuman patience.

So, to exhume a former political prisoner in Russia and have that body reburied in Ukraine was no small task. When Volodymyr sought the necessary permissions to exhume Stus and the other two writers he needed to get signatures and stamps and go-aheads from all manner of offices: the managers of the cemetery, the city sanitation and hygiene committee, ritual committees dealing with corpses, the department of communal services, the local airport, transportation offices, the department of internal affairs, and the local party and government authorities. Each office and committee in Perm and Chusovoy—the small village outside Perm where the bodies were buried—would need to give its consent, in writing. Gathering all the necessary permissions was a logistical feat in and of itself, to say nothing of the fact that exhuming and transferring the bodies of three former political prisoners from a gulag cemetery was politically touchy at best and a sentence in the gulag at worst.

In Kyiv, a team of more than twenty people was making arrangements with the prestigious Baikove cemetery, where prominent writers, artists, and politicians from throughout Ukrainian history were buried. The team in Kyiv also fought an uphill battle. Although the emergent Ukrainian nationalist movement gained momentum in the 1980s, the Communist Party of Ukraine overwhelmingly controlled political life in the Ukrainian SSR. In 1989, the collapse of the Soviet Union was far from inevitable. The Soviet Union remained a global superpower, and reburying Stus—an outspoken critic of the regime and promoter of Ukrainian independence—was not looked upon kindly by many in the Ukrainian political establishment. The people who led the charge for the poets' reburials were people with a new ideology—pro-national political leaders, Ukrainian intellectuals, and Stus's colleagues, friends, and family. Getting Stus out of the ground required overcoming one set of hurdles, out of Russia another, off the plane in Kyiv another, and back into the ground in Ukraine yet one more.

It was a job for someone just shy of crazy. When Volodymyr arrived in Perm on August 24, 1989, he had in hand a signed certificate of permission from V. V. Kazantsev, the head of the department of housing and communal services of the Chusovoy City Executive Committee. The department of housing and communal services was the USSR's centralized system for managing and providing housing, utilities, and related services to the population, and because the exhumation fell under their purview, their endorsement was key. Armed with the certificate, Volodymyr would use it as legal tender to buy his way through the rest of the bureaucratic maze.

He began by coordinating with the Perm airport director to sign off on the transport of three caskets through the airport. From the airport, Volodymyr made his way to his hotel in Perm, where he sweet-talked the manager, a plump and cheerful woman with a jowly smile. She needed to sign off on housing the film crew—already en route from Kyiv—for the duration of their filming. She agreed readily—the arrival of a real film crew all the way from a distant city was a special treat.

Sitting at the hotel buffet with a meal of boiled eggs and seaweed, Volodymyr sketched out a basic plan for filming. Once the film crew arrived, later that day, they would make the two-and-a-half-hour drive to Chusovoy to the abandoned remains of Perm-36, the camp where Stus had been imprisoned and died. There they would film the campgrounds, the cells, and the graveyard. The next day, a team of gravediggers would begin digging up the graves and transferring the bodies to new coffins so they could take the bodies back to the Perm airport for immediate transfer to Kyiv.

Vasyl Stus was born in 1938 in a village in central Ukraine. When he was one year old, his family moved to Donetsk—then called Stalino—where he grew up in the heavily Russified Donbas region. His family, however, spoke Ukrainian at home, and he grew up with his mother singing Ukrainian folk songs to him. Languages fascinated him, and from the time he was young, he played with language as if it were an intellectual puzzle, an opportunity for exploring how grammar, syntax, pronunciation, and vocabulary combined with one another and with culture and ideas. As an adolescent, in mundane local interactions, he spoke Russian, but those close to him assert that he was conspicuously deliberate about which language he spoke and when. By the time he was a student at the institute in Donetsk (Stalino), he spoke only Ukrainian.

He had a head of dark brown hair and full, inquisitive eyebrows, a slight underbite, and a serious, reserved nature. Sensitive and emotive, Stus was also stubborn and unyielding. When he believed deeply in something, he became so uncompromising that some analysts of Stus's work and biography have ventured to call his unwavering nature pathological or even suicidal.

As a young man, Stus began writing poetry in Ukrainian. After Joseph Stalin died in 1953, the Soviet state, led by Nikita Khrushchev, entered a period known as the Thaw—an era of reckoning with the Stalinist past, widespread de-Stalinization in policy and everyday life, and greater freedom of speech. Stus became a member of the Sixties (*shistdesiatnyky*)—a generation of Ukrainian writers, philosophers, and artists who published during the Thaw, exploring the dark history of the Stalinist past free from the constraints of the socialist realism that had dominated Soviet writing for decades. Part of the broader dissident movement in the USSR, the Sixties criticized the authoritarianism of the Soviet regime and called for political and cultural liberalization. They promoted Ukraine's language and history, and they published in prestigious journals and magazines, gaining a well-read audience and contributing to a cultural renaissance in Ukraine in the 1960s.

Rich with imagery and symbolism, Stus's early poetry was vivid and colloquial, concise yet complex. "Stus's poetic voice broke through the conventional socialist realist Ukrainian literature in the 1960s," wrote the Ukrainian anthropologist Natalya Shostak. "His unbleached, deeply touching lyric and intense, often politically charged and yet subtle poetic imagery have not been matched in Ukrainian literature since then." Epithets abound in his poetry— "the shaky path," "angry love," the "hairy embrace of the night"— and he loved to use familiar colloquialisms that bounced off the tongue: "yes and yes, and so and so."

His poetry was rooted in historicity, preoccupied with temporality. He wrote about and to Ukrainian intellectuals who had been killed in Stalin's Terror in the 1930s and those from the previous century. Rich with philosophical allusion, Stus's poetry evoked Hegel and Kierkegaard and was significantly influenced by Rilke. He was among the most sophisticated European poets of the postwar period, according to Bohdan Tokarskyi, a professor of Ukrainian literature at Harvard University.

Of particular historical salience to Stus were the 1930s—a time of unprecedented death for Ukrainians. He wrote specifically of the year 1937, the height of Stalin's Great Terror, in which more than a million people were killed and hundreds of thousands exiled, of whom many were Ukrainian intellectuals. Stus was born the next year, in 1938, as the Great Terror slowed, and the fact that he came into the world precisely then seemed to inform how he engaged with the history of the decade. The past loomed over Stus, and he wrestled with it in his verse.

After Khrushchev was ousted and Leonid Brezhnev became General Secretary of the Communist Party in 1964, the state cracked down on Thaw-era intellectuals. Many were arrested, imprisoned, and killed. In 1965, Stus, along with others, protested the wave of arrests, but his involvement in the protests put him in the party's bad graces. He was expelled from his doctoral program at the Shevchenko Institute of Literature, his poetry was prevented from being published, and, among other odd jobs, he worked on the construction of the Kyiv metro. He continued to speak out against the mistreatment of Ukrainian writers and intellectuals, writing open letters to Soviet politicians and the Ukrainian Writers' Union, and in 1972, Soviet police broke into his family's apartment and dragged him away. After they left, secret police remained in the apartment and tore it apart, rifling through books and manuscripts, opening drawers and cupboards, turning everything upside down. His wife, Valentyna Popeliukh, remembered that it went on until three in the morning: "I was watching them, because it was unbelievable. I never would have thought that they would come to look for something there. What could we hide from them?"

Stus was tried in Kyiv and condemned to five years in camps and three years in exile. The case that the prosecution developed against him was based, among other things, on an open letter he wrote to members of the Ukrainian Writers' Union, complaining that young Ukrainian writers weren't being published anymore— and for telling two jokes that were considered to be anti-Soviet while at a mountain resort in the Carpathians.

In the KGB detention center, a young Ukrainian psychiatrist, Semen Gluzman, shared a cell with Stus for nearly three weeks. When Gluzman came into the cell, he found Stus composed, focused on translating Rilke, and not allowing himself to despair. Gluzman, who was imprisoned for speaking out against the Soviet Union's weaponization of the psychiatric treatment of dissidents, was impressed that Stus was at once deeply feeling and yet possessed of extraordinary mental strength. Gluzman called him "a person without skin," meaning that he felt other people's pain acutely, and when he saw people being mistreated, he was absolutely unforgiving of it.

Though he despised the guards who tortured him and so many others, he wrote of them curiously:

Oh human, I cannot believe your life is
just about looking into my cell?
Does not your life call you?

. . . .

you stand in my heavy sorrow, my aching heart is filled with
  your misfortune
because you are just twice as sad as I am.
I have myself, and you are just a shadow
I am the good, you are the dust, decay
we are both prisoners, that's what we have in common
on both sides of this door, I'm here, you're there
we're separated by these walls of law.

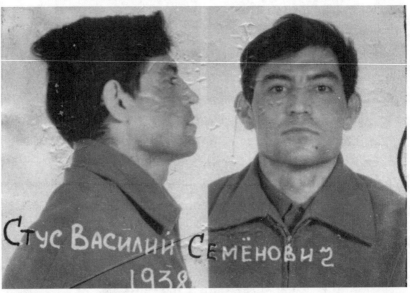

Stus's mug shot after his first arrest in 1972

After several months in the KGB prison in Kyiv, Stus was transferred to labor camps in Mordovia, Russia, after which he was transferred to a gulag in Magadan, Russia, until 1979. There, he worked in mines, extracting ore, breathing through a gauze bandage that quickly became soaked with sweat and dust, until he took it off and worked without any respiratory protection. In a later court testimony against Stus, a neighboring inmate confessed to having urinated in Stus's teapot. Most prisoners suffered from serious malnutrition and had little or no access to medical care, often sustaining major injuries and living with illness for months without care. Stus developed peptic ulcers, which were left untreated. After a number of stomach hemorrhages in 1975, he was taken to a Leningrad prisoners' hospital, where surgeons operated on his stomach, slicing out two-thirds of it in a surgical hack job.

Released from prison in 1979, Stus was arrested again just a few months later, in May 1980. Stus's son, Dmytro, recalled later in his memoir how his father pleaded with him in a letter to maintain his own humanity following his father's second arrest:

Today, my son, you experienced perhaps the greatest humiliation and disappointment in your not-so-long life. I know how painful it is for a man to realize his impotence. It's a pity, as it is for me now, the fact that you see trouble, you see injustice, and there is no way to help. But we have to endure . . . I don't know if we'll see each other again, so I'm only asking you for one thing. Forgive today those people who caused you, me and your mother so much pain. Forgive them, but remember this experience so that you never do anything like it to others.

In his defense speech, Stus's court-appointed defense attorney, Viktor Medvedchuk, offered little defense: he claimed that Stus was guilty of his accused crimes and that they all warranted punishment. Medvedchuk asked the court to consider, however, that in the few months he'd spent in Kyiv since his last prison term, Stus had always met his work quotas.

Stus was given the maximum sentence: ten years of hard labor and five years in exile. The judge additionally imposed a fine of 2,300 rubles for the transportation of witnesses from Magadan who had come to testify against Stus. Mumbling the verdict hastily and closing the trial, the judge prevented Stus from giving his final speech.

"You murderers!" Stus cried. "You didn't even let me make a final speech!" He had never fully recovered from his stomach operation, and he was very ill. Later, after visiting him in his post-trial detention cell, Stus's wife said that he would never survive the sentence.

He was sent to Perm-36, where he lived for five more years. There, inmates were packed together in uninsulated barracks with no pumping or sanitation systems, and food rations were meager. He dedicated himself to a rigorous writing regime; when he was not writing or translating in his cell, he composed in his mind. His poetry kept him sane in the gulag. Guards confiscated his work—as many as eight hundred poems, both original and translations—and told him it had all been destroyed. Stus then began sending poetry home in letters and in the letters of fellow inmates. His collection *Palimpsests* was smuggled out by the sister of one of Stus's fellow inmates and later published abroad. To provide another layer of security, and as a show of solidarity, fellow prisoners—Ukrainians, Armenians, Lithuanians, and Russians—memorized countless of his poems, so that even if the paper was burned, the poems would not be lost until all the inmates died.

In a conversation I had with Bohdan Tokarskyi, who is an expert on Stus, Tokarskyi stressed how intently Stus studied ancient Ukrainian literature and history to become acquainted with the phrases and written patterns of archaic Ukrainian. In the 1960s and '70s, the Ukrainian language was becoming standardized by Soviet linguists and language teachers, modified to sound like Russian. Ukrainian was simplified, stripped of its unique character and historical roots, and Russian words were adopted into Ukrainian, making it easier for Ukrainian speakers to transition to Russian, a shift that was more common in the late Soviet period as Ukrainian was increasingly branded a simple peasant language, a backward tongue.

Stus pushed against this trend, trying to understand the language as it originally was, unaltered by Russification. He scoured old texts searching for forgotten words and phrases, ancient coinages. He pushed himself to work on his own language, writing in both colloquial and classical Ukrainian language that was not lazy, not Russified. The result was a collection of a vibrant Ukrainian full of both archaic phrases and neologisms. When his archive was created in Kyiv in the 1990s, the head archivist who compiled it, Mykhailyna Kotsiubynska—herself a member of the Sixtiers and a close friend of Stus's who was called to testify at his 1980s trial—made notes about Stus's unique language. He was working to rediscover something that had been lost—a version of himself and his people that had been obscured and taken away, slowly over time—the way Ukrainians had spoken and thought and written before they had been conquered.

Stus was preoccupied with death and resurrection, rebirth and metamorphosis. He wrote, as though a common refrain, about life after death, even life *in* death. Stus's poetry shows a concern about his place in the eternities—in time and space. He wrote of both the past and the future and addressed both the dead and those yet to be born. From the darkness and seclusion of the gulag, his poetry reflects a distinct reverie, one in which he returns to Ukraine through his poetry: "My people, I will return to you, and in death I will turn to life . . . As a son, I bow down to you, and I will honestly look into your honest eyes, and in death I will relate with my native land."

He gained a reputation for engaging with his guards' sense of morality, asking them if they didn't feel discouraged about what they did, remarking that they were human, too—why was it that they had chosen such a path? Sometimes just a glance at the guards landed Stus in solitary confinement. In one of his letters, he mentioned that he did not possess any instinct of self-preservation, and in much of his poetry, Stus was deeply pensive on the subject of death and seemed not to fear it. His writings and fellow inmates' memoirs indicate that Stus didn't fear the guards either. Occasionally, prisoners were forced to strip, and the guards checked every scar and crevice on their body. This was a KGB tactic used to humiliate and intimidate prisoners when family traveled to see their loved one in the prison. The physical searches were intended to be so demoralizing that the prisoner would agree to cancel the meeting. Referring to such searches, Stus would say, "They paw you like a chicken," a statement that would get him thrown into the punishment cell. In February 1983, after his gulag diary was published abroad, he was banished to solitary confinement for a full year.

On August 27, 1985, Stus read a book on his upper bunk in the prison, leaning on his elbows. Sitting or lying on the bunk was permitted only eight hours a day, and a guard supervisor named Rudenko, who'd seen Stus reading, remarked that Stus had violated the rules. Stus chose another permitted position, but the next day, Rudenko filed a report that Stus has been improperly using the bunk, and Stus was sent to the punishment cell. Stus was furious and protested, and on his way to solitary confinement declared a hunger strike. When his cellmate, the Russian writer Borodin, asked what kind of hunger strike (solid food, liquid food, hot food, cold food), Stus just said, "To the end."

Stus died on the night of September 4, 1985, in punishment cell number three. He was forty-seven years old and had been in prison for thirteen years.

When Volodymyr arrived in Perm four years later, on August 24, 1989, the prison was closed. All the inmates who had lived there with Stus were either dead or had been released. The guards were gone. The camp was an abandoned relic of Soviet brutality.

Vasyl Ovsiyenko, a fellow Ukrainian who'd been held with Stus, arrived with the film crew to take Volodymyr through the prison. Ovsiyenko led them from cell to cell and relived the thirteen years he spent there. He showed them the four-by-four-meter cells and the bunks on the walls, how they were lowered only at night so that prisoners could not lie down before it was time to sleep. He showed them the *bayan*, a special type of blind on the other side of the windowpane—through it you could see only a small strip of sky. Ovsiyenko himself turned out to be one of the most comprehensive libraries of Stus's poems—he had memorized a host of them. He recited them to Volodymyr and the film crew as they walked through the prison chambers, and demonstrated where he had received poems from Stus, through holes in the foundation or walls. In one, there was still a piece of paper with Stus's writing. It was his personal translation of Rudyard Kipling's "If." "If you can keep your head when all about you / Are losing theirs and blaming it on you," it began.

Volodymyr worried about Ovsiyenko walking through this prison yard. The psychological toll of reliving those years was enormous, and Volodymyr planned to make a stop at a pharmacy once they were back in town to purchase some sort of antianginal medication so that Ovsiyenko wouldn't have a heart attack during the exhumation.

That proved to be unnecessary. As Volodymyr settled into his hotel room that night, he received a call that the exhumation would not be allowed. The town of Chusovoy had issued a spontaneous ban on exhumations, allegedly due to a dangerous epidemiological situation. The city had instituted no other restrictions—no limitation of trade, no closures of schools, restaurants, or catering facilities, and transportation ran as normal. Additionally, it was uncharacteristically cold outside, conditions conducive to safe exhumation.

Volodymyr threw a fit. He petitioned, called, and argued, but the epidemiological and sanitation office prohibited it, and when a Soviet bureaucrat was determined to prevent something from happening, it didn't happen. There would be no exhumation. Of course, an epidemic in Chusovoy never materialized—there was no new flu, dysentery, or anthrax.

Volodymyr was discouraged. Before leaving town, he and the film crew made one last trip to Perm-36 to visit the cemetery. Stus's son, Dmytro, was on the team and had helped to clean up the grave of his father—clearing overgrown grass and weeds, smoothing the dirt around the area. They placed candles on the graves, as well as traditional Ukrainian embroidered towels.

"My own heart was tight," wrote Volodymyr. "I promised myself that we would definitely return, that we would definitely rebury our heroes in their native land. After all, heroes are born on the graves of heroes, and a country without heroes will never become a state."

PART 3

THE
FIRST SUMMER

ANNA

Kolomiya, Ukraine

AFTER LEAVING BEHIND the police academy and parting ways
with her parents in Dnipro, Anna safely made her way to Western
Ukraine. She was lucky to find a job waiting tables in a restaurant.
Soon, as more people flooded the towns and cities of Western
Ukraine, those jobs became scarce. With both her parents serving
in the military, she received a special government allowance, and
she also qualified for some humanitarian aid. With the job in the
restaurant, she was able to pay for a room in a communal shelter,
buy food and transport, and pay for her cell phone, all while saving
a little bit of money.

Her parents, however, were hard to reach. Her mom was in
touch a few times a week at the beginning, but by April and May,
service was spottier, and her mom reached out less frequently.
They spoke on the phone rarely; in April, both her parents called
to video chat for just one minute. During the short call, she could
hardly contain her relief—they were alive, they were together,

they loved her—but as soon as the call ended, the nagging, sick feeling she'd been carrying since she left them in February returned.

Anna didn't have friends in Kolomiya, but she was used to making new friends. Her best friend from Sievierodonetsk had moved to the Czech Republic, but she knew how to engage others and liked the young people she worked with at the restaurant. Online, she found a humanitarian aid program that was helping those who were alone in Western Ukraine, displaced from the east. In May, the program took a group of teenage boys and girls to Bukovel, a beautiful area in the Carpathians known for its resorts and skiing. She met kids her age from Mariupol, Kharkiv, and other cities in the east. They hiked in the mountains, visited waterfalls, rode through the forests on four-wheelers. It was her first trip to the mountains, and she had never seen anything like them before, and when the group left, she dreamed of going back.

Cautious and reserved, Anna wasn't the type of person to take big risks. She wasn't hyperactive or energetic—she liked to lie in bed and think, scrolling on her phone, talking with a friend, following astrological signs, watching a show. She loved animals and had a couple of pet rats she'd brought with her from home. Even after she made some friends in Kolomiya, she spent a lot of her time on her own, carrying with her a heavy feeling of aloneness, a feeling that there was no real safety net for her in the world—there was no one who could help her in a pinch if something went wrong, if she got stuck somewhere or hurt. The feeling weighed on her, and as weeks went on without much communication with her parents, she worried that she'd be alone forever.

In May, her university announced that all students should gather in Ivano-Frankivsk, a larger Western Ukrainian city an hour north, to resume their police training and studies. The university had relocated and was reopening its operations. She gathered up her few things, left the shelter in Kolomiya, quit her restaurant job, and hopped on a bus to rejoin her classmates in the barracks.

Once there, she remembered why she hated it so much. The yelling, the uniforms, the rigidity—she'd despised these things before the war, but now they were unbearable. She didn't have close friends in her unit, so she couldn't talk about it with anyone. She messaged her grandma in Luhansk, but Anna didn't like to weigh her grandma down with her negative feelings about her studies. To distract herself, she started chatting with people online, joining dating channels on Telegram and meeting boys.

She had never started a relationship online. Previously, she and her girlfriends spent time on Telegram, looking at boys and laughing at them. At first it was kind of a joke, something to keep herself occupied in the evenings when she had a few hours of free time. But as she chatted with strangers on the bunk in her room, she could feel that she was searching for something. She wasn't a child anymore. She'd survived the first few months of the war on her own, and it aroused in her a new sense of maturity that she ventured to explore.

She struck up a conversation with a boy from Luhansk—Dima. She was interested in him because he was from the same area and had apparently lived there until recently. He now served in the Ukrainian military, and from his barracks somewhere in the east, Dima and Anna started to chat.

He was nineteen, a year older almost exactly—their birthdays were three days apart in November, though she was a Scorpio and he a Sagittarius. This was a good sign, Anna thought; it suggested compatibility. At first their conversation was mostly banal, focused on their favorite animals and hobbies, teasing each other, flirting. But as weeks passed and they kept returning to the chat, they were sometimes serious. Sometimes they talked about their families, or about Luhansk, or the war.

Out of the blue, Dima would go silent. For a full week she'd hear nothing from him. Later, when he reemerged, he apologized: he had been on some sort of mission and service had been spotty. She understood. She was used to the silence from her parents. But she was grateful that he at least explained and kept coming back to their conversation. As time went on, she would be more open with him about how lonely and miserable she was, or complain to him about her university, and she appreciated his sympathy.

"Why do you stay?" he asked her.

For her, staying was an obvious choice. Gaining acceptance to the university had been difficult, she'd paid a lot of money to attend, her parents were so proud of her, it was useful training and would secure employment. If she quit, she was still liable for the full semester's dues, which she couldn't afford to pay up front and was meeting in monthly installments. But the more she and Dima talked, the more emboldened she felt. He opened her mind to the possibility of quitting, walking away, taking a different path, and it intrigued her. "I believe these are the best years of my life," she said. "I am only eighteen years old and I want to live them in such a way that I remember them, and not in some barracks with a bad mood every day."

Every time Dima reached out to her again after being on the front lines, she wondered why her parents didn't do the same. She heard from them only sporadically, every couple of weeks, and when several days would pass without a word, she often assumed something had happened to them, only to get a message a few days later: "Hello, Anushka"—a diminutive, affectionate nickname—"we are safe, we love you." She didn't know where they were, or even whether they were together, but her mother always wrote "we," which caused Anna to believe that they hadn't been separated. Still, in their silence, she created stories: where they were, what they were doing, why they had left, why they weren't in touch more often.

She was glad when a message from Dima popped up, interrupting this train of thought. It was nice to talk with him. She worried about him on the front, too. When he went quiet, she watched his Telegram profile to see when he was active, how long it had been since he'd checked his phone, just to see if he was still alive. When he came back on, he sent her pictures of himself in his army uniform, and she sent him photos in return. He didn't say much about the trenches, about blasts and bodies and burning; they exchanged funny videos of cats and dogs. They understood each other's humor, and he told her how much he liked her—that she was beautiful, smart, and interesting, that he liked something about her soul. If Dima had phone service and electricity at night, Anna would sneak away to the bathroom in her dormitory, lock the door, sit on the floor in her pajamas, lay her forehead on her knees, and listen to him talk. Often, if they had nothing left to say, they would just sit in silence, but even so, she could hear his breath rattling in the speaker, and she would listen to that as long as she could, knowing she was not alone.

Over the summer, Anna and Dima continued to talk, checking in nearly every day. She liked so many things about him. He was never shy with praise, conversation was fun and involving, and he always showed up in their chats. Sometimes Dima even sent her money. "I initially really liked his generosity," Anna said. "He just threw money at me. He said that he really wanted to spoil me, and I was very grateful to him for that. It was so nice and unexpected. I asked 'why?' And he said: 'I want to make you happy.'" When he thought about her in the middle of the day, he told her. And when she complained about school or that she felt lonely, he told her it was stupid

how they treated her at the university and that she wasn't alone—
she had him.

The fact that they were both from Luhansk and remembered
the beginning of the war eight years earlier was important common ground. They didn't have to explain it to each other, even
though their experiences had differed in many respects. After the
area came under Russian separatist control in 2014, Dima's family
had all stayed in Luhansk, even though they supported Ukraine.
They didn't want to uproot their lives, they didn't have much
money, and they knew from watching all their friends who left
that it wasn't necessarily easier on the other side of that border.
They kept their Ukrainian passports. They buried Ukrainian flags
in plastic bags in the ground. But they didn't talk about politics.
In early 2022, Dima wanted a fresh start. He didn't see a future for
himself in the so-called Luhansk People's Republic, so he decided
to leave and go to Kharkiv. Once the full-scale invasion began, it
would become nearly impossible and extremely dangerous to cross
into the LPR through Ukraine, but if you needed to, you could
go north to the Baltics, east into Russia, then down into Eastern
Ukraine.

Before the full-scale invasion, however, the war was mostly frozen for seven years, and people could go back and forth between
occupied territories and Ukraine with relative ease. Some made
a business of this, carting goods from Ukraine that were no longer available in the breakaway areas. The war in 2014 and ensuing
events led to the destruction of many jobs, as factories, businesses,
infrastructure projects, and schools shut down, and those who
stayed on separatist ground often relied on humanitarian aid or
participated in an informal economy in which they engaged in
small-scale trading. Over the years of "frozen conflict," the local
currency had significantly depreciated, eroding the purchasing
power of regular people, and the region's banking system had all

but collapsed. In the Luhansk winter, electricity and heating were unreliable, because maintaining and repairing energy infrastructure was expensive, and natural gas and heating oil were often in short supply.

Dima was tired of that life, so just a few weeks before the full-scale invasion, after finishing a technical degree at a college in Luhansk, he set off to Ukrainian-held Kharkiv to make a new start. When the war began, many of the kids his age volunteered for service. It was nothing new for him: as he grew up in Luhansk, he'd seen friends from school join the Luhansk People's Republic's army. This was one of the most stable jobs in the region, though he'd never considered it for himself. But in Kharkiv in February 2022, as the city was bombed relentlessly and hundreds of thousands of people fled for safety, he knew it was finally time to take part. He knew it was his turn.

Partway through the summer, Anna and Dima began video chatting, and Anna knew she wanted to meet him in person. They both bemoaned how challenging long-distance relationships were, not because they had ever been in one but because everyone said so. But she hesitated to suggest meeting in person, especially because he was off duty only a few days every month, and traveling to see her in Western Ukraine was a long trip, and it would take up almost all his leave. She wanted him to bring up the idea, but as the weeks went on, he didn't. As the summer neared its end, Dima was stationed on the front lines in the Kharkiv region near the border with Russia. Russian forces continued to occupy the region, where Dima fought and where the Ukrainian army was preparing for a counteroffensive to reclaim lost territory in the northeast.

"Sometimes he would snap at me because he was very scared," she said. "He didn't admit it, but I felt it. I know that it was difficult and scary." Sometimes, when on leave, he would mention how the war had changed him, but he didn't like to talk about it and would soon switch the conversation to something else.

They talked about the foods they liked and didn't like, the funny things they had done as children, all the dreams they had for the future, to travel, to see Europe, to buy a car, to have a kid. They flirted, and when she felt lonely, Anna sent photos of herself to him, and she knew he loved them, saving them on his phone and looking at them in the night in a war bunker. She was a virgin, but she knew enough about sex to know she wanted to have it, and with him.

In August, they broached the topic of meeting in person, and Dima suggested that she come to Kharkiv—leave school and stay there with him—so they could be together during his off-duty time. In the first months of the war, Kharkiv had been one of the hardest-hit cities in Ukraine, with entire sectors demolished. But the city was not occupied, though it was still shelled and bombed several times a week. He told her he'd pay the fine—about nine hundred dollars—for her to drop out of her university if she really wanted to leave. It was a large sum for a young Ukrainian soldier, but he suggested the idea without apparently giving it a second thought.

Anna aired the idea with her grandma and some of her friends, but her mind was already made up. Even when, on August 18, twenty-five people were killed and several dozen injured in a missile attack on two student dormitories in Kharkiv, Anna didn't change course. She didn't read the news much anyway. By early September, Ukrainian forces launched a major counteroffensive in the area, liberating settlements in a major victory for Ukraine. In just five days, the Ukrainian army claimed to have killed nearly three thousand Russian soldiers. Ukrainians bulldozed through hundreds of square miles of occupied territory, exposing the profound vulnerability and incapability of the Russian army. The Kharkiv counteroffensive brought with it a surge of optimism: Ukrainians and their Western allies believed with renewed faith that with the right equipment, Ukrainians could win the war. In a spike of morale, Dima said she should come now. It was the right time.

"He said that he wanted me to be happy, so that I wouldn't cry because of my studies," Anna said. She was grateful and touched by his display of commitment. "Of course, he warned that it was very dangerous in Kharkiv because rockets were flying every day. I didn't read anything about Kharkiv's news. I only knew about it from him, but he was pretty calm. But I said I'd come, because I wanted to, I wanted to spend time with him, and he would take leave for the first time in six months or so, just to see me."

Dima and Anna planned her trip to Kharkiv. She'd come soon—in a week—as soon as Dima could get an apartment in Kharkiv and she could withdraw her university enrollment, plan her route, pack her things. She didn't tell her parents that she was going, and she waited to hear from them, but word never came. As she packed up her stuff, she regretted all the times she fought with them in the previous few years.

Dima gave her money for the trip. She took the train with her pet rats and all her belongings. There were power outages and artillery fire along the road, and it took twenty-one hours to get there. She had been to Kharkiv only twice before, both times with her parents. After the McDonald's in Luhansk had closed in 2014 when the city fell under separatist control, they found themselves talking about how much they missed the French fries and Big Macs and ice cream cones, and they hopped in the car and drove three and a half hours to Kharkiv, which had the closest franchise. It was spontaneous and somewhat out of character for her parents, but for Anna, walking through the park with both her mom and dad and their ice cream cones in a new city, it was one of the best moments of her life.

Looking out the train window and listening to music, she replayed what everyone had told her: her friends and grandma all said she shouldn't do it. "He won't be the same as in the video," they said, promising that she would realize it was a bad decision as soon as she met him in person. He'd probably smell bad, they said, he'll be awkward, and he probably just wants you for your body. She refuted these statements emphatically: "He says he loves my soul," she said.

Her parents weren't in touch, so she hadn't even told them about Dima. But she could imagine that they would discourage her from moving to Kharkiv to be with him. They would try to tell her it was foolish or irresponsible, that young people who had only talked online can't really be in love. Still, she didn't know much about romantic love, but she imagined this was it. And besides, her parents had left without asking her permission. What if she had told them not to go? If she had said, *Mom, please stay with me, don't leave, I am scared, I don't want to be alone*, would her mother have stayed? Would they be together now?

In some sense, she was inspired by her mother—to make such a spontaneous decision that felt right. Creeping toward the city, she thought of Dima. Would they be all right, would he be different from how he was on the phone? From the window she saw burned buildings and heaps of debris that people were sorting into piles. An old woman with a walking stick limped along the side of the road. People were not moving to Kharkiv to start a new life, people were fleeing it to preserve their lives. And yet the trees that were left undamaged were beautifully full of leaves, and the sun shining through them into the train window inspired optimism.

Dima had taken leave and was to meet her at the train station. She hoped he would be kind to her. She hoped she would know she had made the right decision to come to this place. She took in a few deep breaths to calm herself: "I hope he thinks I'm pretty."

TANIA

Mykil'ske, Ukraine

ALL THROUGHOUT UKRAINE there are still old women who remember the sound of German motorcycles sputtering into their village in 1941. They remember the houses those men on motorcycles commandeered, and even after they left, even decades later, the women would warn their grandkids not to go too near those houses, for many years earlier young men had lived there, and while they did, many people in the village disappeared.

Now, in 2022, Russian soldiers were settling in Tania's southern village, but she had already stopped calling them Russians. Like a great many Ukrainians, she called them "orcs" or *rashisty*—Orc, invoking the grotesque nonhuman characters from *Lord of the Rings*, and *rashist* a mix of the words "Russian" and "fascist." After Russians took over the municipal buildings on the first day and installed the Russian flag, a few "permanent" soldiers assigned to the village settled in an empty home. They established a checkpoint at the entrance to the village, and the comings and goings of residents were very strictly monitored.

"We were completely occupied from all sides, and those who left and returned for work went through such terrible tests—they were undressed, they put them on the ground, searched them. Sometimes they shot civilian transport along the highway without warning," Tania said. "I was very afraid to meet the orcs face-to-face. We couldn't know what was in their heads." She and Viktor knew where the soldiers were living, and they made a point never to go near. In fact, in those first several weeks, they stopped going outside almost altogether. They hung dark coverings over their windows and made sure their house looked as though there was no movement or work or life happening there at all.

The permanent Russian soldiers in the village worked to establish themselves among the locals. Moving from house to house, they pounded on people's doors to give their spiel: *Congratulations, you have been freed from the oppressions of the Nazi Ukrainian Kyiv Regime. This village is now controlled by the Russian Federation. If you resist, you and your family will be repressed, but if you work with us, you will enjoy a better life.*

The soldiers demanded that locals provide the keys for their cars and trucks, and then they drove the vehicles off into nearby fields. Later, in early spring, when people wanted to prepare their land for sowing, they couldn't: all the large fields and forest plantations around the village were blocked by stolen village vehicles and Russian equipment—tanks, armored personnel carriers, Soviet BMP infantry vehicles, and BM-21 Grads, known as "hailstorms"— a self-propelled 122 mm multiple rocket launcher designed in the Soviet Union in the 1960s. All the vehicles were parked in the fields, where they were being used for target practice.

When they wished, Tania recalled, the soldiers took fuel and appliances, phones and computers, and when they were hungry, they knocked on the doors of old women and asked to be fed. Such a woman might scurry to the kitchen, trembling, and place a few potatoes and onions into a bag, and the Russians would look at the raw ingredients and shake their heads: "Make something with it; we'll be back in an hour to eat."

They walked through the village without masks, balaclavas, or helmets, and when they weren't taking things, they sat around. Every week or so, a group of higher-ups came to check up on the village. They drove around in an armored personnel carrier with ten soldiers sitting on top. Heavily armed, their faces covered, they went from house to house demanding to see people's phones, scanning through messages and apps to monitor anything suspicious. They rifled through dresser drawers and wardrobes, searched through cellars and basements and sheds. Sometimes they'd take someone's hunting rifle, sometimes they'd take a book of Ukrainian poetry. No one ever knew exactly what they were looking for, and maybe they didn't either.

Several of the locals responded to the Russians' requests for assistance. One of the first prominent villagers to do so was an official of the local elementary school, Oksana. Tania knew her well: they had been in the same school class since preschool. Oksana was from a poor family. Her father died when she was young, and her mother worked as a field laborer. Struggling to survive on almost nothing, Oksana knew that a good education was her only ticket out of poverty, and she did well in school. Their teachers recommended Oksana to the Pedagogical Institute in Kherson, and after graduation, Oksana returned to work at their local village school. She married a well-liked man from the village and gave birth to two children—a son, now twenty years old, and a daughter, now eighteen.

When the soldiers approached Oksana in the first week of occupation, she thought strategically and spoke charismatically. She would not be cold and aggressive like so many of her neighbors; she knew this was hardly ever the way to get what one wanted. Sharing just enough village gossip to win their trust, Oksana justified her burgeoning relationship with the soldiers to other people in the village, suggesting that it was the only way to protect herself and her children. In response, her salary continued to be paid. The soldiers made her privy to certain plans and ideas that concerned the village, and the insider knowledge provided Oksana with a sense of security. Within a few weeks, she had agreed the school would operate under their control, and she worked closely with the soldiers and a handful of other collaborators to acquire new materials for a Russian-based curriculum.

In the summer, when she announced that the school would now operate in accordance with Russian law, almost all the staff immediately quit. But she recruited new staff. Although there were many people in the village who would rather struggle through privation than kowtow to Russians, there were also many anxious for the security of a job. Similar events unfolded at the local daycare: the head of the school gathered her staff and announced that it would now function under Russian rules.

At the elementary school, "Almost none of the previous employees supported [Oksana]," Tania said, "but she recruited a new team, and they were all paid. They were bought. As I understand it, she wanted a good future for her children and herself, but she didn't think that this was bloody money. She did this under the guise of wanting to help people—us—but she was a traitor."

Creating incentives for collaboration proved to be one of the most powerful tools of Russian occupation: it gave the occupiers access to a concrete social network within the local community and prevented that community from unifying against the occupiers. Oksana was exactly the type of person the Russian occupiers sought out. They wanted to work with elected officials, business owners, directors of schools and universities, and bureaucrats—people who had sway and could lead others along with them, all while providing valuable insight into the social and political dynamics of the town.

Another man in the village, a relatively wealthy farm manager with a strong business sense, started working with Russians to coordinate a new supply chain. In the first weeks of the full-scale invasion, it had become difficult to get goods into the village. Medicines and hygiene products were in especially short supply. Whatever was available cost several times more than usual, and people began paying for their goods in patchwork ways—partially in cash and partially with credit, or by bartering.

The farm manager worked out a new arrangement: if he was allowed to pass easily through the checkpoint with coveted merchandise, he'd give the soldiers a cut of his profits. He began privately arranging for essential goods—medicines, toilet paper, soap, toothpaste, salt, cooking oil, coffee, packaged foods—to be shipped to the village. Though some of these items were meant to be provided as humanitarian aid, he sold them and set the price at up to ten times the market value. Over the course of a few months, he opened four stores and made a killing.

"This is easy money," Tania said. "And he and the Russians were all friends, hugging, kissing on the cheeks, sharing goods. Before the full-scale invasion, he had a beautiful house and was able to pay for his children to be educated." Why he needed more, especially at the cost of his integrity, made no sense to Tania. "But this is greed."

Many people who collaborated were greedy, but others found themselves collaborating because they were poor and relied on those in power to give them options for survival. Single mothers offered houses and practical help to occupiers, in hopes that it would increase the chances they would get jobs under the new administration. Sure enough, they were often the first in line to work as daycare teachers. Villagers who chose not to collaborate didn't feel as betrayed by this echelon of collaborator, but villagers marked them out nonetheless. Under occupation, power in the village tipped in favor of a hodgepodge group of bureaucrats and businesspeople, teachers and farmers, single moms and destitute old people. They hung Russian flags with their own hands in the school and at the post office, and although they said all the lines—"We are for a United Russia!"—collaboration seemed less to expose people's political inclinations than to reveal who was desperate. Collaboration, it seemed, had less to do with principles than with the lack of principle. And when Oksana began to strip Ukrainian textbooks and literature from the school's shelves, replacing them with books on Russian history, Tania surmised it had little to do with her loving Russia and more to do with the fact that as a little girl, she had had to pick food off bushes and trees when she was hungry.

After several weeks, Tania was fed up with the Russians and with herself, and she decided enough was enough: she would go back outdoors and continue with her life. She couldn't stay sequestered in the dark house crying for the rest of her life, so she peered out, slipped on some work pants, slid on her shoes, zipped up a jacket, and went to the garden. She'd tidy up and make sure everything stayed in order. "I will learn to adapt," she thought to herself. "I will distract myself." Keeping busy with their farm and animals, she would live as though their small plot of land was her entire world.

The Russians stole livestock from several people in the village and neighboring villages, taking chickens, cows, and pigs for food, and as spring neared, Tania and Viktor knew they needed to figure out what to do with the pigs before it was too late. Food was becoming a problem. Because very little was delivered to occupied villages around Kherson—and the cost of delivered goods was hyperinflated—by April, people were scrambling for nourishment. Clients who had purchased Tania and Viktor's pork in the past messaged them constantly, asking for insider information on when they would be slaughtering a pig, submitting advance orders for

anything they'd be willing to sell. At first they resisted: they wanted
to preserve the pigs until they could travel to the market to sell the
meat. But they also knew that the longer they kept the pigs alive,
the more likely it was that the Russians would confiscate the pigs
for themselves.

Finally, they decided that they would slaughter several pigs at
once in a few batches over the summer. This was a big risk, because
if word got out that they had hundreds of pounds of meat, it would
almost certainly be confiscated. Before the war, they'd sold their
meat exclusively at an open-air market in the neighboring village,
but traveling to the market was now dangerous, especially because
it was across a strategically important bridge, right on the front
lines of fighting. To ward off the danger, they chose to sell their
meat only to customers who were willing to pick it up at their house.
Tania and Viktor marked down the price significantly so that the
meat sold quickly. After each sale, Viktor would make a dangerous
trip into Kherson to exchange the Ukrainian hryvnia for dollars;
when he came back, they'd stuff the dollars into jars and bury the
jars in the ground.

Explosives ripped through the air every day of the spring and
summer, rattling the ground. Once, in the night, phosphorus incendiary bombs rained down on fields near the village. "It was almost
like fireworks, only a thousand times worse. I lay in bed, closed my
eyes, and thought it was the end," Tania wrote. Because they were
on the front lines, bombardment came from both directions, as
Ukrainian and Russian forces traded volleys. But they learned, over
time, to distinguish what was Ukrainian: if the explosive hit a clear
target, they knew it was launched by their own.

They feared for their pigs, who were becoming wild with the
never-ending thundering. The animals were terrified, moving er-
ratically in their sty, trembling and grunting, their high-pitched calls
reaching Tania in the house as she hid for cover. Shrapnel and pieces

of shells often fell in their yard, and they worried it was only a matter of time before their pigs were either killed or hurt.

By summer, they decided to begin selling again at the market, where they would move the meat faster and avoid bringing business to their house. They'd take as much to the market as they could, making the extremely risky trip over the bridge and back. Once they'd sold everything, they could breed more pigs when the situation was more stable. In some sense, going back to the market was a matter of principle: they would not sit at home and cower; they would go on with their lives and resist the fear tactics the occupiers used to manipulate people. When they approached the checkpoint on their way to the market, they wouldn't talk with the occupiers, would say only the word "market" when the officer asked where they were headed.

In June, they made their first trip. The weather had turned hot and dry. The line at the checkpoint was often long, and they tried to get there by six. In the early summer morning, the smell of exhaust wafted through the open car windows. The back seat of their car was full of wrapped-up pork. When it was their turn, they pulled forward, and a Russian soldier walked up to the driver's window.

"Where are you going?"

"To the market."

"Identification." Viktor's passport was ready. On the front of the Ukrainian passport is printed the Ukrainian trident, a three-pronged symbol used as early as the tenth century in the Kyivan Rus' Empire. The symbol was reappropriated after the collapse of the Russian Empire in 1918, when Ukrainians declared their independence and created the Ukrainian People's Republic. The founders of the republic used the trident as the new state's coat of arms. When Ukrainians declared independence again in 1991, the trident reappeared. Passing the passport back and forth always felt like an exchange of messages more than a routine check.

They made the trip a few times a week until, in July, the bridge connecting their town to the market was damaged by the Ukrainian army, which was seeking to limit Russia's movement in the region. It was impossible to move from town to town in the area without bridges. The Russian occupiers responded by building a floating pontoon bridge, connecting a series of floating planks with supports held up by the water's buoyancy. But getting to the market over the pontoon bridge was a big hassle and an even bigger risk. Russian soldiers put it up in the morning and took it down every afternoon to ensure that it wasn't destroyed and to limit traffic. They drove large equipment and tanks over the river atop the floating pontoons and allowed limited civilian transport.

To get to the market, Tania and Viktor would now need to wait in line at the pontoon bridge for three hours. They sold their meat quickly, within an hour, and then rushed back to the bridge so they could get there before it was dismantled and closed for the day.

Once, at six in the morning, they drove up to the crossing and stood at the front of the line when suddenly the bridge came under fire. Shells flew, dirt exploded on the banks of the river, and gravel sprayed like water. Viktor realized quickly what was going on. He revved up their small car and spun it behind a large Russian vehicle for cover. The ground shook and broken-up rocks pelted their vehicle. During a reprieve, they sped off back toward their house. When they got there, Tania sat in the car and clutched her head in her hands, shaking with fear.

A few days later, when they'd composed themselves, they went back to the market again, then again and again, coming under fire occasionally but always slipping through unscathed. Tania never told her daughter, Vika, in the United States the perils of the market trips, and when they talked every few days, Tania insisted it was relatively quiet, despite the fact that Russians lived just a few minutes from them, and Oksana and her team were working to Russify the school.

But one day in early September, Tania and Viktor decided they would not cross the bridge to the market anymore. They would not go anywhere anymore: just a couple of minutes after they arrived home from the pontoon bridge, the bridge was attacked, and three people died, and most of the village was too scared to attend their wake.

YULIA

Dnipro, Ukraine

IN EARLY APRIL, just after Yulia was sped from the hospital in Kramatorsk to a larger one in Dnipro, doctors met her at the ambulance doors, rushed her on a stretcher to another operating room, and immediately amputated her right leg. They took care to shorten and smooth her femur bone so that it was covered by an adequate amount of soft tissue and muscle—this way the bone was protected. With her left leg, they worked decisively to reassemble what they could, eventually securing it in an external fixator, a device used to stabilize and secure surgically corrected bones. Finally, they amputated her middle finger, closing off the wound with the remaining skin.

After the operation, nurses wheeled her to a room of her own in the post-op ward. It was the middle of the night. The dark Dnipro sky loomed through a large window. When the nurses asked where she'd like her bed positioned, Yulia chose a spot in the corner of the room, as far from the window as possible. Even in her post-anesthesia grogginess, she was looking for a safe place. By early morning, Oleg and the girls arrived in Dnipro, having driven through the night. They waited by her bed for her to wake up. Oleg brought homemade broth from home, as well as mashed potatoes with fish. He helped her wipe camphor alcohol all over her body to prevent bedsores.

Yulia lay in the hospital until summer, sharing her fifth-floor room with two other women who had survived the Kramatorsk train station bombing. Surgeons operated on her regularly for months. In addition to her leg injuries, she had large open wounds all over her body from shrapnel. Only two weeks after the explosion did she learn about a piece of tissue, the size of two palms, that had been torn from the back of her thigh. To perform skin grafts, doctors cleaned and prepared the wounds using a vacuum-assisted therapy that helped drain excess fluid and reduce swelling around the lesions. They took skin from near the wounds for the grafts and left them to heal for a week. Although she feared that the skin transplants would fail, her body accepted everything.

Oleg and the girls settled in Dnipro. Yulia's sister had a friend who lived in the city, and he helped them find a place to live. Although Dnipro was still an eastern city, just 130 miles from Donetsk, it was relatively far from the front lines and had become a major hub for displaced people from the south and east. This friend worked for an internet company, which rented an office in a residential building. Since everyone in the company was still primarily working remotely, they allowed Oleg and the girls to live in the office. They pushed the desks to the periphery of the room and brought in rollaway beds. With a small kitchen and bathroom, the office was suitable as a temporary apartment.

For six months Yulia wore the eternal fixator on her salvaged leg, screwed into the bone. It was bulky, cumbersome, and uncomfortable, and it prevented her from adjusting her position or sleeping well. Without the ability to bend or put weight on her leg, she stayed in bed and watched the time pass by observing the apricot trees outside the hospital window—their first blossoms opened soon after she arrived, then fell to be replaced by leaf buds, followed by leaves and clusters of tiny fruit. By the time she was discharged, the fruit was almost ready to harvest.

From her fifth-floor window she thought about the yard and animals back home, the gazebo and patio. There was often shelling there, occasionally missiles, and she worried. On a Telegram channel for residents of Konstantinivka, people she knew posted photos of shattered windows, caved-in roofs, pieces of shrapnel lying in yards. But Yulia's neighbors sent assurances that so far everything was okay. They watched over the house and the yard. Every day they hopped on top of the wall that separated their yards and climbed down a ladder Oleg had put up on the day of the railway station bombing. They fed the chickens and pheasants, gathered eggs, left food scraps for the cats, and made sure no debris had found its way into their house. When Yulia's trees bore fruit in the late summer, the neighbor harvested and preserved some of the yield, placing jars of tomatoes, pickled cucumbers, peaches, pears, and apricots in the cellar.

When her doctors removed the external fixator, Yulia began moving around a bit more in a wheelchair or on the top of the bed. Sometimes she was startled to look down and see no leg. As she began rehabilitation to rebuild muscle and strength in her thigh stump, she found herself unable to picture the amputated leg in her mind's eye. This posed a problem: without imagining her former leg attached to the thigh stump, she had no ability to control the stump—as though it could not move without her acknowledging what was missing.

She found, over time, that the only way to prod awake those nerves was to close her eyes and picture herself moving the lost leg, imagining that it was still attached, and—in her mind—wiggling those toes, rolling her ankle, pointing the foot, bending the knee, lifting the leg, turning it in and out. As she did this, the thigh stump began to tingle.

When she was discharged from the hospital, she moved to the office apartment with Oleg and the girls. As she lay in bed in the unfamiliar apartment, phantom pain at the site of her amputation kept her awake through the night. It felt as though she had stuck her foot and leg inside an anthill, with a prickly, painful sensation reverberating sometimes as far as her fingertips. Painkillers had no effect, and to keep herself from going insane, Yulia pictured everything she could about their home. She imagined the drive up their street, the familiar bumps in the road, their tiled driveway, which Oleg had spent days laying to get just right. She listened closely in her mind to the way the gate creaked when it opened, the sounds of their birds in the back part of the yard as she stepped in, their faint squawking and rustling. Her blooms, which she had never missed in twenty years, would be dying by now, and she tried to figure out how she might sweep them up without her leg.

The office apartment had served them well, allowing them all to see one another every day while she was in the hospital. But it did not feel like home, and their ache for their land, animals, and house became acute. Oleg also missed home. In Dnipro, he found work with a handyman who worked construction, helping him with electric wiring in apartments, tiling walls, laying laminate flooring, and making drywall partition walls. He knew how to do all this work after renovating their own house and working at a factory workshop for over twenty years. The work in Dnipro helped them survive, but it wasn't much, and Oleg—a homebody and a creature of habit—became depressed.

Oleg's mind wandered back to the railway bombing often when he was not thinking about something else. He thought about the moment the rocket hit, about trying to find Yulia, screaming her name. Before he got to her, he saw the body of a young boy, eight or ten or twelve years old, he didn't know. It was hard to age a corpse. The boy's skull was broken, and Oleg saw the boy's brain, that distinctive pink, winding tissue most humans only ever know from photographs. But Oleg saw it firsthand, and he couldn't forget it. Even while he carried Yulia to the car, her legs in pieces, he thought of that boy. Still, months later, the boy came to his mind while he laid laminate flooring or heard laughter in the park, and as more time passed, that little boy, whom they never knew beyond a body and brain, lived a new life in their memories.

One evening in the late summer, Yulia had the energy to get out of the house, and they decided to stroll in the large park near their apartment. The park was beautiful, lined with full, majestic oaks that in a few weeks would turn their seasonal orange and red. Oleg lifted Yulia from the wheelchair to a large rock and sat next to her. She wanted a picture, which Sonya took for them. Once they were home in Konstantinivka, she thought, when all this was over, she might want to look at that picture to remember these days. Perhaps it would feel distant then, a painful memory that was somehow imbued with a certain strained nostalgia. From the wheelchair, Yulia gathered acorns and took them back to the pot Oleg had brought from home. She planted the acorns in that soil. Maybe one will grow, she thought, and I will plant it next to the juniper tree.

By early fall, they decided that Oleg should make a short trip home, even though fighting had approached Konstantinivka over the summer. Yulia worried about him in Dnipro. Oleg was a happy and gentle guy by nature. But in Dnipro, he was discouraged and melancholy, and they thought the trip would be good for him. He'd stay a few days to check on the animals and the house, do any necessary repairs, and bring back whatever they needed.

Driving along those narrow highways into the heartland of the

Donbas steppe region, weaving through grassy fields and over small rivers—a route his father had traveled in the late 1940s to escape the secret police—Oleg approached a bloody front line with every passing second, hoping to find healing in their home. When he arrived, he talked to their birds and animals, held them in his hands, stroking them as much for himself as for them. He thought again of the boy at the train station. The new windows that they had purchased over time to replace the old ones were now covered in a thick dark rubber, and very little light shone through. But even in the dark with the sounds of shelling outside, he loved those walls. Even after all that happened, he felt a vague confidence in his walls: that somehow they would keep him safe from anything that threatened to hurt him.

MARIA

Mukachevo, Ukraine

AFTER THEIR ESCAPE from Mariupol, Maria, David, and Maria's sister's family jumped from place to place for a couple of months before they settled in a small town at the foothills of the Carpathian mountains in Western Ukraine. The town, Mukachevo, had switched back and forth between different polities for a century—from Austria-Hungary to Czechoslovakia, then back to Hungary, then to Nazi Germany. In the early twentieth century, nearly fifty percent of Mukachevo was Jewish. Situated on the southwestern edge of the Pale of Settlement—a region in the newly annexed western areas of the Russian Empire that Catherine II had established to keep the Jews contained—Mukachevo is known for its importance to the early history of both Hasidism and Zionism. In 1925 there were more than thirty synagogues in town, and the first secular Hebrew-language high school in Ukraine was built there.

By the time Maria arrived in Mukachevo in the summer of 2022, there were only about a hundred Jews left. Eighty-one years earlier, in August, most of the Jews in town were killed in just a couple of days. The event became known as the Kamianets-Podilskyj massacre, in which more than twenty-three thousand Ukrainian and Hungarian Jews were murdered; a month later, an additional twenty-eight thousand were shot in a single day in Vinnytsia, a Ukrainian city several hours northeast, and a few days after that, thirty-three thousand were killed in Kyiv. Most of those who survived the Kamianets-Podilskyj massacre were shipped to Auschwitz three years later, and after the war, Mukachevo was incorporated into Soviet Ukraine. The native Hungarian population was forcibly expelled, and new people—mostly Ukrainians and Russians—moved in, transforming the town in a decade—along with many others in the region—from a diverse Jewish, Hungarian, Polish, and Ukrainian settlement into a Soviet one. And just a few decades later, in the summer of 2022, the town was flooded with internally displaced people like Maria, a Ukrainian, who showed up speaking Russian.

Her first day in Mukachevo, Maria went to the pharmacy to buy some medicine. A pair of middle-aged women in white pharmacists' jackets stood behind the counter, and Maria mumbled her order in Russian.

"They looked at me so wildly," Maria said, "and I didn't understand why they looked like that." She repeated her request—again in Russian—and the women answered in Ukrainian. Only then did she realize that they spoke only Ukrainian, and they expected Ukrainian from her.

For decades, Western Ukraine had operated as a Ukrainian language stronghold. Though Russification policies had begun in the 1940s, the language was still perceived as an outsider tongue, unlike in Eastern and Southern Ukraine, where a significant percentage of the population were ethnic Russians who had moved to the area for work and where Russification policies had been in full effect for well over a hundred years; there, even the ethnic Ukrainians—as well as

Jews, Greeks, Serbs, and others who had settled in the region—had largely become native Russian speakers.

Through the twentieth century, official Soviet rhetoric and cultural bias branded Ukrainian an unrefined, undesirable language, significantly inferior to Russian. Although many people spoke Ukrainian at home, in public they switched to Russian, the Soviet lingua franca and the de facto "cultured" language of the region. The Ukrainian language was associated with the village—illiteracy, backwardness, and provincialism. Many Soviet Ukrainian parents did not want to disadvantage their children by giving them proficiency in Ukrainian only, so they sent them to Russian-speaking schools, which were increasingly commonplace as the Soviet Union neared collapse, despite Ukraine's burgeoning national revival movement. In Western Ukraine, however, Ukrainian speakers remained the majority. After independence, in the 1990s and early 2000s, the Russian language became increasingly obsolete in the west, even as the population of Eastern, Central, and Southern Ukraine—especially in cities—still overwhelmingly opted for Russian.

The Russian-speaking Ukrainian populations of the east and south did not necessarily feel that they were victims of Russian colonization, cultural subjugation, and forced assimilation. They were just Ukrainians born into Russian-speaking families and towns. They never chose to be born Russian-speaking, just as they never chose to be Ukrainian. Both were aspects of their identity that had been assigned to them, more or less, at the time of birth, and they never felt they were making overt political statements by continuing to speak Russian in their daily life. It wasn't a problem for them at the household level—they could switch back and forth between Ukrainian and Russian easily. But they were often bothered by politicians who chose to make it into something it wasn't: their choice to speak Russian wasn't about pandering to Russia, and it was not a rejection of Ukrainian nationhood. For them—and millions of other Ukrainians who continue to speak Russian as their first language—it was about familiarity, it was about feeling at home in the words they spoke.

But with the outbreak of war in the Donbas in 2014, many Russian-speaking Ukrainians decided they'd had enough, especially those who were displaced or saw their family members flee their homes. At home or in public, they began speaking Ukrainian to demonstrate their opposition to Russian separatism, a shift that accelerated in 2022. By March of that year, millions of Ukrainians who grew up speaking Russian had switched entirely to Ukrainian to show their resistance.

Many of Maria's friends who had abandoned Mariupol—a predominantly Russian-speaking city—had made this lingual shift, even those ethnic Russians whose grandparents had relocated to Mariupol after the Second World War to work in heavy industry. They had all learned Ukrainian in school, though they very rarely used it outside the classroom. Like them, Maria's Ukrainian was rough and unpolished; she had used it only in occasional formal settings. She thought and dreamed in Russian—and this wasn't a choice she had made; she was born into a Russian-speaking family, just like her parents and all her friends. Her Ukrainian was less automatic: She had to think marginally more as she spoke, which added an extra layer of inconvenience and mental strain. "It is very difficult for me speak Ukrainian when I'm nervous or when I'm very angry. I believe somehow that my anger doesn't deserve Ukrainian," she said, chuckling.

She stumbled through her order at the pharmacy and ran home. It was clear that if she was going to live here in the relative safety of Western Ukraine, she'd need to start speaking Ukrainian, and as Leonid was held captive by Russians, she suddenly didn't mind. Maria didn't consider herself so principled that she'd never speak Russian again—for example, she and I spoke primarily Russian when we communicated—but most of her social media posts were now in Ukrainian. The exception was when she was angry and found herself posting scathing rebukes of pro-Russian acquaintances who remained in Mariupol.

Although Russia ostensibly began the war to protect Russian speakers in Eastern Ukraine from the Ukrainian nationalists who were allegedly seeking to oppress them, the conflict ended up ameliorating Ukraine's east-west divide: many of the Eastern Ukrainians who fled to live in the west had once spoken Russian and felt sympathy for Russia, but no more. They responded to the war—fought in the name of their language rights—by choosing a new tongue.

As the summer passed, Maria felt unsettled at having done very little to assist with Leonid's release. The government promised that the soldiers would be returned within a few months, and as the months passed without word, Maria panicked.

In late July, Russians bombed one of their own occupied prisons in Olenivka, Ukraine—a small village in the Donetsk region. A single barracks building in the prison that housed POWs was blown to pieces. At least fifty-three people died and more than a hundred were wounded. Later, it was revealed that most, if not all, of those housed in the barracks were prisoners taken from Azovstal. There was no information released about the prisoners who survived the strike. Later investigations into the attack, which Russia blamed on Ukraine, indicated that Russia had planned it, transferring prisoners to the barracks and preparing for its obliteration. Ukrainian officials also noted that satellite images showed graves Russians had dug on the periphery of the prison camp prior to the bombing.

"I understood that I made a big mistake, that I had done absolutely nothing to return my husband," Maria said after the first months had passed. The realization sank in, as it did for thousands of family members of other Azovstal POWs, that they could not rely on the state alone to bring home their captive family members. They had to organize and make demands.

Maria started calling every organization she could think of—POW, military, government, humanitarian—asking for any information about Leonid. For several weeks, she could not find him even listed in any database, and she knew nothing about where he was located. She had only basic information: Leonid Kuznetsov, his birthday (December 14, 1996), and his unit: National Guard of Ukraine 3057, 12th Brigade.

She learned that the Red Cross had been involved in caring for wounded soldiers taken from Azovstal. She called them every day for weeks, sitting on hold, giving a callback number, and speaking with operators. Finally she got through: they had him listed as missing. Maria realized that if Leonid's name was not on every single POW list, he would be forgotten.

She made it her mission to get his name into the world, by any means possible, to ensure he was not a nameless body in some POW camp in Russia but someone remembered, known, and searched for. Connecting with other family members of Azovstal soldiers in captivity, she helped form a coalition called Family Members of Azovstal, and they lobbied politicians, contacted journalists and foreign aid workers, and called military organizations throughout Ukraine to make sure that every soldier was registered.

In September, after a major exchange of prisoners, more than two hundred Azovstal defenders were released. But no word of Leonid. In exchange for the Ukrainian prisoners, Ukraine turned over fifty-five Russian prisoners and one pro-Russian politician: Viktor Medvedchuk, a personal friend of Putin who had been held under house arrest since the previous year on charges of treason and financing terrorism. An oligarch and politician, Medvedchuk had started his career as a lawyer in the 1970s. One of his first high-profile cases was as the sham defense attorney for the poet Vasyl

Stus. In Stus's defense, the then young Medvedchuk claimed, "All of Stus's crimes deserve punishment." Fifty years later, Medvedchuk was being sent to Russia in exchange for many of Leonid's commanders.

That month, after the exchange, Maria made contact with an exchanged POW who had been Leonid's cellmate in captivity. He informed Maria that Leonid had been injured in Azovstal—he'd been hit with shrapnel and had a concussion—and was still recovering. As far as the soldier knew, at that time, Leonid and fellow POWs were located in a small border town in western Russia.

Maria took to social media, posting old photos of Leonid, telling their story. In one post from the late fall, she shared a photo of her and David. "David needs his dad," she wrote, asking people to share the message.

When I saw the Instagram post a couple of months later, I was surprised to see several hundred comments on it. A few came from people offering condolences and solidarity, but hundreds were from Maria herself, tagging Volodymyr Zelenskyy, his wife, Olena Zelenska, the president's chief of staff, and the commanding general of the Ukrainian army. In the middle of the night, or chasing David at the park, or riding on the bus, Maria tagged the profiles of leaders over and over again. Someone important, she hoped, would see the post and share Leonid's name, so that the next time they were negotiating an exchange, they might bump him to the top of the list, they might pull strings to bring him home.

POLINA

Lviv, Ukraine

RUNNING THE CHURCH shelter in the early weeks of the full-scale war, Polina and John watched the emergence of dozens of small-scale, ad hoc Ukrainian aid ventures, and they began working with many of them closely, securing food donations for the shelter or helping to gather materials to send to vulnerable cities in the east. They were impressed with these spontaneously formed organizations. Many of them sprang up in the first days of full-scale war as people rallied to solve problems immediately before them: their cousins in Kharkiv didn't have food, or their aunt's water supply had been cut off, or displaced children had nothing to keep themselves busy all day. Hundreds of formal and informal organizations developed, dedicated to filling some specific niche.

Ukrainians responded with striking creativity to solve obvious needs. In a small town in Western Ukraine that was flooded with displaced people, one woman I corresponded with began a cookie decorating program for displaced children. Through the night she baked gingerbread cookies in the shape of Ukraine and the Ukrainian trident, then during the day, she gathered dozens of kids and older people together to decorate them with icing before packing them into bags and boxes to ship to wounded soldiers in hospitals. For an hour a day, the kids could forget about the war. "I can't hold a weapon," she said, "but I can fight with what I know best—that is, making gingerbread. So, I decided that this should be my way of approaching victory . . . helping those children who are experiencing stress due to their existing circumstances." One friend told me about a group of old women in Kharkiv who gathered after all their homes had been destroyed to sew adaptive clothing for wounded soldiers and specialized gloves for Ukrainian snipers. On old treadle sewing machines from the early twentieth century, they sewed gloves of their own design, with three fingers, that would keep soldiers' hands warm while still allowing them to keep their thumb on the back of their gun and their index finger on the trigger.

As time went on, it became clear that those small volunteer organizations, especially those that worked to supply critical aid to frontline areas in the south and east, were doing real work to help Ukraine win the war. And yet these organizations often got little attention and struggled to find access to reliable funding. Europeans and Americans who were moved to donate resources in the first months of the war often sent funds to well-established aid organizations that set up camp in Western Ukraine or in Poland, attending to the needs of millions of displaced people. While their efforts were important, quite often they did not meet the most urgent needs or were burdened by costly overhead that prevented funds from being used to benefit the maximum number of people. Several Ukrainians have commented that the better an aid organization looks, the less they trust it. If there's a robust PR team, they know it may be at the expense of relief.

As Western Ukraine, and especially Lviv, became the nexus of humanitarian efforts, a new problem arose. Because there were far more people willing to bring aid to the western borders than to transport it through Ukraine to areas under bombardment or near active fighting, the aid often got stuck. Warehouses in Lviv full of food and medicine and other supplies kept shelters and displaced people in the west well stocked, while the many hundreds of thousands of people in the most severe conditions rarely benefited.

Through the spring and summer, tens of thousands of Ukrainians began responding to this problem, organizing pathways with their friends and colleagues to get the aid from Western Ukraine to hard-hit areas. These ad hoc Ukrainian-run aid networks proved to be efficient and effective but remained largely unknown to Western donors and media, because they typically had no PR teams (beyond potentially an inconspicuous Instagram account or a Telegram channel) and no budget, operating on small individual donations from other Ukrainians. Their operations were run on cell phones alone—no offices, no boards, no infrastructure—just a couple of guys in their thirties, for example, who made it their mission to get body armor from Poland to the eastern front. They were scrappy and productive, and many of them sent accountings to every single donor on how their money was being used. For example: "We bought 900 hryvnia [about twenty-five dollars'] worth of potatoes, rice, eggs, and diapers for several families in Kharkiv region. Thank you for your donations! Every cent is used to help our people."

They worked unofficially and informally, something that larger non-Ukrainian aid organizations couldn't do, because to operate in Ukraine, they needed formal registrations and certificates and approvals enabling them to do their work. This bureaucratic hurdle proved a significant barrier for many non-Ukrainians trying to get humanitarian goods into the country. Ukrainian bureaucracy was an especially thorny obstacle for people working to provide military aid. Going through the process took significant time and resources, and items like body armor and individual military-grade first aid kits—tourniquets, hemostatic bandages, and other combat trauma gear—were some of the most pronounced deficits in the late winter and early spring of 2022. Such items were significant because although soldiers were given a gear kit upon enlisting, many of those vital items became damaged or destroyed and were not automatically replaced. It quickly became difficult for many people to outfit themselves for war.

To bypass bureaucratic obstacles, many volunteers began driving across the border, picking up shipments of body armor in Poland, then driving back without declaring anything and shuttling the armor as close to the front lines as possible.

As aid bottlenecked in Western Ukraine throughout the spring and summer, Polina and John started to shift gears. They decided to leave the shelter in the hands of other volunteers who had begun running it alongside them. Polina and John worried about Polina's younger, teenage sister, Hanna—the only of her siblings who could legally leave the country, as her brothers weren't permitted over the border. Polina's parents agreed to let Polina take Hanna back to the United States, while John went to Kyiv to begin establishing new aid networks. For Polina, saying goodbye to the shelter and to her family was not simple: there was a unique solidarity among Ukrainians who stayed in the country—or returned to it, as she did—after February 24.

On May 19, they sent their last message from the church shelter in Lviv: "Hi. Today is our last day in Lviv, we are going home to Kyiv to help more. These 2.5 months were very eventful, we helped about 2,500 people. Costs for today's food: 2661 UAH ~ 89$."

Over the summer they began working as middlemen—John in Ukraine and Polina in the United States—helping to connect American donors with Ukrainians who could make sure of supplies.

In June, they coordinated the delivery of 50 combat application tourniquets, 330 water purification sets, 5,610 hydration sticks, 18 body armor sets, 40 helmets, 50 pairs of tactical gloves, and a pair of night vision binoculars. They developed a small team—Polina's brothers and several friends—who traveled to dangerous regions in the east delivering donated goods that Polina and John helped to ship from the United States. Over the summer their extended team and partners went to Kramatorsk in the Donetsk region three times each, among other cities, and delivered a total of five tons of goods, helping around four thousand people obtain food. On one occasion, their team came under artillery fire. In July, they connected with an orphanage and its staff who had been evacuated from the city and were now hiding out in a remote monastery in Western Ukraine and supplied the orphanage's seventy-five children with several months of nonperishable food, medicine, clothing, and toys. In the heat of the summer, Polina and John began collecting donations to provide water to Mykolaiv, a Southern Ukrainian city in the Kherson region that had been under constant shelling since February. Its water supply lines had been destroyed, and residents of the city relied on jugs and bottles, which volunteers brought to the city in the back of vans. A one-dollar donation provided fifteen liters of water—enough for one person to drink for a week—and in a few days, Polina and John's team, notably John's former mission companion Parker, raised seven thousand dollars—enough money to provide drinking water to thirty-five hundred people for three weeks.

Over the summer many Ukrainians began pivoting from strictly humanitarian aid to military aid, especially as the armed forces prepared for counteroffensives in the south and the east. By then the United States, the UK, Canada, and the EU had approved tens of billions of dollars' worth of assistance, providing crucial weapons systems, training, and intelligence to Ukrainian commanders.

The need was acute. Despite suffering embarrassment in the early months of the war, Russia's military was one of the most powerful in the world, with several times the reserve troops, tanks, artillery, and missile launchers. Just before the full-scale invasion began, military analysts estimated that Russia's military had just under 1,900 combat aircraft. Ukraine had 160.

Some critics in the West suggested that Ukrainians relied too heavily on acquiring weaponry from abroad rather than manufacturing it themselves. In the first months of the full-scale war, Ukrainian manufacturers scrambled to pivot, while volunteer networks improvised their own solutions.

A friend of mine living in Kriviy Rih, a small industrial city in the southeast, told of an eighteen-year-old neighbor who had enlisted in the army in the first days of the war, been wounded, and returned home on leave. Infuriated by the military's lack of armored vehicles, he got to work. Before the war, he'd labored at a local factory. Familiar with the factory's machinery, he crowdsourced money to buy an old city utilities truck, called a Kaz, parked it in the factory warehouse, and began outfitting it as an armored vehicle. He, along with a group of local guys, welded AR500 metal plating to the exterior, added a turret tower, and secured whatever military offensive equipment they could get their hands on. It was a powerful, lethal machine made by a teenaged wounded soldier in the outskirt warehouse of a small factory a hundred kilometers from the front lines. He made the vehicle for thirty thousand dollars of donated money—a truck that on any black market would cost several times that. The problem was that once the homemade armored vehicle was ready for the front lines, he was not willing to hand it over to the military to station it wherever it pleased. He wanted the truck to go to his guys, his friends, his hometown schoolmates, specifically.

The young man's combination of ingenious dedication to the

Ukrainian cause and more local loyalties was not uncommon. After fashioning the truck, he and his associates began making drones to assist in medical evacuations. Eventually they took the truck to Kyiv and established a partnership with a company that could provide the resources they needed to obtain proper licensing and continue building armored vehicles and land drones.

By the end of the summer, Polina and John had returned home to the United States and were also shifting their work toward military aid. They began calling their small group the KLYN Foundation, inspired by the word *klyn* in Ukrainian, which means "wedge." They hoped a wedge might symbolize what their efforts could become: a small intervention with latent leverage, capable of a profound impact. But Ukrainians of all stripes did not waste much time wondering whether their tiny interventions might make that kind of difference: many simply did what they believed they had to do.

Volodymyr—1989

RETURNING TO KYIV without the three poets' bodies, Volodymyr was irritated. The epidemiological "situation" was clearly pretense, and it had cost him and others valuable time and resources. Back in Kyiv, he set to work again. This time he would take precautions for every possible contingency. For nearly the entire autumn of 1989, Volodymyr pounded the pavement. He sent letters to all the offices in Perm that might have anything to do with the reburial, and in return he received written approvals to travel back in November to finish what they had started. He received these approvals from everyone but one office: the Perm Regional Sanitary and Epidemiological Office, whose dubious epidemic claims had halted their work in August. They didn't refuse him—in fact they sent a telegram assuring him that there were no epidemics in the area—but they withheld a stamped and signed certificate attesting that the epidemiological condition of the area was fit for an exhumation.

Through September and October, Volodymyr tried pulling every string he could. He called up all his friends and acquaintances in the USSR's storied unions—the Writers' Union, the Union of Cinematographers, the Artists' Union, and others. Creative workers' unions had a unique power in the USSR, with their members often populating the highest ranks of the Communist Party. Even if they weren't in power themselves, key members constantly interacted with those who were. During perestroika, as political control was decentralized and the Communist Party weakened, these creative unions remained powerful because of their ties to the political elites and their participation in national movements, as well as the prestige they enjoyed among the public. Appealing to his friends in the unions, Volodymyr asked them to pester the Perm sanitation office with appeals for a certificate of permission, as well as to threaten to write to local media outlets if Stus's reburial was not allowed.

While he waited for approval, he planned the filming and reburial down to the minute. They would be on a strict schedule, and any deviation could throw off the mission. He would fly into Perm one day before the film crew, and then give the go-ahead for the crew to come. Once the crew arrived, they would have forty-eight hours to drive three hours to the cemetery, dig up the graves, transfer the bodies to new coffins, and get back to the Perm airport. Those funding the reburial could afford to send the whole crew for only two days. If anything went wrong—if there was any bureaucratic mishap—they'd fail.

Finally, in late October, the sanitation office capitulated, but only partway: Volodymyr, they wrote, could come with his film crew and plan for the reburial, but he would have to visit their office when he arrived in Perm and pick up the certificate of approval in person. Volodymyr straightened his tie and set off for the second time.

The morning after he arrived, he went straight to the Perm Sanitation and Hygiene office to pick up his certificate. Volodymyr got to the office early and waited at the door for the office workers to show up. He even brought his own sheets of paper, in case someone claimed that they couldn't issue the certificate because they were out of paper.

When the head doctor came into the office, Volodymyr jumped to his feet and introduced himself.

"Hello—I am here from Kyiv for the permission to exhume our poets," he said.

"Yes, that's right," the doctor replied, shifting nervously on his feet. "Give me a moment." He stepped quickly into his office.

Volodymyr followed him, and the doctor shuffled around. When Volodymyr pestered him for the certificate, the doctor waved his hand and walked into a hallway. Volodymyr followed him again, and halfway down the hall, the doctor stopped abruptly and faced Volodymyr. He whispered sharply, inching closer to Volodymyr's face: "Don't you understand where you are going?" he said, referring to the abandoned prison site. His eyes were wide. "What does the Sanitary and Epidemiological Station have to do with it?"

He stared at Volodymyr seriously, and now it was clear to Volodymyr: whatever the office had said about an "epidemic" in August, the idea had not originated with them. The doctor moved his head in the direction of another building a few blocks away, and Volodymyr's stomach dropped. The doctor was gesturing toward the "deep drilling office," as Soviet citizens mockingly called the KGB. If Volodymyr was going to get his certificate, he would first have to trudge over to the KGB building, where officials had worked closely with the Perm-36 labor camp for all those years. Volodymyr would need to get their approval in writing, and he'd need to do it in person.

He nodded to the doctor and walked backward slowly. It was freezing, and reddish-brown snow covered the ground. Volodymyr trekked for a few blocks through the center of Perm, arriving all too soon at a large, imperial-looking building with those terrifying three letters on an iron plaque near the door. He stepped inside. It was quiet and cold, and Volodymyr took care not to make too much noise. He looked around. In the darkened lobby a dozen portraits of former KGB leaders looked down from the wall.

Coming to a front room where workers sat plunking away at typewriters and scribbling on files, Volodymyr cleared his throat.

He'd like to talk with the boss, he said. Out came a Major Chentsov, a white-browed man with a hollow face. "He was trimmed and licked, unsmiling and unremarkable," Volodymyr wrote.

Chentsov greeted Volodymyr like a long-awaited guest but without any emotion. Chentsov had expected Volodymyr. The major took the folder of petitions and certificates from Volodymyr's hand and they stepped into his office, windowless, devoid of embellishment. Thumbing through the files in Volodymyr's folder, Chentsov took care to look briefly at each one—Volodymyr's ID, the certificates from other regional Perm offices, the letters from all the important people a thousand miles away. Chentsov sighed, and a tired smile slipped onto his face.

"What brought you to our region?" he asked, something in his eyes twinkling.

Volodymyr thought for a second. If he answered incorrectly, could he end up like Stus, in some prison cell somewhere for the rest of his life? Perhaps he should suggest that he'd come only to retrieve the remains on behalf of Stus's family, so they could conduct religious rites and a proper burial, and that he, Volodymyr, would do his best to keep the operation under wraps. Volodymyr remembered his August visit to Perm-36 and listening to Ovsiyenko describe his treatment there, and he shuddered. He also thought of Stus, writing letters to his son inside those cells, losing weight and deteriorating from illness. Volodymyr wondered if Chentsov had known Stus personally. Volodymyr glanced at Chentsov's face and felt that, at the very least, he owed Stus a truthful answer.

"This is a debt we owe to our tortured heroes," Volodymyr said quietly.

Chentsov was not happy with that. "And what do we have to do with it?"

"Well . . . you are here," Volodymyr said cautiously, ". . . in business!" Chentsov let out a huff, somewhere between a laugh and disgust. "And some have said that it was you who managed Stus's case," Volodymyr added.

Chentsov stiffened. "We sometimes had preventive conversations," Chentsov admitted, by which he meant that he had interrogated Stus himself.

"And how did it go?" Volodymyr asked.

"It didn't help."

Volodymyr shifted the conversation. "Tomorrow I have to call a film crew who will film the exhumation process. But the Sanitary and Epidemiological Office is afraid to issue a certificate of permission. Obviously, this fear is not from an epidemiological threat." He showed Chentsov the telegram he had received from the office confirming that there were no epidemics.

Chentsov looked at the telegram and back up at Volodymyr. "We have no influence on the sanitary service!"

Volodymyr responded with a smirk. "Then the affairs of this state are miserable if you don't even control the sanitary service anymore!" he said. Chentsov seemed to like that, and smiled, but he wasn't impressed. The conversation was going nowhere, and Volodymyr felt that his chances for success were slipping away. He'd have to pull out his only weapon.

"If I am not able to call the film crew tomorrow to give the go-ahead," Volodymyr warned, "then the day after tomorrow, the newspapers of the three creative unions of the USSR and of Ukraine, as well as newspapers of the Ukrainian diaspora in Europe, Canada, the United States, and Australia, will be forced to publish the headline 'Major Chentsov Is an Enemy of Perestroika.'" He spoke firmly, not breaking eye contact. Volodymyr's tone was almost sympathetic. "This mechanism is already in motion."

Chentsov was angry. No one ever spoke to him like that.

"Don't you think this reminds you of . . ." Chentsov scoffed, nervously.

"Blackmail?" Volodymyr readily suggested. "But it's worth it, believe me."

Volodymyr had struck a nerve—times were changing in the USSR. An "enemy of perestroika" was a term people had used throughout the late 1980s to describe those conservative old-timers who resisted the liberalizing reforms ushered in by Gorbachev's new program. Within just a couple of years, perestroika caused dramatic shifts in the composition of the Soviet ruling elite; it had led to the forced retirement of the old Soviet guard, the conservative, dogmatic Soviet has-beens Gorbachev's administration was weeding out swiftly and openly. Just two months earlier, the general secretary of Ukraine, Volodymyr Shcherbytsky, known for opposing perestroika, had been publicly ousted at a meeting presided over by Gorbachev himself.

Chentsov stood abruptly and turned to leave the room, taking with him the stack of petitions, certificates, and references Volodymyr had brought. He placed a book in front of Volodymyr on the table. It was a new American book that had just been translated into Russian, one of the first in the wave of glasnost imports, and it was *the* book to read in the late eighties in the Soviet Union: Dale Carnegie's *How to Win Friends and Influence People*.

Twenty minutes passed, then Chentsov came back in and got straight to the point: "Our management said that we are not against reburial. We will even help!"

"It would be quite enough if you just didn't interfere!" Volodymyr said, jumping from his seat. After a call from Chentsov, the sanitation office dutifully issued their certificate. Volodymyr set off to send a telegram to the film crew in Kyiv: *Get here quickly, we're digging up the bodies.*

PART 4

THE
FIRST FALL
AND THE
SECOND WINTER

VITALY

Borodyanka, Ukraine

IN THE FALL, enormous piles of rubble still lined many streets in Borodyanka. Overwhelmed with the demands of waging war, the Ukrainian government was forced to set aside pressing issues. In remote areas with little traffic, demolishing destroyed buildings, hauling rubble, and cleaning up were low on the wartime to-do list. Vitaly complained about this regularly. That the Ukrainian state was doing so little to rebuild his town fomented feelings of resentment in him. "When this war ends, people will have a lot of questions for the authorities that they won't like, but they'll have to answer them."

After weeks of helping clear Borodyanka's streets, Vitaly began taking loads of metal, wood, and plastic to recycling plants. Though brick, tile, and metal are often more valuable, transportation costs made paper Vitaly's most profitable material. He paid collectors to bring him big loads of scrap paper and books and pamphlets and manuals, tied together with string in heavy stacks. The collectors had scavenged the paper from various garbage dumps—a job that

Vitaly himself had done for years. Vitaly didn't have a car—he rode his bike everywhere—but he rented a van every week to take the paper to the recycling plant.

In his years of recycling, Vitaly had inadvertently kept a finger not on the pulse of Ukrainian reading preferences but of Ukrainian indifference. He saw what books people threw away, and since he dealt with thousands of pounds of them at a time, he could gauge broad trends. In the 1990s, everyone was throwing away Soviet books, manuals, pamphlets, propaganda—handbooks on Soviet ideology, Soviet magazines, and socialist realist novels about young Communists who overcame the odds to become devoted party members, such as *How the Steel Was Tempered*. In the fall of 2022, it was Russian books. Not just piles of works by undeniable Russian chauvinists like Dostoyevsky, Solzhenitsyn, and Ivan Ilyin, authors who had overtly criticized the Ukrainian national project or equated Ukrainians with Russians. Vitaly hauled away vans full of books by anyone who was Russian or represented Russia, even if they had never said anything about Ukraine.

Vitaly grew up in a dual-language household. His father spoke Russian, but his mom spoke Ukrainian. His dad usually called the shots, so they defaulted to Russian. Vitaly began to prefer Ukrainian in 2014, switching entirely in 2022. By April 2022, his position on Russian had hardened, even though Vitaly himself did not speak pure, educated Ukrainian. His language was populated with Russian words or idioms, not intentionally but because for him, as for many Ukrainians, the two languages ran together almost as one. After his home and coffee shop were destroyed, he started trying to disentangle the two languages in his mind, disciplining himself when he felt himself hankering to use a Russian word to describe something.

"I think there should be two languages in Ukraine after the war," Vitaly said, "Ukrainian and English." His inclusion of English may have been pandering to me, but it also may have been rooted in the somewhat popular idea that in order to join Western Europe,

Ukraine needed a lingua franca that would connect Ukrainians with citizens of other NATO countries. "As for Russian, after everything they did here, not even their spirits should be here. I really don't like it when Ukrainians speak Russian, and I believe that soon we will all speak our native language."

Still, like most Ukrainians, Vitaly understood the practical nuances of how people spoke. He knew it often had little to do with their ideological convictions, and he sent me a video on Facebook of a middle-aged professional woman from the east who, after being displaced in 2014, then displaced again in 2022, joined the army. "I have been trying to escape the Russian world for eight years," she said, "and now I'm fighting against it." She spoke in Russian.

"See?" Vitaly said. "She is from the east, and I am from outside Kyiv, and we think the same."

Only a small fraction of the prewar recycling plants operated, and Vitaly could sell his material for just one twentieth of its prewar value. A kilogram of scrap metal sold for just two and a half Ukrainian hryvnia, about seven cents. For a thousand kilograms of wastepaper, he'd earn $73. After he paid the wastepaper suppliers and the rental car, he had an extra $13.50 in his pocket, just enough to buy some cheap food and medicine and pay for his cell phone for the day.

His money never went to alcohol or cigarettes—he didn't smoke or drink—but he often bought antianxiety medication such as benzodiazepines. "I don't sleep very well, because I am constantly thinking about what to do next and how," he reflected. He's constantly moving. A poor student in school, he probably had undiagnosed ADHD, which made it hard for him to engage in schoolwork with focused attention. But he never stops working. "I don't have any kind of rest," he said. Only when he takes a pill to calm down can he sit and take a few deep breaths.

In the summer, he and his family were selected among others who had lost their homes to receive a few hundred dollars monthly from a humanitarian aid project sponsored by an American donor. And so he decided to have another go at the coffee shop. In August, he rented a space in Borodyanka's city center, which was relatively well preserved and where rent was dirt cheap. Nonetheless, he would still have to repair the new shop's windows, ceiling, and walls. He collected a couch that had been abandoned in the rubble of a building, as well as a free table and some chairs. He cleaned them up, brushing out dirt, pounding the cushions free of dust, and sewing up patches.

In a few weeks, the coffee shop was ready and with some of the aid money he came into, he bought a new espresso machine. While half of Borodyanka sat charred, Vitaly wrote that by the end of September he was "brewing coffee and making smoothies, mojitos, milkshakes, hot dogs, hamburgers, and paninis." He could sell an espresso for twenty hryvnia, about fifty cents, and although, after costs, he earned just a few cents per cup, he found some personal relief in packing down the coffee grounds and sweeping the excess off with his finger. It forced him to slow down, just for a second.

Many days he lost money on the coffee shop—most of Borodyanka's residents had not returned, making patronage inconsistent, especially as the weather cooled and people stopped strolling outside as much. He relied on customers coming in from the highway, and his day-to-day earnings varied. But reopening the shop, even at great cost and high risk, was the only thing that kept him going through the fall.

"The coffee shop is for me, for my soul," he said. People come to a coffee shop to begin the day, to say hello, to wake up their brain with a shot of caffeine before they're on their way to all manner of tasks and jobs. A coffee shop means people keep on living and that there's life there to live. A coffee shop defies war. So, even in desperate economic straits, when his suppliers came by to tout their wares, he ordered something from them for the shop. "But I don't order much in advance," he said. "That's what this war taught me."

YULIA

Dnipro, Ukraine

SHELTERING IN DNIPRO, Yulia and Oleg's sixteen-year-old daughter, Sonya, quickly found a group of friends and formed a band. Since the full-scale invasion, and especially since moving to Dnipro and watching her mom lose a leg, Sonya had gained an appreciation for heavy metal. She began taking guitar and bass lessons to prepare for playing in a rock music bar on the weekends. She wore black clothes and painted her eyes with thick dark eyeliner.

"Sonya's friends sometimes come to our apartment and play and sing until the evening," Yulia said. "I don't bother them, but sometimes they cover songs that I remember and used to really like. And from the other room I sing along."

Yulia and Oleg went once to support Sonya and her friends at the bar and see what it was all about. Yulia liked it—the walls covered in posters and old album covers, neon signs, and graffiti. Mostly she liked seeing Sonya play hard, focused, her lips pursed seriously in black lipstick.

Since the full-scale invasion began, Ukraine's underground music scene had seen a surge in popularity. Between air raids, young people poured into music venues to release stress, meet new friends, and find solidarity. The music became angrier and more overtly political, and was no longer performed in Russian. In late August 2022, a Kyiv DJ—sporting a military uniform—played electronic dance music for a crowd of about a hundred young people. The people closest to the stage jumped to the music under fluorescent lights and artificial smoke. Farther away from the stage, partygoers gently bobbed their heads as they drank beers and smoked. Occasionally, a handful of the more aggressive men formed a mosh pit. Organizers rolled a barrel painted with a Russian flag onto the dance floor, and people kicked it and took turns beating it with a baseball bat.

Sometimes Yulia and Oleg worried about Sonya's new persona, but Yulia saw it as temporary, a reaction against the difficult circumstances of war. "She is a very soft and gentle girl, though she tries to seem tough on the outside," Yulia said. All told, she was glad to see Sonya trying to cope with the war through creativity, even if the songs demonstrated a clichéd juvenile angst. Yulia understood this impulse herself—although she was not interested in heavy metal music, she kept busy by writing poetry about her dog, Happy, and taking on small crafting and art projects.

For years, she brought in decent money with her felting. But now, since the full-scale invasion, she could not make her cat houses anymore; it was a long and physically demanding job to prepare the wool, stretch the felt, lay it all out, cut, paint, and design. "It is unlikely that I will be able to do it on a prosthetic leg. But if it works out, then of course I will return to my favorite pastime," she said. In the meantime, she turned to embroidery and smaller projects—felt flowers, wall hangings, and hats.

Before the war, she was part of a felt crafting guild that met at a wool store in the neighboring town, Bakhmut. The store was run by a woman named Natasha—a crafting enthusiast who was very skilled at using wool. Natasha organized the guild, and people came from all over Ukraine and Russia for retreats and gatherings. Sometimes Natasha invited a "wool master" who would teach new techniques and approaches. Sitting around a large table, Yulia and her group fashioned felt ornaments and plush toys, flowers and jewelry, banners, buttons, and teddy bears.

They learned how to make dresses out of wool using the felting method, ensuring that it had the stretchy properties of knitwear. Or they learned how to make a landscape, with specific techniques to create airy textures and wispy movements in grass and clouds. Some women worked only with dry wool, some were expert at needle felting. Others—like Yulia—specialized in wet felting, skillfully dampening and agitating the raw wool to create designs. "Each woman has her own secrets," Yulia said. "And we shared them at our meetings."

Yulia still spoke regularly with one woman from the felting guild. She lived in Zuhres, a tiny town a hundred kilometers to the south that since 2014 had been occupied by the separatists. "We never even thought of confronting each other politically," Yulia said. "On the contrary, when she needed help, I was ready to shelter her, but she could not come. Now her husband has been mobilized, and he is fighting on the side of the DPR [Donetsk People's Republic]. She has had almost no communication from him. I hope he wasn't killed."

As fall went on, Oleg continued to make regular trips to Konstantinivka, where he'd stay for a couple of days, then return to Dnipro. His homesickness drove him back, even though the three and a half hour drive each way consumed a lot of gas, which was not cheap. Of course, money was tight for Oleg and Yulia. The state provided Yulia her medical care and rehabilitation services for free, but by the end of the summer, the company whose office they had been living in did not renew their lease, and Yulia and Oleg were forced to move to another apartment.

Rent in Dnipro was expensive, and paying it every month took creativity. Oleg worked odd jobs throughout the city, and Yulia sold her small felting and embroidery handicrafts, though they didn't bring in much money. It often wasn't enough. On his trips home, Oleg began sorting through their garage in Konstantinivka. He rounded up a compressor, a bicycle, an electric motor, a chain saw, and a bunch of aluminum pots left by his mother, and he listed them for sale on an online sellers' platform.

In early October, Bakhmut—the neighboring town, five kilometers away, where Oleg had gone to college and where Yulia's crafting guild met—was assaulted by the Wagner Group, the private military company funded by the Russian state and controlled by Yevgeniy Prigozhin, a close friend and ally of Putin. Within a week, Bakhmut had become the bloodiest spot on the war's front lines. Russian and Ukrainian forces spilled through the city, digging trenches and constructing fortresses in abandoned office buildings and grocery stores and nail salons.

Yulia was exactly the kind of Russian-speaking resident Putin ostensibly waged war to protect—an ethnic Russian, born of Russian grandparents who'd settled in the Donbas after World War II. But Yulia found this line of reasoning abhorent. "Justifying the war based on the protection of the Russian-speaking population has nothing to do with reality," she said. "On the contrary, it is mainly the Russian-speaking regions that were previously loyal to Russia that have suffered in this war. Such perfidy will never be forgiven."

Though Yulia spoke Russian as her native language, she was schooled in Ukrainian and could switch over easily. When she met someone who initiated conversation in Ukrainian, she, too, spoke Ukrainian without even thinking about it, and often, Ukrainian speakers did the same for her in Russian. "The language problem does not exist between people at an everyday level. But it is effectively used to create conflict," Yulia said. "It is used as a political lever. It's an artificial tension."

Just like the Russians, Ukrainian lawmakers politicized the issue as well, but in the other direction. Yulia perceived many Ukrainian lawmakers riding the wave of wartime Russian backlash, issuing new bans on Russian-language literature, music, and videos to gain popular support. This angered Yulia, who saw the policies as shortsighted and strategically unsound: "This plays into the hands of Russian politicians, because [the Russians] can again and again rely on these newly adopted laws in our country to say that the Russian-speaking population is being humiliated and needs to be protected, as if the ground is being laid specifically to justify Russia's invasion of Ukraine." Many Ukrainians, however, especially young ones, support language restrictions as well as curbs on Russian-sympathizing politicians and parties. Since February 2022, the Party of Regions, For Life, and the Communist Party, which historically comprised Ukraine's pro-Russian political tribes, have largely been eliminated from the political scene.

Yulia was far from pro-Russian. Rather, her allegiances and identity may underscore a point that moderate Ukrainian philosophers, political scientists, sociologists, and historians have argued since the 1990s: there is no need to pursue a singular Ukrainian identity in order to form a successful Ukrainian nation, just as there are no homogenous states in Europe, and just as the tendency toward regionalism remains very strong in the United States. The test for Ukrainians is to embrace the tensions inherent in their nation: it's a country composed of people who believe different things, who come from different places, and who speak different languages.

Those thinkers have argued that righting the historical wrong of discrimination against the Ukrainian language was never something that could be accomplished by force or edict; the renewal of the language had to be something that Ukrainians chose, and as the war raged on, more Ukrainians did.

Even Yulia, who continued to speak Russian as she went about her daily life, began translating her poetry into Ukrainian. Her daughter Olya, who was now displaced and expecting a baby, lived in Western Ukraine not far from where her paternal grandfather had fought with the UPA against the USSR. Though Olya had been raised in the heart of the Russian-speaking Donbas, since moving to Western Ukraine, she spoke Ukrainian almost exclusively.

On Oleg's trips home in Konstantinivka, a soundtrack of explosions and firing played constantly, booming with particular force whenever a big rocket was launched, like those from a BM-21 Grad.

"Of course, it's noisy here," Oleg wrote me from Konstantinivka, "the front is ten kilometers from us. But as long as there is a house, electricity, gas, and water, I need to keep coming back, because soldiers and people fleeing Bakhmut are constantly trying to get into other people's homes to squat for shelter."

Not knowing who was gone permanently and who was away for just a short time, Ukrainian soldiers made a practice of setting up camp in empty houses a few miles from the cataclysm in Bakhmut. One of Oleg and Yulia's neighbors who was sheltering with family in Kyiv came home to collect some items they'd left behind, only to find a squad of soldiers cooking in their kitchen and sleeping in their beds. The squad let the man come in to get his stuff, but they didn't permit him to go in every room: they had set up a small hideout, and the weapons, plans, and maps were highly sensitive.

Oleg took meticulous care of his house, and though he supported the army, he wouldn't allow them to squat there, at the very least because letting soldiers move in would mean that he and Yulia weren't returning, at least for a long while.

In the months since they left, Konstantinivka had changed. Before the war, the town had a population of seventy thousand people. Thousands had left—many moving farther west for safety, but many others moving to Russia, where they had family. A close friend of Yulia's who had two young children was among those who relocated to Russia, to live with and care for a great-aunt who was old and sick. That they had moved east was a sensitive topic in our conversations. Yulia assured me there was no ideological tension between them—that she was relieved the children would at least not hear constant explosions. They had gone with the belief that they would someday return home and took nothing with them except clothes. But now there was nothing left. Their hometown—Chasiv Yar—was an increasingly hot battleground and everything there was being destroyed.

Still, several thousand remained in the area. Yulia and Oleg's neighbors—a couple in their late sixties, who continued caring for their birds and plants—had no intention of leaving even as the front lines drew perilously close. People stayed because they saw no other options, or because their sick parents stayed, or because, even though the sounds of war shook them to the core in the first month, by autumn they were used to it.

Government offices closed and moved to towns in the neighboring region. If you needed to renew a passport or a license, or to register a birth or a death, you couldn't do it in Konstantinivka. Schools closed. Parents who chose to stay kept their children home with them and let them attend school online. The internet, however, became unreliable as fall moved to winter, so many children had no school at all, playing outside all day long until an explosion shook in the distance and their mothers would holler for them to get inside quickly.

Stores closed and buses ran only in the morning. Those who didn't have cars mostly stayed home. By late fall, there was only one dentist left in town, and he dealt only with emergencies. If something wasn't working around the house—if there was a plumbing problem or the refrigerator broke down—residents had to wait weeks, often months, for a repair person to come. Sometimes, a repair person couldn't come at all, and with appliance and electronics shops in town closed, the family with a broken refrigerator would have to start storing their food in boxes outside.

One resident created a group on Viber—an online messaging app—for people who stayed in town, called "Konstantinivka WE ARE HERE!!!" It had nearly nine thousand members. There, people asked the group if there were any hairstylists left, where one might procure firewood, who had the number of an evacuation van, or the number of the veterinarian in the next village over— "my cat is sick and has thrown up four times today and isn't eating anymore." Some took it upon themselves to alert the group when power was out in a section of the city, when there was a missile attack nearby, or when one of the remaining grocery stores had a sale. The moderator tried to keep the group focused on logistical needs, but sometimes it devolved into angry political discussions.

Other times, at night, old women sent out digital graphics—cats hugging each other, sparkling flowers and birds, or misty, glowing reindeer standing in front of a full moon with the text: "May you dream sweet dreams! Good night!" There was nothing ironic about the photos; the old women hoped that their neighbors, surrounded by the war, might see the images and not feel so alone.

Everyone in the group, almost without exception, wrote in Russian. But Oleg made a point of telling me, "Those who are sitting and waiting for the 'Russian world,' I will tell you, there are very few such people."

According to Oleg, their town was now half civilian, half military. "They don't sell alcohol here anymore. They introduced a dry law. You can't legally buy it anywhere. This is in order for soldiers to have a sober head . . . And the soldiers, of course, also help ordinary people, bring them some food, grains, potatoes. They give them to people who sheltered them, to somehow share with them."

In the background of the WhatsApp voice recordings he sent me from their house, I could hear the dull rattle of shelling in the distance. He told me that the windows trembled with every explosion. "Trenches and dugouts have already been dug around Konstantinivka. They are preparing the city for defense."

"But despite this, people live, and even babies are born in our maternity hospital in Konstantinivka, sometimes ten newborns per week, because people come from the surrounding villages to give birth here."

Family members and friends asked them, incredulously: What kind of life is there in such a place? Like all the people who stayed behind in Ukraine's war zones, they were terrified to live there, but they had somehow adjusted: When a road was destroyed, they walked somewhere else. When another family fled, they bade them goodbye. When someone was killed, they held a wake.

Soon, the thought of leaving the one thing they had left, the one thing that never left them—the house and the land it sat on—was more terrifying than being killed there.

ANNA

Kharkiv, Ukraine

WHEN ANNA ARRIVED in Kharkiv in August, Dima met her at
the train. He had rented an apartment in the center of the city
where they could live together. They knew what the other looked
like—they'd exchanged plenty of photos and had video chatted—so
Anna expected she'd be able to pick him out. She told him which
car she was traveling in, and he stood on the platform and waited.
As the train slid to a stop and passengers exited, Anna gathered
her belongings and filed down the aisle, her fingers trembling and
heart racing. Stepping off the train, she caught a first glimpse: He
was not particularly tall, and his head was shaved—a typical military
look—but the hair growing in was a dishwater blond. Acne peeked
through fuzzy facial hair. He was trying to grow it out, but it was
patchy and sparse. To anyone else, he might look completely average, but as Anna stepped off the train and walked toward him, he
glowed.

He spotted her, and a smile spread across his face. Approaching him, she watched his body language carefully. Was he nervous or shy? Did he want to be close to her? Before her trip to Kharkiv, their conversation had often focused on Anna's looks—and she was quite pretty, with soft features, defined cheeks, and striking green eyes. "He was worried that I wouldn't live up to his expectations," Anna said, and as she neared, he stepped toward her and pulled her into a firm hug.

"You're even better than on the phone and in photographs," he said, smiling.

She felt his approval and adoration, and she loved it. Her emotions overwhelmed her as they walked from the train station and through Kharkiv. To Anna, the city, even though much of it had been bombed, was beautiful, and walking through it with Dima was a thrill, though her stomach lurched with nervousness. Yet somehow she didn't feel scared.

She liked how he talked. He was gentle but sociable, comfortable taking the lead in conversation. Anna was naturally more reserved. After many months of chatting online, she had found a rhythm in their exchanges and had shed some of her shyness. But now, in person, she felt herself stiffen slightly. Turning the key in the lock of their apartment, Dima pulled the door wide open and slid her suitcase inside, waving for Anna to follow. She stepped in. It was nice, cozy, and somehow it felt safe. She grinned, and he was relieved to have made her happy.

She looked around: *Okay, this is where I live now.* Anna was surprised at how doting he was. He'd rented a small studio apartment located right in the center of the city. Normally, a nineteen-year-old enlisted private in the Ukrainian military would never be able to afford a renovated studio in central Kharkiv, the second-largest city in Ukraine after Kyiv. But after the city had been assaulted for months, hundreds of thousands of people had left, and apartments were cheap. Their small studio had been left intact, and although it was in an old, small pre-Soviet complex, the apartment had undergone *evro-remont*—European-style renovations that made it Western and modernized, with new cabinetry, a small dishwasher, a tile backsplash. The apartment was next to lots of shops and not far from the Kharkiv National University, an impressive campus that—before the war—was one of the most beautiful in Ukraine.

The university was founded in the Russian Empire in 1804 as a vocational school, offering courses on Enlightenment ideas and preparing men for bureaucratic state service. The university's faculty—many of whom were Western Europeans—spread variants of the nationalist thought becoming popular throughout Europe, and by the 1820s, as university students began to reflect on Ukrainians' former autonomy, the beginnings of Ukraine's national movement had been sparked. Intellectuals criticized the marginalization of the Ukrainian people in the Russian Empire, and the university boomed with projects of cultural reclamation. Students set off into villages to record Ukrainian folk songs, stories, and dialects, and the university published anthologies of Ukrainian literature. Many of Ukraine's first modern works of literature, history, and ethnography were published there, as well as the first newspapers and journals in imperial Russia–ruled Ukraine. The city became an important and influential education and publishing hub, not just in Ukraine, but throughout the Russian Empire. A cultural renaissance brewed in Kharkiv in the mid-nineteenth century, and its distinction traveled far.

In the late 1800s, as Ukrainian nationalism came under attack—with the language outlawed, nationalists imprisoned or killed, and universities under pressure to teach imperial histories and language—a network of secret societies dedicated to the issues of nationalism called *hromada*s popped up throughout the city, laying the groundwork for Ukraine's first, short-lived modern independent state, from 1918 to 1921.

In the first months of the war, Kharkiv was disproportionately targeted by Russian assaults; explosions continued without breaks. Kharkiv was a strategically valuable city for the Russians, in the northeast of the country not far from the border, and Moscow seemed intent on leveling it into submission. Within a month of the war beginning, no building at Kharkiv National University remained intact. It was one of the most obvious instances of Russians targeting sites of Ukrainian national significance.

Anna looked around the apartment: a bathroom, a kitchen, a small dining table, a couch that folded out into a bed, some pillows and blankets, a small mirror. The curtains were not particularly stylish, but they seemed nice enough, and after living for months in shelters and barracks, Anna was not complaining.

Anna felt a pang of awkwardness. She had never lived with a boy before, and she felt possessed by a new sense of privacy. He prodded her to not feel embarrassed or timid. "I didn't understand how to behave," she said.

She was relieved when Dima pulled her in for a kiss. Feeling the warmth of a body near her, she felt even more acutely just how alone she had felt for so long, and she thought this was why she had come, to remember what it felt like to be cared for by someone else. Later that night, they told each other that they loved each other.

It was the end of summer and the apartment was stuffy, and one night, when Dima got up to open the window at four in the morning, he saw flickering outside. "They are launching Iskanders nearby," Dima said, referring to a mobile short-range ballistic missile system used commonly by the Russians, and the words terrified Anna. A missile landed not far away, and a plume of smoke rose outside the window. Dima made her promise that when he was away and rockets flew outside, she would run into the hallway or to the basement. But that night they just stayed in bed and listened to the bomb shake the earth around them.

"But somehow we survived it," she wrote, "and we had a very

good time, we liked each other so much, and despite everything, I have been here since August, and I don't regret being here."

In August and September, Anna grew up a lot. She woke up to the rumble of explosions, but as long as the collapse of bricks and metal, the shattering of glass, and the car alarm sirens were not too close, she felt this was a step up from the shelter in Western Ukraine, where she was completely alone and where it always smelled dank and soiled and she slept clinging to her backpack in a bunk bed in the same room as seven other people.

She was proud of herself for successfully moving her life across the country amid war. She was making adult decisions—where to be, how to live, who to love.

And yet she was still young. She was a virgin when she arrived in Kharkiv; in fact, Dima was her first real boyfriend. When he wanted them to have sex for the first time, Anna said, "I didn't dare." She was self-conscious and nervous for the first several weeks, though eventually, she said, this wore off. Soon they talked about having kids and a family together.

Though she didn't hear much from her parents—a text message from her mom now and then—as the summer turned to fall, Anna felt happy. She liked the city, and she was content knowing that she was nearer to her parents—on the front lines—than she had been in the west. When Dima was home, she loved his company, and when it was time for him to leave again, he put on his army clothes and combat boots, and carrying his helmet on his wrist, made his way back to his platoon to begin fighting again.

Even with Dima at the front, Anna remained content. Dima was stationed on the border with Russia, just north of Kharkiv, about twenty-five miles away. At the end of a shift, he could come home for a day off, or sometimes he could hop on a bus in the evening, stay the night, and leave early in the morning for the base. Every couple of months, he got a longer vacation—a few days or maybe a week—and regardless of the length, they spent all his off time together.

Dima was not a natural soldier. When the full-scale invasion had begun, he had been living in Kharkiv for only a few weeks, and he wasn't inclined to military service. He'd grown up around war in Luhansk—he'd seen his friends join the LPR military to earn a wage, he saw how miserably they all lived, he knew the smells of military vehicles, he understood the weight of a gun strapped on your chest. It wasn't for him, and he left Luhansk to escape it.

But when the full-scale invasion began, Dima saw so many men, even older men, standing in line to join up that he felt a pang of responsibility. He woke up one morning, on the third day of the war, the city burning, his heart in his stomach, and walked to the nearest enlistment office and filled out all the questionnaires about who he was and his body and health, and a doctor had him strip down in a room with other guys where he checked their heart and lungs, and then someone issued them uniforms based roughly on their body sizes, which they slipped into for the first time. Knowing that some of them would die in those clothes, the recruits avoided eye contact, uncomfortably shifting their weight from side to side as they took oaths. They were given guns they didn't know how to use, put on buses, and sent off to learn all the things most of them had never wanted to learn. A few hours away, in his hometown, Dima's classmates who stayed in Luhansk were drafted to fight on the other side, for Russia. Dima had just turned nineteen.

Those first weeks of the war were lonely. He was among the youngest anywhere he went, and he was small for his age anyway. He put on tough faces and spoke crassly to seem unaffected, but he was shaken to his core to be so far away from home, to go weeks without speaking with his mom, to listen to so much talk of killing and dying and destruction. He'd started talking with Anna in April on a public chat room to distract himself, but as their exchanges continued, something about her seemed familiar. She was from Luhansk, yes, but more than understanding where he was from, she seemed to understand him, and he liked her quiet, gentle disposition. She didn't like drama, she was subtle and sweet and occasionally funny. When he had a hard day, she wanted to help him feel better, sending love notes and hearts and assurances that she cared for him. The more they talked, the more he thought about the future.

When he was away, she enjoyed the privacy of the small studio apartment, and she passed the time by chatting with her grandma in Luhansk or her best friend from Sievierodonetsk, who had moved to the Czech Republic. "We talk, but we don't dwell on war anymore. We are just waiting for the end of the war, because everyone is already fed up, everyone wants to go home, although we have nothing left from either my house or my friend's house. We just want the war to end so that a time of peace would come, and everything would be restored as it was before, or maybe even better."

Initially, Dima was stationed somewhere in the Kharkiv region, which had recently been liberated, and he was not directly in the center of the fighting. But by December, he'd been moved to Bakhmut, the town adjacent to Yulia and Oleg's, where tens of thousands of Ukrainian soldiers confronted the infamous Wagner Group—by now many of the militia's recruits were convicts who'd been released from Russian prisons to go and fight.

Previously, when Dima was stationed in the Kharkiv region, he'd gotten in touch every day, if he was lucky to have cellular service. Once he went to Bakhmut, the contact became less regular—once or twice a week.

"When we talk, we talk about the war," she said, "because it is important for me to know how he is, whether everything is fine with him, or his comrades, since I know some of them . . . He'll tell me about how everything is going, how they engage in battle. At the moment no one storms anything, and in principle, thank God, there are minimal losses." But that changed day to day. In one conversation he told Anna that he and other troops came under fire at their position, and one soldier near him was severely wounded, while another was hit by shrapnel in the head and died right next to him.

"Sometimes we talk about his moral condition, and I often support him, because it's hard for him," Anna wrote. In Ukrainian, the word "moral"—*moral'no*—connotes something more than a moral or ethical condition; when Anna said she and Dima spoke of his moral condition, she also meant his psyche, his soul. "But I try not to talk about my problems . . . I'd rather tell him how I went on a walk or how much I love it in Kharkiv. I just hope for the best, and I am waiting for him to come home alive."

POLINA

Kyiv, Ukraine

BY THE FALL, Polina and John had begun working with a couple of young Ukrainians, around their same age, who supplied weapons and tactical gear to the front lines. The couple was looking for a way to outfit a company of two hundred Ukrainian soldiers with thermal gear, and Polina took up the project.

She thought a lot about winter, as did most Ukrainians in the fall of 2022. The first full winter of the war would be a challenge for soldiers if they were not properly outfitted, and Polina, who was trained as a fashion designer, was drawn to the challenge. She would put together complete military winter clothing kits and deliver them to Ukraine herself. She had been back in the United States since summer, and she was itching to get back home.

By then, in the United States, it seemed to Polina that many people were already tired of talking about the war. After running the shelter in Lviv and living on pure adrenaline for several months, she fell into a depression in Utah, where they stayed, where there was no indication that anything was wrong anywhere in the world. She stopped wanting to go outside, and she didn't want to let anyone know she was back home. On the Fourth of July, the sound of fireworks sent her into a tailspin. Occasionally, people would congratulate her or her little sister for making it safely out of Ukraine, but she herself couldn't make sense of why all she wanted was to be back there.

"We came home fundamentally changed, and yet no one else was," Polina said. For months she couldn't talk to people. "We heard attacks, we lived through attacks. We witnessed so many people who went through horrific events and lost so much of their lives," she continued. "And that shaped me."

Polina began researching military-grade thermal clothing in earnest, consulting with former US soldiers and army gear manufacturers. It would need to include four different layers. First, a base layer of moisture-wicking underwear, often made of merino wool or synthetic blends, necessary to wick sweat away from the skin and keep the body dry and warm. Next, an insulation layer, like long thermal underwear and fleece jackets. The outer layer would be a waterproof shell, like Gore-Tex, protecting against wind, rain, and snow while remaining light and breathable. Finally, gloves, neck gaiters, wool socks, and balaclavas.

They were on a strict donation budget, and to fully clothe two hundred soldiers for winter was not cheap. She bought some items from an American army wholesaler, in addition to fifty tourniquets and chest shields, and tactical medical equipment. But many of the materials she needed, such as fleece jackets, she couldn't find for a good price in the United States, so she packed up what she had and decided she would find the rest in Ukraine on her own, hoping to find a better price and support Ukrainian manufacturers. John would stay in the United States this time, and Polina would go on her own to transport the goods, find additional thermal materials, assemble the kits, and see her family.

The day after she arrived in Kyiv, a drone attack there blew up critical infrastructure in Ukraine's power sector. She and her family ran to the basement, and the electricity was shut off for several hours across the city. Little did she or anyone else know that it was the first of thousands of Russian drone and missile assaults that would continue to target Ukraine's energy infrastructure throughout the fall and winter, causing sweeping blackouts and critically impairing the distribution of heat throughout the country.

Across most of the former Soviet Union, being cold was a collective fear. In Ukraine, as in other Eastern European countries that experienced the harshness of winter during the Second World War, a collective memory contributed to a kind of cold trauma, which prevails in the contemporary Ukrainian psyche. Everyone had heard stories of people freezing to death—how they first became numb in the cold, then stopped speaking to conserve energy, their hearts eventually halting—or how children became sick in the winter and never fully recovered, even in adulthood.

In wintertime, Ukrainian kids are still swathed in layers upon layers of sweaters, jackets, full snowsuits, scarves, gloves, hats, and boots. If you want to make a scene, step outside in the wintertime with an improperly dressed child, and old women will descend upon you in feverish fits, rushing you back inside with a lecture or meeting you with a blanket of their own. You are likely to be served room-temperature drinks at a restaurant (ice cubes are out of the question), or to be shoved into house slippers the moment you remove your shoes inside someone's house, lest you catch a chill on the cold floor. It's not uncommon for older people to be wary of air-conditioning.

As the power went out across the country, leaving Kyiv and

other cities entirely in the dark and cold, many—especially older Ukrainians—began to panic. It was a cruel Russian strategy to exploit a Ukrainian psychological trauma that Russians themselves shared. But the panic was not only about the cold. The power outages disrupted every aspect of daily life in Ukraine. The government scrambled to supply switches, transformers, and generators to stave off a total collapse of its power grid. The word of the season in fall 2022 was "generator." Usually running on gasoline, a generator's engine starts up like a lawn mower, and it generates mechanical energy through a rotational motion that is transformed into electricity. Businesses that couldn't afford generators either collapsed or made do without power, using battery-powered lamps, serving cold food, and working in the dark. One friend told me about her nail salon in Kyiv, which didn't have a generator and could provide only old-fashioned manicures—no gel or acrylic manicures that required LED lamps to cure. Most women got their nails done after work in the late afternoon or evening, but since it was autumn and dark, manicurists wore battery-powered headlamps as though they were working in a mine shaft.

Spontaneous power outages left the city in constant dysfunction. Businesses and restaurants shut down, Wi-Fi networks were wiped out, and stores and pharmacies assumed new, irregular hours to take advantage of brief periods of power. An older woman with whom I corresponded wrote to me of her adult son who had developed severe epilepsy after suffering meningitis as a baby. He was mentally disabled, and the power outages frightened him. To prevent a grand mal seizure, his mother had to ensure that he took medication twice a day at very specific times. She had lived for nearly twenty years under that undeviating regimen, going to the pharmacy at specific times on specific days to ensure they had the medication right when they needed. If they didn't, he would usually seize, lose consciousness, and fall to the ground, his body jerking on the floor. He was often injured during a seizure, and watching him convulse and turn blue, foaming at the mouth, was traumatic for his mother. With the power outages, the supplies and schedules of pharmacies became unpredictable, and they could no longer keep to their strict medication regimen, though she begged pharmacists to dole out more pills than allowed just so she'd be sure not to run out. In the end, they simply lived in fear, running between pharmacies all day long, trying to get enough pills to prevent a seizure.

Working in the dark as the weather cooled, Polina first sourced good fleece. A year earlier, Polina had worked for BEVZA, the prominent Ukrainian high fashion designer, and she had become especially expert at fabric sourcing, finding luxurious, high-quality fabrics that draped well and created clean-cut silhouettes. She reveled in the challenge.

Finding the fabric and pattern and seeing her work come to life—it all motivated Polina. Since she was a little girl, she had loved keeping her fingers busy with scissors, cutting and pasting and folding. And she was proud of her tiny creations, which only developed sophistication as she grew up. In her twenties, she still felt the same pride looking at her work. BEVZA was the only Ukrainian designer to show at New York Fashion Week, and when she attended the event in September 2021, just before the full-scale invasion, her heart swelled with satisfaction.

Polina found a local fabric store that contracted with a factory manufacturer at wholesale prices. The factory, an hour southwest of Kyiv, produced the kind of fleece she wanted. She drove down to check it out, inspecting the material's weight and weave. She ordered hundreds of yards of the fabric and had it delivered to a sewing shop outside Kyiv, where seamstresses sewed two hundred jackets and hats from patterns they'd been using to outfit soldiers on the front.

None of the jackets, however, would be finished while Polina was in Kyiv: the massive power outages delayed production of the fabric, and the sewing shops worked at reduced hours when electricity was turned on. When an order of jackets and hats was finished, Polina's siblings would pick them up and, after school, assemble the kits in plastic bags and deliver them to the guy who would take them to the front lines in the east. She was disappointed that she wouldn't get to see the completed jackets before she left. But she had come home to Kyiv for another important purpose.

Just before she left, she had taken a bus to a clinic, one she had visited since she was a child. She went alone. The clinic ran on emergency generators, and after a urine sample and a blood draw, she climbed atop an exam table and waited for the doctor to come in. When she did, the doctor rubbed warm jelly all over Polina's stomach and moved a Doppler around searching for a sound. After a few seconds, the doctor found what she had been looking for: that unmistakable thump, the sign that life goes on, a rhythm that changes everything forever.

She had taken a pregnancy test a few weeks earlier, but now, after hearing the heartbeat, Polina walked back to the bus stop slowly, confidently, even under threat of another drone attack, as though with two heartbeats inside her, she would live forever.

TANIA

Mykil'ske, Ukraine

AS THE WEATHER cooled and the local farmers in Mykil'ske began dodging the military equipment in their fields and gathering whatever last yields remained, a small group of Russian soldiers and collaborators began knocking door-to-door. They carried folders of paper ballots with one question: "Are you for the incorporation of this territory into the Russian Federation?" At the bottom were two boxes: yes and no. The referendum vote proposed formally incorporating all of occupied Ukraine, around fifteen percent of the country, into Russia. The voting took place over five days throughout the areas occupied by Russia in Donetsk and Luhansk, as well as in Zaporizhzhya and Kherson, all together a territory approximately the size of Portugal.

The former mayor of Kherson, Vladimir Saldo, helped to stage the vote. Saldo had also served in parliament as a member of the pro-Russian Party of Regions. Now he was announcing the referendum on the messaging platform Telegram, writing that he hoped the region would become "a part of Russia, a fully fledged subject of a united country."

The paper ballots gave the impression of a legitimate vote, that the will of all the people who received the papers and marked yes or no would determine the outcome. Tania and Viktor and everyone else knew this was a joke; that countries were not annexed by slips of paper but by tanks and the people in them—they had seen it with their own eyes. In the first few months of the Russian occupation, Kherson locals rallied against the Russian occupiers. Hundreds of people took to the streets in protest, waving Ukrainian flags and chanting in Ukrainian "Kherson is Ukraine." But in time, Russian secret service officers acquired the names, addresses, and phone numbers of those who led and participated in the protests, and the officers showed up at those people's houses and threatened them in front of their children.

By the time of the referendum in September, there were no longer demonstrators, though many protested the vote by locking their doors and refusing to come out or by not going to one of the town's designated voting stations. Many locals who were sympathetic to the Russians or, at the very least scared of falling into their bad graces, helped facilitate the vote.

In Tania's village, Mykil'ske, one local young woman—Sophia—assisted in the referendum. She was a former classmate of Tania's daughter, Vika. Mykil'ske was a small village, with just a few thousand people. Most everyone knew one another or of one another, and Tania recalled that Sophia had given Vika trouble in school—fighting and bullying, rallying people against Vika when she went to study as a foreign exchange student in the United States. Sophia was raised poor by a single mother who worked in the fields, just like Oksana—the school official who also collaborated—and when Tania saw Sophia outside the window handing out referendum ballots, she felt a flare of anger but also shook her head in pity. "Healthy, normal people wouldn't do this," Tania wrote.

The referendums were widely condemned as a sham and went unrecognized by the international community. But Saldo, the former mayor, claimed victory on social media with an 87 percent yes vote. "It's already clear that the vast majority of people supported the issue of secession from Ukraine and joining Russia," he wrote. A week later, he, along with the Russian-installed leaders of the Donetsk, Luhansk, and Zaporizhzhya regions, went to Moscow to shake Putin's hand on a job well done. Russia declared Kherson Russian, just as it had done three hundred years earlier.

Tania and Viktor went on with their life as best they could. Ever the pragmatist, Tania kept her nose to the ground, working hard, even as the weather started to change. The fall was usually mild and pleasant, and the cooler temperatures after a hot summer came as a relief. The village was relatively quiet, though tense, until October, when news began to spread of Ukrainian troops approaching. They were retaking villages and small settlements every few days, advancing across the wide steppe as Russian forces retreated from villages they had occupied since March.

After the whirlwind counteroffensive in the Kharkiv region a few months earlier, everyone watched the movement of the front lines in the Kherson area with bated breath. That fall, Putin conscripted an additional three hundred thousand recruits to fight in Ukraine, something Russia had not done since the Second World War. The mass conscription, Putin claimed, was "in order to protect our motherland, its sovereignty and territorial integrity, and to ensure the safety of our people and people in the liberated territories." Russian army commanders recruited actively in prisons, offering pardons for six months of service in Ukraine. Russian soldiers and mercenaries fighting in Syria and South Ossetia were redirected to battlegrounds in Southern and Eastern Ukraine. That fall, the United States, the UK, and EU countries provided Ukraine with long-range weapon systems en masse, enabling Ukraine to hit Russia's ammunition depots and command-and-control centers, leaving Russia significantly weakened.

Russia dug in its heels and threatened nuclear war if the West did not curtail its support of Ukraine. Russia's war, according to Putin, was with the whole West. While Ukrainians asserted that they fought a war of decolonialization, Putin suggested he did, too: his was a war that would free Ukraine—the heartland of Russia—from the hegemony of the West. And if the West continued to stand in his way, he would wage war on it as well.

Putin's war on Ukraine, of course, has only intensified Ukrainians' support for an alliance with the West, and the relevant reforms required. Over the last decade, Ukrainian society has pushed against an often corrupt or overweening state in productive ways, requiring tangible reforms to reduce political graft and improve Ukraine's democracy, striving to transform Ukraine into a more likely future member of the European Union. Politicians responded by reforming the public tenders system and implementing and enforcing a system of income declarations for state office holders and politicians to keep them in check. When change has been slow, Ukrainians have responded fairly decisively: as the political scientists Maria Popova and Oxana Shevel have written, "It was disappointment with this slow pace of change, in part, that led many voters to choose Zelenskyy in 2019." They went on: "Ukrainian civil society and Europe have kept pressure on Zelenskyy's administration over the last two years [from 2020 to 2022], and it has been paying off." Zelenskyy made big promises—as Ukrainian politicians have for decades—about curbing corruption, and his government has, in fact, made notable improvements. After his election in 2019, Zelenskyy engaged in a pointed "de-oligarchization" campaign, attempting to separate oligarchs from politics, a move that significantly weakened Russia's control over Ukraine, as many Ukrainian oligarchs leaned east.

Zelenskyy's approval rating at the beginning of the war skyrocketed when he refused to leave the country. Since then, approval has remained relatively high, though many Ukrainians—especially intellectuals—are skeptical of Zelenskyy's ability to govern, which seems consistently overshadowed by his ability to perform effective PR. Many became still more skeptical of Zelenskyy when he later postponed presidential elections, with the justification that it was unconstitutional to hold them while Ukraine was under martial law.

That said, the anticorruption measures established in Ukraine in the previous half decade have proven relatively sturdy. Popova writes that at the beginning of the war, when military aid and other types of aid started flowing to Ukraine, many people postulated that illegal smuggling of weapons across the border and the disappearance of aid funds would become commonplace, based on the country's corrupt track record. And yet reports of arms smuggling remained few, and the news of financial scandal, Popova argues, is actually encouraging, because it shows that Ukraine's anticorruption institutions are robust enough to allow exposure and to punish those who misappropriate funds or resources. Ukraine's democratic institutions have proved surprisingly resilient, yet many Ukrainians feel that the government could be doing significantly more to curb corrupt spending and allocate money more judiciously, especially when it comes to social and veteran welfare.

Throughout October of the first fall, the Ukrainian army steadily approached Tania's village of Mykil'ske, fulfilling Zelenskyy's announced goal to redraw the battle map by winter. The writing on the wall was becoming clearer: Ukraine would be able to retake large portions of the Kherson region, but just how much would depend on military aid from Western allies.

At the end of October, Saldo announced that the remains of "His Serene Highness Prince Potemkin" had been removed from St. Catherine's Church and taken to safer territory. Potemkin was revered by Putin, and his bones were of paramount importance to

Russia and its imperial myth. After nearly 250 years, Potemkin left his New Russia for the old one, under the smoke of shelling.

Soon after, the Russian occupiers in Tania's village started packing up. Unsure of either their next destination or Russia's larger strategy, they made the most if it. They went door-to-door appraising the value of different items as though they were at a garage sale. They came in groups, removing paintings from people's walls, carrying rugs over their shoulders, with microwaves tucked under their arms. They strapped upholstered furniture to the top of the cars and tucked perfumes and shoes and a little kid bike into the trunks. Collaborators prepared to leave, too—the school official, the leadership of the kindergarten, the man who prospered by marking up goods for sale. They packed their cars as though for a long vacation. Threatened with serving a prison term if they stayed around, most of them retreated alongside the Russians into Crimea or across the Russian border to the east. Collaborators whose work was not well known could blend in with the larger refugee population and flee to Poland or westward. But many more low-level collaborators remained.

"They justify themselves that they did it for the sake of money," Tania said, before adding: "Something went wrong in the lives of these people and their lust for money."

But even if their motivations were financial—even if those people were not ideologically anti-Ukraine—they were left with an indelible mark. For them, social survival in the village after liberation would become very difficult. People didn't want to help them with donations or volunteer work. Although Tania is a non-confrontational person who hates conflict—and chooses simply not to communicate with these people in any way—the hatred was suffocating. According to Tania, members of the SBU, the Ukrainian security service, came to the town immediately after its liberation and extensively interrogated those who collaborated.

Sophia—the girl Vika's age who helped at a low level to carry out the referendum vote—also ran away, but whether to Russia or Poland, Tania does not know.

Oksana, the school official, fled to Russia. But she and others who left in Russia's retreat kept in touch with people in the village on various messaging apps. They wrote angrily of people's foolishness for not embracing the Russian soldiers, adding that Russia would return eventually—and probably soon—and when they did, everyone who pushed them out would be sorry. Their messages reverberated throughout the village; people gossiped about what Oksana and others had to say, and many were scared they were right. Tania shook it all off dismissively. She had known Oksana since she was a child, and the tantrums didn't faze her. "I don't want to bother with all this nonsense," Tania wrote.

Two days after their retreat, on November 11, as the Russians crossed the river to the other side of Kherson, they blew up the Antonivsky Bridge over the Dnipro River, as well as the small bridge spanning the Inhulets River, which connected Mykil'ske to the villages around it and was the only road providing access to highways leading to reclaimed territories. Early in the morning, from the vantage point of their house on a grassy, fertile inlet between the Inhulets River and the Dnipro, Tania and Viktor could hear and see everything—explosions, smoke, the roaring of planes and tanks, the firing of missiles. The clamor exceeded anything they'd heard before. "There was such an explosion that we thought we would be blown away," Tania said.

The now destroyed Antonivsky Bridge had played a key role in Russia's strategic calculations. It was the primary transit route for supplies between Crimea and occupied Kherson, and Ukrainian forces had consistently targeted it. But Ukraine had been careful not to destroy the bridge, and they presumably intended to use it to pursue retreating Russians on their way out of Kherson. Now that was impossible. Russia had left Kherson for Ukraine's taking, retreating to—and regrouping in—territories on the south side of the river.

The day the bridge was blown up, a neighbor came running to Tania's house: "Our people are in the village," she said, "driving an armored personnel carrier along the upper street."

Tania leaped forward. "I was crying with joy, I was trembling all over," she said, and she ran with her neighbor to the entrance of the village in hopes of catching a glimpse—"at least to see what kind of guys our guys were."

As the soldiers came into the village, a crowd met them, cheering and crying. At the town's main entrance, Ukrainian soldiers parked their cars in the middle of the street. They stepped out and awkwardly unrolled a Ukrainian flag. People started to gather, and old women kissed the soldiers and cried. Two thousand people gathered on the streets—nearly the whole remaining village. Many remarked that they were surprised to see so many; people had been so afraid to leave their houses for eight months that no one actually knew how many had remained in town.

"They were so handsome," Tania said. "You couldn't take your eyes off them." Tania and other villagers were spellbound. Later they recalled the experience vividly, commenting on how clean and well-groomed the soldiers appeared, how polite and refined their manners were, and their superior kindness. "They asked us to excuse them," Tania said, "that it had taken them so long to free us from the *rashisty*."

Ukrainian soldiers moved into the houses abandoned by fleeing collaborators or soldiers. Those first several days, people from the village flocked to the soldiers with flowers and various homemade delicacies—breads, cakes, soups, dumplings. Residents organized volunteer kitchens and began cooking meals for the military. This was true in every nearby liberated village in the region. "We all coordinated and brought food there," Tania recalled. "Kitchens prepared up to one hundred meals a day, and others baked and fried hand pies and boiled dumplings. The soldiers were very pleased and said that they did not expect that they would be met like that." They were just normal guys, but they had become mythologized: they were the gods who saved the village.

The Kherson counteroffensive in late 2022 liberated thousands of square kilometers in Southern Ukraine and dozens of villages and settlements, a major shift in the war that was in large part credited to the artillery systems, guided munitions, and long-range rocket launchers that the United States and other Western allies had provided to Ukraine. Since February of that year, Ukraine had regained about half the territory Russia seized in the first days and weeks of its invasion. With more military aid, Ukraine could have pushed farther and turned the tides of war, as it hoped, before the Russian army could dig in and fortify a long line of defense in its other occupied territories in the south and the east. But Ukraine's counteroffensive eventually stalled after the bridges were blown up. Ukraine suffered immense losses liberating Kherson, and the region was now split: the northwestern side of the Dnipro River was controlled by Ukraine, while the other side, in the direction of Crimea, remained under Russian occupation.

Tania's village now sat directly on the war's fault line. Although the village was finally liberated and under Ukrainian control, liberation brought a new onslaught of violence, as the town was assaulted continually by Russian artillery from the other side of the river. Soon, water and electricity would disappear for months. Beginning in the late fall, as the weather cooled, Tania and Viktor and everyone else began surviving on well water, outdoor fires, and generators. They washed their clothes in water they carried from the river in buckets, set up barrels to collect falling rainwater, and bathed themselves with washcloths and a bowl of water heated on a fire.

With both bridges destroyed, selling anything at the market-place was out of the question. Villagers now had no ability to leave unless they could drive several miles northeast and circumvent the rivers—an extremely dangerous route that took them just several hundred meters from Russian occupied land, through territory that was under constant fire. Alternatively, they could row across the river, an even more dangerous route, as rogue or poorly aimed projectiles landed regularly in the water. In an open rowboat, unlike a car, there was nothing separating its operator from direct impact, and artillery and metal fragments fell on the river like rain.

It was as though they lived on an island, cut off from the world. Electrical and water line repair teams were too scared to venture to Mykil'ske, so residents were left on their own without power or functioning pipes as the weather turned cold and the land began to freeze over. Tania and Viktor survived on preserved food and the money they'd made from selling their pork in the summer.

But they knew this couldn't last forever. Soon those resources would run out, and they would have to find another way to survive.

MARIA

Mukachevo, Ukraine

WHEN DAVID TURNED two years old, in late November, Maria knew that it was high time to stop breastfeeding him, but she couldn't give it up. Two years earlier, she'd been in labor for almost two days before nurses wheeled her to an operating room, an anesthesiologist put her under general anesthesia, and another doctor sliced open her abdomen and removed the slippery baby, then stitched her up. Leonid was the first to hold David after the doctor and nurses checked him. He was the first to feed him formula in a bottle, while Maria came to as the anesthesia wore off.

The emergency C-section wrecked Maria. It took her twenty-four hours after delivery to come to her senses, and even then, she was not herself—loopy, tired, overwhelmed, and in pain. The nurses and doctors urged her to practice standing up and begin some basic exercises, which would help her heal in the long run. But she couldn't—the pain at the incision, the anesthesia still running through her body, and her weakness after nearly forty-eight hours of intense labor had all left her limp. When the nurses brought David to her bedside in a transparent plastic bassinet, she looked over at her red, swollen baby sleeping beside her. He didn't look like hers. Had they made a mistake? Leonid and all the nurses assured Maria that he was indeed her baby. In the evening, she wanted to hold him, but hospital policy required her to practice standing up before holding the baby, to ensure that she was stable, and just the thought of pushing herself to her feet made her shrink into the bed and drift back into delirium.

A few hours later, in the middle of the night, she heard a baby cry from the nursery. "For some reason I knew that this was the cry of my child," she said, "and at four in the morning I woke up my husband and said, 'Help me get up.'" She was already moving herself to the side of the bed. Leonid shot up from his cot and moved next to her, gripping her hand as she put her feet on the floor and stood on them. Her legs trembled. "I was in so much pain," she recalled. "I really remember this pain."

She told Leonid to get the doctor immediately, and when the doctor saw Maria standing up, she brought in David immediately and laid him on Maria's chest, and Maria recognized his cry from the nursery. "I feel like that's when I became a mother," she recalled.

Because they had waited a few days to begin breastfeeding, David did not latch on to her breast well initially—but when he did, it felt like a small victory. She loved breastfeeding him, and as he grew older—past the normal age for weaning—she couldn't bring herself to stop. She knew she needed to teach him to fall asleep without nursing. But especially once the war began, once Leonid was gone, and once she found herself alone in a new city, she came to see breastfeeding as the only activity reminding her that she was still the same person she was in Mariupol. So she wouldn't give up on it—not yet. She benefited from the endorphins, anyway, and she appreciated the closeness of David's body.

Now that he was two, Maria's relatives and neighbors all said she should put David in a nursery school for a few hours each day so that he could socialize with other kids and she could get some time to herself. David still knew only one word—*papa*—and the socialization, people said, would help him become more verbal. Theoretically, she could afford the relatively inexpensive nursery. Even so, it scared her to be away from David, who, after everything he'd heard and seen in Mariupol, flew easily into hysterics and could be difficult to calm down. Pacification was another advantage of breastfeeding.

As time passed, Maria became paranoid and jittery. Her anxiety ran wild. In moments of quiet, left without an immediate problem to solve, she could convince herself that conspiracies and betrayals, bombings, kidnappings, and death were near. Even when she and David were together at a playground, she couldn't let him out of her sight, and she ran herself ragged caring for him at all hours of the day and night, without a break.

Leeched of spare emotional and psychological resources, Maria was unable to keep herself or David on any sort of consistent schedule, simply because enforcing it was too overwhelming. She fed David potato chips for breakfast. She handed over her phone so he could watch cartoons for as many hours as he would take it. If David cried or behaved defiantly, Maria lashed out, and then she hated herself. How could she do that to him?

Her mind jumped from worry to worry. She had lost the ability to think deeply, to concentrate. If she knew there was food and they were safe and warm, she would then just feel empty, as if her insides had been carved out. She stopped wearing makeup. Before the war, she'd painted her nails, put on eyelashes, had her eyebrows done. There was no energy for that anymore. She flipped her hair up into a bun most days and didn't shower regularly. She stopped exercising altogether. Many months after she left Mariupol she said: "I don't even know what my body looks like anymore."

Even before they left Mariupol, Maria responded to David's pleading for his dad by saying, "Papa is at work, he will come home when he's done with work." As the fall wore on, Maria stopped worrying whether what she said was true. She would believe it—that Leonid was at work, a job that must be done for Ukraine, and he would come home when it was finished. She would believe that Leonid was alive, and when he was released, they would resume their life together. In my communications with Maria over the course of many months, she never wavered in this, always saying "When Leonid returns" and never *if*.

She missed the proximity of Leonid's body. Not necessarily sex, but physical contact. When she had extra cash, she bought Leonid new clothes for when he was released. When she left Mariupol, she brought with her his cologne instead of her own perfume, and sometimes she wore it, giving her the sense that he was with her— just beside her or behind her, though out of sight. Leonid began to occupy the part of her mind that was made of memory, not present reality, and this shook her. But sometimes she got so close to a memory she could feel herself inside it. "I can remember, almost tactilely, how his hand felt in mine," she wrote.

Sometimes she imagined the scene when Leonid came home. She usually tried to discipline herself, to avoid hypothetical nonsense, but sometimes she indulged, picturing what it might be like when she saw him again. She had seen videos of other soldiers released from captivity—she could re-create the scene to her liking.

That fall, she lived somewhere between daydream and memory, imagining life when Leonid returned and picturing life before he'd left. In Mukachevo, she remembered the first apartment in Mariupol she and Leonid lived in together—the studio room with a basic burner stove and no real kitchen. They worked so hard in those days, trying to earn and save money so they could get a better place. Working opposite shifts, they sometimes wouldn't see each other all day. "But still, we were so . . ." she trailed off. "When we had days off, we were each other's entire attention. At the cinema, at the sea. Of course, we quarreled. But now I remember our quarrels with warmth."

What could she make of those memories now? That apartment building had been ransacked sometime in the summer and she couldn't know what became of it. Many people from Mariupol suffered similar disorientation. One woman I corresponded with wrote: "Today, the neighbors from Mariupol sent a video of how the occupiers are destroying our apartment building . . . you see, on the right, in the smoke, is a small white balcony, which will soon become a pile of garbage. This is the balcony from which, as a child, I used to reach for a ripe apricot growing on a branch under the house. Now there is no apricot, and soon there will be no home."

On nights when Maria felt especially low, she wondered what of it was real. Had they really been so happy? Had they actually loved each other the way she now remembered they had? Somehow the breastfeeding helped. As she felt the tingling of milk descending into the duct of her chest, she remembered how, in the early months of David's life, Leonid would take a bottle of freshly pumped milk from her hand, scoop up David from his bassinet, and lie next to her in bed, the three of them learning how to be a family in the early hours of the morning. Since then a lot had changed. But her body still made that same milk, and as long as David sucked, it kept coming, a tiny stream connecting who she was then to who she was now.

VITALY

Borodyanka, Ukraine

THE COLDER IT grew, the more concerned Vitaly became that he might actually freeze. He was living in the same old, drafty apartment that he'd settled into when he came back from Western Ukraine in the early spring, and without reliable heating, the nights were frigid. He slept in a thick wool sweater and under three heavy blankets, and in the morning, without any hot water, he skipped a shower many days and ran straight to the shop to begin brewing coffee for any clients who might come in. He had been able to procure a small generator, which meant he could stay in business through the winter. It also meant he could stay warm. The generator also brought in business: when it buzzed, there, too, would be warmth and food, coffee and friends.

The happiest moments of the war for him were in the evenings when he got back from a hard day of recycling or picking up supplies and could sit down and enjoy a cup of coffee with whoever happened to be at the shop. Even after he switched off the generator to save gas and lit a few candles, Vitaly stayed as late as he could, cleaning everything meticulously, putting every cup back in its place, before locking up and meandering home. There he'd light another candle and draw until he was too tired to keep his eyes open, or he'd memorize a patriotic poem he would then record and send to his friends.

On a short visit home from the front lines in late October, Artem visited with his three-year-old son, Yehor. Vitaly sent me a picture of the three of them sitting together on the refurbished couch that used to sit in someone's living room, Yehor drinking hot cocoa with a straw, and Vitaly's arm around Artem, still in his military greens. Artem was tired and stoic. He had been fighting in Eastern Ukraine for six months already, and it had taken a toll on him.

As a kid, Artem had been rambunctious and silly, and he loved Vitaly, thirteen years his senior and very cool, though never too cool to let him tag along. Now, looking at Artem on the couch with his kid, his eyes dark and sunken with a heavy expression, Vitaly remembered when Artem was in middle school and was always trying to be the class clown. In one chemistry lesson, Artem swallowed a dry alcohol tablet that the class had been using for an experiment. His teacher nearly fainted from worry, but he was fine, and all the boys around him roared in admiration. His cheerful disposition was nearly gone now, but still Artem could find it in him to make a joke now and then.

A few weeks later, in early November, Vitaly was surprised to find journalists crowding into his former courtyard, where an image of a young boy using karate to flip an adult had been painted on the wall of his dismantled kindergarten. While Vitaly had brewed coffee across the street, he had seen the artist and a small team out there applying black spray paint. Vitaly had assumed they were just some hooligans spraying graffiti.

Talking later with the journalists, Vitaly learned that the iconic

British artist and activist Banksy had come to his building, and that the boy was understood to symbolize Ukrainian resistance. Vitaly had never heard of Banksy but was assured he was a very big deal. That night, Vitaly wrote: "Some famous artist came here and painted on the side of the kindergarten walls." He chuckled to himself.

He thought it over: Banksy was one of the most famous living artists in the world, well known even in New York City, the homeland of everything Vitaly perceived as cool. "And he came to me," Vitaly thought, "to my courtyard, to the rubble of a building my dad built." "Maybe this will help someone rebuild that kindergarten, where at least three generations of kids learned that they were Ukrainian," he wrote. Forty years had passed since he was a student there himself, pretending to be a Cossack, and when he thought of how fiercely his people had fought that year, he sometimes smiled; he was pleased to know those childish games proved prophetic.

In December, Vitaly visited Kolomiya to see his family, who remained there in a shelter. With Orthodox Christmas coming, they prepared a package to send to Artem on the front lines. They collected warm socks, soap, shampoo, a razor and shaving cream, and some food—homemade cookies from Vitaly's sister-in-law, and a jar of homemade preserved fish and meat from Vitaly's mom. Vitaly threw in the chocolates he knew Artem loved most. They mailed it from Kolomiya to a post office close to the front lines.

Watching the postal worker stamp and mark the package, Vitaly thought about Artem as that blond kid from the courtyard. His sister, Natalka, Vitaly's first love, had immigrated to New York City in 2015, soon after the war began in Eastern Ukraine and the economic situation in Ukraine had become extremely difficult. In the years since then, Vitaly and Artem made plans to visit her. Watching the postal worker place the parcel on the stack of other Christmas packages headed to soldiers in the east, Vitaly thought: "You know, if I survive this war, I really think that I will see the Statue of Liberty someday."

He celebrated the New Year with his family in Kolomiya before going home to Borodyanka and the coffee shop. A couple of days later, the package to Artem traveled to the front lines—near Bakhmut—where it was to be deposited at one of the few remaining operational post offices. Vitaly messaged Artem the address and date it should arrive—January 5, just two days before Orthodox Christmas. But when Artem went to pick up the package, it was still en route. He'd have to get it after his next mission.

"I'll try again in a couple of days," Artem messaged.

A dozen Merry Christmas messages were the next to appear on Artem's phone, which he never saw. On January 7, Christmas Day, after a round of active fighting, Artem ventured to retrieve a wounded man and was killed by a sniper, not far from where Dima fought, not far from Oleg and Yulia's home. His soldier brothers retrieved his body and took it to safety. The soldiers called Artem's parents, who called Vitaly. When Vitaly heard the news, he collapsed to the floor of the coffee shop and stayed there the whole night without the generator running.

At the front, soldiers asked what they should do with the package for Artem. *Keep it for yourselves*, Artem's parents told them— a gift for their service, a gift for retrieving Artem's body, for being the last to care for him. When Artem's body was transported back to Borodyanka for burial, Artem's classmates returned home to walk alongside him in his final procession into the earth.

On Orthodox Christmas evening, somewhere outside Bakhmut, two groups of soldiers gathered. One group crouched on the floor of an abandoned elementary school to open a package they knew was not meant for them. Inside they found homemade cookies, home-preserved meat and fish, and chocolates placed there by Vitaly. They ate in silence until one of them repeated a few phrases Artem often said, and they all nodded.

Nearby, another group of soldiers sat in a basement bunker around a simple Christmas meal—open-faced sandwiches and pomegranate juice—and an aid worker marched down the stairs with several boxes, passing out plastic sacks. They ripped the packages open, pulling out fleece jackets, thermal layering garments, hats, and gloves. Holding up their new warm clothes, they posed for a picture—big smiles, thumbs up. Some of them would die in that fleece.

On his way out, the aid worker sent the photo to Polina back in the United States, and she stared at it for a long time, examining each face, looking at the fabric they held in their hands, trying to remember its texture, trying to imagine what it would feel like when the soldiers slung their arms through the sleeves and slipped on the hats before going back into the January night, with the thunder of artillery marking the start of another year of war.

ANNA

Kharkiv, Ukraine

"HALF AN HOUR ago it was exactly 365 days, exactly a year, when the war began," Anna messaged me from Kharkiv early in the morning on February 24, 2023. "I lit a candle at four in the morning for all the dead, for every warrior who defends us, for a peaceful sky overhead."

Dima fought somewhere in Bakhmut that night. The combat had intensified, and he and Anna talked less frequently, once a week or so. Their conversations had changed in the last couple of months. He'd become distant and occasionally agitated. After he was transferred to the front lines, he had come under heavy stress, and back in Kharkiv, off duty, his mood was darker and his temper was short.

She started worrying about the relationship, because they began quarreling more regularly, often over silly, simple things.

"At first I thought that I was the reason," she said, "but no, his mood changed sharply. He could be aggressive, even if I didn't do anything wrong. Many things irritated him, and I didn't under-stand, because I had no experience in relationships with a military guy, but also I had no experience in relationships in general."

Once, Anna became frustrated, and she ignored him, not an-swering when he pestered her with questions. This infuriated him, and, approaching her angrily, he hit her, hard, across the face. Anna gasped, her eyes wide and horrified. She cried and cowered away, and he held his face in his hands, ashamed, then went toward her to apologize. But she wouldn't let him close to her, and she cried on the bed and kicked him off, and he sat alone, angry and disgusted and confused.

By evening, Anna had softened and they made up, but through-out the winter, he continued to get angry or pull away and occa-sionally he struck her. Anna was often anxious and perplexed. She felt nervous, sometimes unsafe. But he promised her that he was changing, that he would never do it again, and they made up—several times.

He spent all the time they weren't together firing guns, sitting in trenches with other men, talking about killing people and then try-ing to do so. When she ignored Dima and treated him dismissively, something flared in him.

"He was under deep psychological pressure from his command-ers, the war, everything," she said. "It affected him. And he took it out on me. Then he apologized, and I forgave. I had a kind of dependence on him."

Once, on a break from combat, he brought Anna a special sur-prise to keep her company while he was away. He knew that she had wanted a dog for years, and he found a wide-eyed four-month-old mutt whom Anna named Jessy, and who slept with them in the same bed. Anna adored the dog, caring for her as though she were a child.

Dima could never stay long, just a couple of days or a weekend before he went back. When the battle for Bakhmut began in August, it mainly involved artillery and air strikes, but as the weather turned cold, the combat operations became grueling. In some places there was trench warfare and in others urban-style combat with soldiers navigating complex streets and alleys. The Wagner forces fought brutally, often forcing waves of convicts to charge armed with nothing but basic tools like shovels, compelling Ukrainians to expend their ammunition. Then, by the fifth or the sixth wave, fully armed Wagner soldiers—who had fought in Ukraine since 2014, or in Syria or Libya—would attack, overrunning Ukrainian positions that had run out of bullets.

"He's been there for a year and he really wants to go home," Anna said. "He tells me almost nothing, so as not to hurt me with what he sees. Only this: how his mother or father is, the weather, something neutral. And I tell him how my day went."

While Dima was in the trenches or hiding out in abandoned buildings or slogging from house to house searching for a kill, Anna and Jessy took walks together in the morning, and Anna called her grandma in Luhansk. She and her grandmother spoke on the phone every few days, or whenever her grandmother had an internet connection, which was often poor.

Her grandma's life in occupied Luhansk was slow and uneventful—she prepared food, took the dog out, and called up relatives. "When the seedling season comes," Anna said, "she plants a small vegetable garden in her yard, and she talks about how she plants tomatoes there, cucumbers, all that kind of stuff. She talked about the books she's read, the news, and Ukrainian TV shows. But basically, I don't hear anything like that from her anymore. When we call each other, I mostly tell her about myself, because my life, as a rule, is more urgent."

Her grandma worried herself sick over Anna alone in Kharkiv, especially because Anna's parents so rarely got in touch, a point that was painful to talk about, especially as her grandmother was opposed to Anna's mom—her daughter—having gone to fight in the first place. Neither of them fully understood why Anna's parents didn't reach out more regularly. After weeks of silence, it was reasonable to begin wondering if perhaps they had been killed. But then a message would come, something short and sparse, a communication that both brought relief and reopened a wound.

"My grandmother is probably the kindest person in my life," Anna said. "She and I have always had such a warm relationship, and will always have one, and I am waiting for the end of the war to finally go see her. Quite often, the Russians say that no one is waiting for Ukrainian forces to return to the occupied cities, but in fact this is not true, people are simply afraid that they will be abducted if they speak. They have no freedom of speech, so they say they don't have an opinion, but there are people like my grandmother, like Dima's family, who hide Ukrainian flags in jars in the ground. My dreams are, first of all, for the war to end, second, to see my grandmother and, of course, start my own family."

While Anna walked Jessy through Kharkiv or lay on the bed in the middle of the afternoon or tried a new recipe to keep herself busy, she made plans with her grandma. They talked about what it would be like when Anna was able to go home, what they would do and see together, how they'd spend time together in the garden, make jam, boil dumplings, about how Anna would bring Dima and her grandma would finally meet him. "It's not clear when this will be," Anna acknowledged. "Even if the war ends, it is not a fact that those territories will be under the control of Ukraine. [And] if they are not in Ukraine, then I still won't be able to go there personally, and she is already too old to travel long distances to Kharkiv or anywhere else."

"She's afraid that she will leave us without ever seeing me. And this is also my main fear."

Anna and her grandma were separated by less than two hundred miles, but although, before the full-scale invasion, some crossed those borders casually, the risk was high, and her grandmother was scared to leave. They hadn't seen each other in nearly a decade, since Anna was nine years old.

Her grandmother dreamed of having a great-grandchild, and Anna dreamed of this, too. Even after Dima had started hurting her, she pictured herself pregnant with Dima's child, how they would make a family together, take walks in the park. They'd drive to Luhansk, and Anna's grandma would hold the baby and wonder if she had ever in her whole life seen such a beautiful little girl.

As the snow melted, Anna had not heard from her parents for a long time, and sometimes she would go a full week or ten days without hearing from Dima. She feared that at any moment, she might learn that something had happened to them, and every time an unknown number flashed on her phone, her heart raced.

But sometimes she was surprised to find that she worried less and less about Dima. "It was no longer the same as before," she said. "My eyes didn't burn when I looked at him, and I became less worried about him. Maybe it was out of resentment, telling myself that I didn't care."

And yet she worried about what would happen if he was gone. She felt dependent on him, almost trapped in their relationship—not financially, but psychologically. "I understood that I am alone in Kharkiv," she said, "and besides him I have no one. And it was very difficult to understand that he could disappear at once and that's it. He has money, he can rent an apartment, find a girl, and I—I'll be left alone."

Loneliness scared her more than anything else, and she stayed with Dima just to have a person who she knew was there.

"One day he tore the necklace chain off my neck," she said. "I thought he was coming to choke me or something like that, but no, he just tore it off, threw it, broke it." They made up again, but something changed for Anna after that experience.

In early spring, Anna messaged me that she and Dima had broken up. She didn't share more details, and soon she stopped responding to my messages altogether, and we lost contact.

For the many months we had communicated, her messaging pattern was consistent and reliable. For weeks, I found myself up in the night thinking about Anna. Was she okay? I mapped out the missile attacks and shelling in Kharkiv, trying to determine how close they were to her apartment. I sent more messages—"Hi, are you all right? I hope you're safe"—and I started to feel a small fraction of what Anna had been experiencing all along, the uncertainty, the lack of closure, the dark reality of war that she knew as well as anyone: that people disappear, sometimes into thin air, and you make up stories about how they're doing and where they are, trying to convince yourself that everything is fine, that they're okay, and that you will be, too.

Volodymyr—1989

TRYING TO SCHEDULE a gravedigger proved a problem. Leaving the sanitation office with his permission certificate, Volodymyr called the local gravedigging services in Chusovoy and surrounding villages, but no gravediggers would agree to the job. They were scared. Having grown up in the area, the gravediggers were familiar with Perm-36. Even if they didn't understand the extent of its horror (much was kept secret, even among locals who worked in the camp), they'd heard enough vague, whispered rumors as children to know it was somewhere they should avoid, especially if they were there to dig up the bodies of former prisoners.

Volodymyr and his film crew would have to dig up the graves themselves. After one last refusal from a gravedigger, Volodymyr hitched a ride to a communal farm outside town to procure crowbars, ropes, shovels, and an ax. An old collective farmer led them through the farm's various buildings to scrounge what they could, but the farm was in its own straits—it was poor and remote, and farmers weren't interested in handing off valuable tools to strangers who wandered in. Volodymyr managed to obtain only four rickety shovels, so he moved on to the village, where he went from house to house begging for the rest.

By the time he had all the tools he was going to get, it was night. Volodymyr got a ride back to Perm and hauled the tools into the hotel. Starving, he went down to the hotel's cafeteria and gathered a plate of boiled eggs and seaweed. He cut up the rubbery egg whites and crumbled the cold gray yolks into a bowl of hot water and plopped in half a bouillon cube. The warm broth settled in his stomach, and having sipped the bowl clean, Volodymyr lay down on the bed and floated into sleep.

He dreamed of Stus. The eyes on the front cover of Stus's *Palimpsests* seemed to follow Volodymyr through his dream, watching him. After a short nap, Volodymyr woke up with a start. He was sweating, feverish. What did Stus need to tell him?

Again Volodymyr listed to himself all the steps he'd take: "I have the tools, I have the rope, the coffins were ordered long ago in Perm and should be ready, the transport boxes for the coffins were ordered here and have already been made." He had protective gear he'd brought from Chernobyl in case there were dangerous pathogens when they transferred the bodies from the wooden coffins to the new ones—hats, masks, gloves, and respirators. The coppersmiths he'd need to seal the new zinc coffins were confirmed.

"But wait," Volodymyr thought. He hadn't made plans for the main event—how to actually transfer the bodies from the wooden coffins to the zinc coffins. "They can simply crumble in your hands because they have been in the graves for over four and five years," Volodymyr said. "And this is not just horrible—it is barbaric." They would be performing this action in just a few hours, and he needed to think quickly.

He sat and pondered for just a few seconds. The solution came instantly, as if Stus himself had revealed how he needed his body to be moved. In his mind, Volodymyr watched himself cover the coffin with a thick cloth, pulling it taut. Half their team would hold the coffin, half would hold the fabric. Those holding the coffin would, in one movement, flip it upside down, letting the body fall onto the cloth. If the fabric was kept tight, the corpse would fall only a few inches and remain, he hoped, more or less intact. They would then cover the back of the body with another cloth, lift the body into the zinc coffin, and slowly pull the fabric to turn the body face up.

Just before midnight, he met the film crew, including Stus's son, Dmytro, at the airport in Perm. First thing in the morning the crew set off for Chusovoy, where the poets were buried. Volodymyr went to a fabric store in Perm. A cheerful woman, expert in her field, helped him pick twelve yards of a heavyweight fabric, after which he went to pick up the coffins. As soon as the coffins were loaded in the van, he and the driver would meet the rest of the crew at the cemetery. Digging was to begin promptly at two o'clock so that the exhumation would be complete by early evening. Then they'd seal the coffins, get back to Perm, and sleep before leaving for Kyiv early the next morning.

When Volodymyr showed up at the coffin workshop, he knocked hard on the door. No answer. After knocking repeatedly, yelling through the door that he was there for an order, a teenage appren-tice cautiously peeked out through a thin slit. He was scared. The head tinsmith had been knocked unconscious in his stairwell the evening before and had lain there for hours before being taken to the hospital with a severe head wound. When the teenage boy showed up to work that day, his boss will still in the hospital.

Volodymyr seethed with anger. He knew this was no coinci-dence. Someone—and he assumed it was Chentsov—was trying to sabotage their mission. Volodymyr asked if the boy had seen how his boss had upholstered the first coffin. He had.

"Then close the door," Volodymyr said, slipping inside the work-shop. "We'll do this ourselves."

Volodymyr, the driver, and the boy knelt on the floor of the workshop gluing padding and tacking fabric inside the coffins. By ten o'clock they were ready, and after loading the coffins in the van—the glue still drying—Volodymyr and the driver were on their way out of Perm to Chusovoy.

On the highway leading out of the city, the driver spotted a checkpoint up ahead. When they came to a stop, the police officers said they'd been radioed to look out for this vehicle, whose pas-sengers, they were told, were dangerous and suspected of a serious crime. The officers circled the van, searching inside and out, and one officer covertly slashed the rear tires. Volodymyr and the driver were told to park on the side of the road near the checkpoint and wait for clearance to leave.

"How long will this take?" Volodymyr demanded. The officer shrugged callously and disappeared into the roadside station.

Volodymyr's blood pressure rose. He could see the officers in-side doing absolutely nothing. He eyed his watch every few min-utes. Hours passed. They'd had no contact with anyone from the crew since the crew left the hotel for Chusovoy in the morning, and he knew they'd be confused, maybe even scared, when Volodymyr, the driver, and the coffins didn't show up on time. He hoped they wouldn't give up and return to Perm.

Finally, at two o'clock, just when the crew was supposed to begin digging the graves, the officers emerged and said there had been a mistake. With the wave of a hand, they were sent on their way. They limped off on deflated tires, which turned their three-hour drive into four.

By the time they arrived, night had fallen. They pulled onto the dirt road leading up to the overgrown cemetery, their headlights illuminating frozen fields. As they approached the grave site, they caught a glimpse of a distant figure, then another and another. It was the crew—they had stayed, huddled by the graves for hours. When they saw headlights bump up the road, one yelled, "Our guys are here!" and they all jumped to their feet.

In the afternoon, when Volodymyr hadn't shown up, they'd decided to dig the graves anyway, just in case he came late. Stus's grave was marked by an inconspicuous tin plate with the number 9, nailed to a wooden stake. If Volodymyr hadn't shown up with the coffins, they'd have filled the graves back in and left Stus and the two other poets to lie in Russia. But when Volodymyr did show up, they were ready.

The graves had been open for hours when Volodymyr hopped down from the van. He peered into the holes. There rested the wooden coffins, soiled and damp. They needed to work quickly.

They lowered straps into the ground, and a member of the crew descended into the first grave to pull the straps underneath the first wooden coffin. Men on each side hauled the coffin up until others could lift it onto the ground. A member of the crew used a lever to pry the lid open. They all held their breath, watching until every nail was pulled loose and the lid could be flipped to the side.

The skeletal remains of a body lay there, exposed. Much of its soft tissue had broken down and fully decayed. A withered head and face, still with some hair and tilted slightly to the side, looked up at them.

"It's Dad," Stus's son, Dmytro, said, staring into the coffin.

Volodymyr had never seen Stus alive but had no doubts. He recognized him from the cover of *Palimpsests*—and from the dream he'd had the night before in which Stus told him how to move their bodies.

"This is Stus," Volodymyr said confidently.

Customarily at burial, family members or friends place important personal belongings on the chest or stomach of the deceased.

On Stus's stomach, the prison guards who buried him had laid his work boots, the ones he had worn through all those years of imprisonment. His arms were not crossed over his chest but laid down at his sides.

The crew filmed Stus's head and body for the record. There was a lesion on his head above his temple, contributing to a theory that Stus was actually murdered by a guard and had not died of hunger.

Volodymyr covered the body with the heavy fabric he'd purchased that morning. They hoisted the coffin up and swiftly, decisively flipped it over. Bodily dust and shavings fell out, and as gravity pulled the body away from its wooden bed, the corpse released itself from the coffin with a dull thud and hung down on the cloth. They laid the corpse in the new coffin, and after placing another length of fabric on its back, they softly pulled the fabric to turn the body face up. They repeated the process with the two other poets, closed the coffin lids, and transferred them to the van.

The crew threw the remains of the wet wooden coffins back into the graves and knelt to push dirt into the holes with their hands. They worked fast, almost frantically, as though, suddenly, they could not leave that place quickly enough. The drivers revved up the vans, everyone piled in, and they sped away from the cemetery, the prison camp, and the village toward the highway, a chill shivering on everyone's neck that dissipated only after they had left that field well behind.

They got back to the hotel in Chusovoy after midnight, and Volodymyr and the driver went to a garage to seal the coffins with nails. They slid the coffins into the wooden boxes Volodymyr had built several weeks earlier, then patched up the van's tires that had been slashed by the police outside Perm.

When he returned again to the hotel in the early hours of the morning, an hour before he was to leave for the airport, Volodymyr's heart was beating so fast he worried he would have a heart attack. He had not had a decent night's sleep in three days. He felt as though he hadn't taken a breath since he drove up the bumpy road to the cemetery earlier that evening. Hopping into the shower to try to calm down, he took one of the nitroglycerin pills that he had kept on him in case someone had a nervous breakdown at the graves. He leaned against the side of the shower to keep from falling over. His fingers trembled with adrenaline. Afterward, lying on the bed for a few minutes before departing for the airport, he tried to calm down, deep breaths in, deep breaths out.

At the airport, the airport manager, whom Volodymyr had met in August during his first attempt at reburial, kept his word and made sure the coffins were loaded onto the plane to Kyiv. Volodymyr watched from the gate window as the boxes were lifted into the cargo space of the aircraft, and soon he and the crew boarded the plane, took their seats, and let out a deep, tremulous exhale. Resting his head on the back of the seat, Volodymyr closed his eyes and tried to drift into sleep. The poets' bodies lay just a few feet below him. They were all going home.

PART 5

THE
SECOND SPRING

TANIA

Mykil'ske, Ukraine

THE DAY IN November when Ukrainian troops liberated Mykil'ske was euphoric for most villagers, but after liberation, life was even more difficult than it had been under occupation. Water pipes and electrical lines had been destroyed. The village was shelled nearly every day. People were killed in explosions, and more families moved away, especially those with children, even though with both bridges bombed, the available routes out of town were regularly under fire.

Where there were more than three thousand people before the war, there now remained just over a thousand, a hundred of whom were children. Projectiles flew over Tania's roof and fell into the yard nearly every day, and collecting shrapnel became a regular chore.

The money they made selling pork sustained them until December, after which Viktor got a job as a security guard in a neighboring kindergarten, working every other day and making just over $150 per month. They used eighty of those dollars to pay for their utilities, which at the time was gas only. The rest of the money they used for groceries.

Once every seven to ten days, Tania and Viktor hooked a small trailer up to their car and stacked it with eight forty-liter cans to fill at one of the village wells, helping to distribute the water through the village. But it was not enough. The town's two or three wells were far from sufficient for a thousand people, and Tania and Viktor, along with most of their neighbors, trekked almost every day to the river—even in the dead of winter—to do laundry, wash their dishes, and bathe. They would haul their stuff over their shoulders or in bags balanced on bicycle handlebars, across frozen ground, down to the riverbank. The river was frozen over, and they and other villagers cut holes in the ice to gather what water they could. Often they plunged their clothing and dishes directly through the ice hole because it was easier to carry the laundry than the water.

As the operations on their farm dwindled to almost nothing, Tania threw herself into volunteer work. One fifty-nine-year-old woman in the village, Valya, enlisted the help of various churches and charitable foundations and the Ukrainian state to bring aid to the village. Along with Valya, Tania set to work helping to deliver food, especially to old women who couldn't walk far.

Repair crews were afraid to come to the village to restore the electricity and fix the water pipes, but in the spring, a handful of local men organized themselves to do the job. They had only rudimentary electrical skills, but still they set up ladders, climbing up to splice broken wires and repairing transformers as best they could.

"Thanks to these people, we periodically have power," Tania said. "For two days there was no power; today the guys spent the whole day making repairs, and an hour later there was another shelling and we were without power again."

By May, Tania messaged me: "Glory to god, the water was turned on." International relief programs had afforded the village two powerful generators with which they were able to pump water from wells and the river and restore periodic running water, rationed by household, a couple of days a week.

As the weather warmed, Viktor wanted to breed more pigs, but Tania couldn't bring herself to agree; it felt irresponsible. "God forbid you have to run away, and they must be left," she said. Besides that, to grind their feed using the generator was expensive.

If they weren't going to breed more pigs, and if they were unable to travel to a market to sell produce from their farm, sometimes Tania wondered why they stayed. "I don't even know how to explain this," she said. "I ask myself these questions, why are we sitting here? There is a war going on, there were shellings just yesterday. We went down to the basement, and there has been no electricity for almost half a year."

In the 1990s, as newlyweds with a young baby, they had staked their future on two piglets and one ton of grain when Viktor was laid off. They'd worked nonstop, learning how to cut and package meat and stuff sausages, both of which for two decades had remained in high demand throughout their region. They built their house and farm with their own two hands, Tania mixing cement and carrying stones and nailing slate to the roof, and over time they proved something to themselves, which even during war they struggled to give up: a belief that they had some control over how they lived, and if they worked hard and stayed the course, they could earn the life they wanted, far from the impoverishment of their childhoods. Somehow, even while wringing her clothes in an ice hole in the river, Tania believed that if they persevered and didn't leave, once things were quiet, they could build it all again.

YULIA

Dnipro, Ukraine

IN THE SECOND week of the new year, Yulia was fitted for a prosthetic leg at the rehabilitation hospital in Dnipro. What remained of her left limb was measured to create a mold made out of plaster and fiberglass bandages. From the mold, the manufacturer created a positive model. In several weeks, the prosthetic template would be ready for a fitting. Once it arrived, she'd try it on, putting pressure on the leg stump inside the prosthetic to feel how it fit. Afterward, doctors could make a few more alterations to ensure it was comfortable, and then she would begin rehabilitation therapy in earnest. Rehab would be intense and time-consuming; she and Oleg would need to travel to the rehab center a couple of times a week, and Oleg's now somewhat regular trips to Konstantinivka would have to become less frequent.

Their neighbor back home assured them she would continue to monitor everything. She had proved a faithful friend through it all—climbing the ladder over the fence every day to check on the birds, scatter feed in their coops, maintain a clean and healthy environment for them, and gather the eggs. A few weeks earlier, she had promised Yulia and Oleg that she would let the rooster into the coop as spring neared to ensure that the flock was strong by later in the season.

Life in Konstantinivka had not been easy for those left behind. The front lines continued to constrict throughout the fall and winter. In neighboring Bakhmut, the fighting had become even more relentless, with increasing daily losses and unabating artillery fire. The Russians shelled Ukrainian positions hundreds of times each day. If Bakhmut fell, the next strategic goal would likely be Chasiv Yar, which was perched on a hill, within artillery range of neighboring Kramatorsk and Konstantinivka, one of the hills that Yulia had climbed as a child, exploring the flowers and plants. The week Yulia was fitted for her prosthetic leg, her elementary school in Chasiv Yar, where she had read every book in the library as a girl and where her grandmother had taught for decades, was blown up. It burned for days.

"Rockets just fly back and forth," Oleg said. "But in spite of everything, the city lives its own life, public utilities clean up the garbage, and after these attacks they bring a tractor, the tractor digs a huge hole, fills everything in, and life goes on."

One of Yulia's best school friends from her elementary school years, Irina, had stayed in Chasiv Yar until 2017, when she moved with her adolescent son to Tver, Russia, where she'd found a work opportunity. Yulia kept in touch with Irina. By now Irina's teenage son, who'd grown up in Chasiv Yar, had entered a Russian military institute in Kazan.

"Of course," Yulia said, "I understand, this is his choice. But I can't get my head around how this fits together in her life. I asked her, what will happen when he graduates? What if he is sent to Ukraine to fight? Will he shoot his grandmother?" Yulia shook her head with a shudder. "But she waves it off. 'God forbid,' she says. Or she says that by then it will all be over. These are the paradoxes that exist. At once she, of course, does not support the war. But her son is a future officer in the Russian army."

The rest of Irina's family—her mother and brother and his family—stayed behind in Chasiv Yar when Irina moved to Tver, but by winter 2023, they hadn't been seen or heard from for several weeks. Yulia searched on the lists of wounded people published by hospitals, but she never found their names.

In the year since the Kramatorsk railway attack, confined most of the time to a bed, Yulia had gained weight, and sometimes this worried her. She had always been slender and active, and the extra weight was hard on her weakened legs.

In general, Yulia had been able to manage her emotional and psychological distress remarkably well. She had been on an anti-depressant since leaving the hospital, which had helped her immensely. She was calm and gentle by nature, and while she didn't shy away from difficult topics, she regularly said things like "The most important thing in such difficult situations is not to give in to despair," or "You can choose the passive oppression of your body and soul, or you can work on yourself, correct your body and thoughts from negative to positive. I allow myself to cry sometimes, but not for long." She said many times to me, unironically, that her favorite book was *Pollyanna.*

Of all my interlocutors, Yulia wanted to know the most about me. She asked me often about myself, my opinions, my daily life. I could tell she grew tired of talking about the war, and she often changed the subject to other aspects of life she enjoyed—parenting, crafting, home decorating, gardening. I often sent her photos and videos of my children. Once, she gave me advice on how to keep them from drawing all over our apartment walls, and we engaged in a conversation about the hazards and delights of toddlers for a couple of days, until it suddenly stopped. She went silent for some time, though I could see that she had seen my messages. When she returned to our conversation after several days, we didn't talk about children drawing on walls or jumping on furniture; Konstantinivka was being shelled again, which was no longer news in itself, but this time the activity was so near their house that all the windows in their gazebo were shattered, and one of their birds had been killed by a shell fragment.

A week or so later, Yulia wanted to talk about other things again, but hanging over our conversation was the understanding that we lived in different worlds, that she had been touched by war and I had not. Once she mentioned that in their town, just a few kilometers from the center of the carnage, some people still sold pumpkins from their gardens at an outdoor market. When a building on the market's street was shelled, those farmers helped to clean up the mess and then went back to work. When the market itself was shelled, they found a new place to sell their pumpkins. Despite the danger, they tried to live an ordinary life. And I sensed this was what she did in our conversations, too. Oleg, in his own way, did this as well, driving back home to Konstantinivka month after month.

Just before he set off on one such trip, Yulia sent me a video of her rehabilitation work. Oleg grinned in the mirror while she held on to parallel handrails and began the process of relearning how to walk, taking very short steps, heel to toe. The therapists promised that over time, once she was walking in everyday situations, she would develop the skills to navigate stairs, curbs, uneven surfaces, and hills. Over time she would again walk confidently, with long strides. Her life would never be as it was, but with a new prosthetic leg, she would be able to bend, kneel, and crouch. Perhaps someday, she dreamed, she would return alive to her native Donbas and plant the acorns she had gathered in Dnipro. Maybe by then the sky would be safe, and they would grow into tall, sturdy oaks.

POLINA

Utah, USA

BY THE ANNIVERSARY of the full-scale invasion, Polina and John's savings were completely drained. They were settling into a small rented apartment in a suburban neighborhood in Utah, and Polina was seven months pregnant. They had sold or given away all their furniture when they left for Ukraine, and this was the first time that they'd settled down since leaving for Ukraine a year earlier. For John, there was no returning to his fancy design job in LA, but he found work as the creative director for a local solar energy company. It took them a few months to piece together some furniture, and with every paycheck, they saved to buy a crib, a stroller, and a car seat.

They kept busy with their various aid projects, though the urgency seemed to have diminished, a fact that unsettled them. But even people living in Ukraine admitted to growing weary of thinking only about the war. Occasionally people found their minds playing tricks on them, and they'd forget about the war entirely for a few moments. One woman in the northern Ukrainian city of Chernihiv wrote, saying: "The mood in the city is unique, wavelike. Today I found out that a man blew himself up with a grenade almost in the center of the city, and another, a young guy, hanged himself. People can't stand the tension, they seem to give up . . . and yet, at the same time, I see many happy families, children on scooters, they chirp and smile, as if they do not know that there is a war now. And I sometimes catch myself also thinking this on those rare days without anxiety; I forget about this terrible word—'war'—and live as if nothing had happened."

Others commented on the discomfort of knowing different scales of distress. Yes, there was a terrible war, and the collective pain of it was acute, and yet individual people continued to endure their own unique problems—loneliness, family dysfunction, poor health—and to respond proportionally to diverse sufferings and predicaments was a challenge. For example, on the day of a serious bombing that killed several people, one young mom found herself worrying all day about whether her newly potty-trained child would have an accident at daycare.

After coming home from Ukraine, Polina and John felt a persistent unease about giving themselves over to new concerns—buying furniture, preparing for a baby, thinking about the future. "It felt like we were able to finally come back to the life that we had," Polina said. "It's warm. We have a bed, we have a table, we have all the things to be comfortable in this apartment." And yet none of it felt like before. It was not just that they now saw a peaceful life through a new lens; it felt as though their eyes themselves had been changed. They came back to the United States with a kind of night vision, enabling them to perceive what lives in dark registers that they had never even known existed.

They never regretted their decision to return to Ukraine, affirming that they made that choice with more clarity than any other in their lives. John said that during those first few days of the full-scale invasion he felt as though he was in an elevator watching the doors close just as someone rushed to catch it. It was as though he was watching himself carefully to see how he would behave reflexively: he'd either put his hand out or he wouldn't. "In that moment, when the doors are shutting, you have an opportunity to let the doors shut, or to reach in and open that elevator back up. And if you don't, you are betraying yourself, and you have to live the rest of your life justifying why."

"In some ways," he reflected later, "it was easier to go than to endure that dissonance."

Of course, Polina and John's relatively minuscule efforts could hardly have a decisive impact. But as the war drags on, and the problems facing Ukrainian society become more complex, the small interventions individuals make are more than ever among the most important assets Ukraine has. Polina and John were inspired in the first few days of the war to join the civil movement they saw millions of other Ukrainians joining, and, like many Ukrainians, after just a few months of war, Polina said: "I became unafraid. I started to sort out what I'm scared of, what matters and what does not. I lived through war, and now I live my life differently."

Throughout her pregnancy, Polina said, "I felt like this baby knew why he's coming." She added: "He has Ukrainian blood, and he understands what's happening. And during the pregnancy, I didn't have any fear." In April of the second spring of the war, two weeks before his due date, Polina delivered a healthy baby boy.

Polina and John gave their baby an old family name after one of John's great-grandfathers, a Swiss man who lived in Odesa, Ukraine, for a time in the nineteenth century. They called him Serhiy, a Ukrainian name derived from Greek, meaning protector, or servant.

MARIA

Mukachevo, Ukraine

A YEAR AFTER they fled Mariupol, Maria's sister and parents were accepted into a resettlement program in Montreal, Canada, through the Canada-Ukraine Authorization for Emergency Travel. In March they left Western Ukraine for a new home far away. Maria easily could have gone with them, but she couldn't bring herself to leave Ukraine, not out of a profound sense of patriotism but so that she would be there the very hour Leonid was returned home. After his release, he'd need to stay in Ukraine awhile to undergo therapy and rehabilitation, and she wanted to have a home there for him, a place where he could feel secure and stable.

At the end of winter, most of her close friends from Mariupol had also left Ukraine—for Poland, Romania, Sweden, or elsewhere. With her family now in Canada, Maria and two-and-a-half-year-old David were alone in Western Ukraine.

Though she was still in her country and much was familiar, Maria couldn't kick the feeling that she was an outsider. Ukraine's tendency toward regionalism has always been pronounced, and she felt it acutely. The Mariupol of her adolescence and Mukachevo had different traditions and cuisines and distinct sensibilities. It was as if she were a girl from Cleveland who suddenly found herself alone in rural Louisiana. She had never spent time outside the Donbas, and she was often surprised at how foreign her new home felt. Even after more than a year there, and after it had become clear that returning to Mariupol was impossible, she resisted calling Mukachevo "home."

For over a year she had lived in survival mode—securing housing, finding food, jumping when her phone rang, searching for safety, trying to sleep. For months, she'd blocked off the feelings that she didn't have to address immediately, pushing away the anger and sense of abandonment she harbored against Leonid and a vague regret at having left Mariupol at all. Over the last year she had wondered, only sometimes, whether leaving had been the wrong choice. Had they stayed, would Leonid have come back before he was trapped in Azovstal? Might they have left together? If they survived the bombings and the air raids and the hunger and cold, might life in Mariupol have somehow been more manageable than this?

"But a year later," she wrote, "my subconscious has begun to come to its senses," and she started to see things for what they were—that Mariupol was completely destroyed and that those who remained there were now subjects of a new regime, unable to speak openly about what they had seen and experienced. Only after a full year was she able to accept that there was no reasonable counterfactual narrative for her; leaving behind her husband in the city she'd known her whole life had truly been her best option.

In March, it had been a year since David had last seen Leonid. "And you know what people say to me?" Maria asked incredulously. "That he no longer remembers [his dad]." Maria insisted those people were wrong. "[David] comes across photographs," Maria said, "and he immediately says 'Papa, papa.' He remembers." He was just two and a half years old, but Maria believed that he understood a lot, much more than she knew. "People say he looks mentally older than his age because he understands too much," she said.

But still David spoke very little. He said few words other than *papa*, and Maria worried about a speech delay, because even in war, mothers stay up in the night worrying about such things. *Perhaps once Leonid is home*, Maria thought, *David will start speaking.*

When her sisters called to talk to David, they always asked, playfully: "And where's your papa?"—thinking that if they talked about him enough, perhaps David would internalize that Leonid was a real guy. In time, David began to answer them: "At work."

What kind of "work" Leonid was doing, they couldn't know. Maria had her theories about where he was and what was going on, but "until he's freed, I won't talk about this," she said. The families of Azovstal prisoners continued to organize rallies in cities across the country. Since the Red Cross ostensibly cared for captured soldiers taken from Azovstal, the families of POWs were told by the Ukrainian state to appeal to the organization for information. When they did, the Red Cross often redirected them, suggesting they instead appeal to the Ukrainian state. As time went on, it became obvious that no one with any information on the captured prisoners was willing to share it, and families continued to live in the dark. Where their husbands, fathers, sons, and brothers were held in captivity no one really knew. And whether they were starving or tortured, if they were alive at all, was a question that followed the families everywhere, like a gray shadow. On the anniversary of the soldiers' capture inside the steel factory in late May, Maria and hundreds of other families were devastated when the government did nothing to mark the occasion.

"A year ago," Maria wrote, "everyone in the world rallied for the Mariupol Garrison. Everyone screamed for Azovstal. Every second person knew the pain of Ukraine. Now a year has passed, and it seems everyone just fights for themselves."

After she suffered a panic attack in the spring, Maria met with a psychiatrist and got on an antidepressant. This helped her. She eventually decided to send David to a small preschool in town, which was a big step for her, because for over a year, she was too scared to let him out of her sight. At the preschool, David started meeting with a speech therapist.

Walking down the street, she began to look around at other people and see them in a new way, "even the grandmothers who are sitting there selling flowers," she wrote. Before the war, if she was to buy flowers from an old woman, she would haggle for a better price. "But now I just calmly give them the money, because I understand how hard life is for them now."

As it got warmer, she decided it was time to go to the hair salon. For almost a full year, she had been wearing a bucket hat. Her hair was long and fine, and it tangled easily. She didn't want to cut it all off, but she did not have the energy to brush it consistently, so she just plopped the bucket hat on her head everywhere she went. Over time, a matted ball of hair had formed on the top of her head. When she went to the hair salon, the stylist picked at it with her fingers and a comb.

"What the hell is this?" the hairstylist asked, surprised.

Maria was only a little embarrassed. "I've been wearing this hat for basically a year and a half," she said. The stylist worked through it, trimmed the edges of her hair, rubbed Maria's scalp. She had not been taken care of in so long.

She watched herself in the mirror curiously, as though observing a stranger. She did not look at herself much. At home, she had just a small compact mirror and she could see only pieces of her face, fractured angles of her eyes, her chin, her cheeks and jawline, as though she could never get a complete picture of who she was. At the hair salon, she watched herself. Her face somehow looked completely different, though she couldn't put her finger on exactly what had changed.

Leaving the hair salon, Maria decided it was time to buy a mirror.

ANNA

Kharkiv, Ukraine

IN MAY, I saw Anna's name flash across my phone for the first time in many weeks. She reached out again, this time with distressing news: Dima had been seriously injured. In an attack on their position in Bakhmut, the man next to him was hit directly by a shell and blown to pieces. Shrapnel tore through Dima, and the blast force threw him through the air. When other soldiers retrieved him, they discovered that the explosion had ripped off Dima's hand and crushed the bones of his arm.

He was transferred to a hospital in Kharkiv and underwent surgery. When he regained consciousness, he asked the mother of one of his friends to call Anna, to ask her to come.

"I came running," Anna said. Inside the hospital, wounded soldiers lined the hallways. Dima, she told me, was in the purulent surgery department, "purulent" referring to a state in which wounds continued to weep pus. More accurately, Anna clarified, he was in the hallway of this department. The ward was overcrowded, and hospital staff put the most severely wounded patients there, presumably so that they could be attended to easily.

When she first stepped into the department corridor on her way to meet Dima, she was rocked: "No arms, no legs," Anna reflected on what she saw when she first arrived. "They screamed, constantly cried, because everything hurt them, their amputated limbs. It was a spectacle."

Approaching Dima's bedside, she saw him lying there, bruised and cut up all over. Where there was once a wrist there was now only a stump. Seeing him in that condition, she said, "was my biggest fear." She tried not to cry when she was there, but as she left the first day, emotion overcame her. As the hours passed, Dima became despondent. It would have been better if he had been killed, he said.

But all things considered, Dima was relatively lucky. That it was just his hand and arm bones was extremely fortunate. All through Ukraine there were thousands of men wandering hospital hallways with severe burns and bleeding internal organs, with crushed jaws and eye sockets, with pieces of metal still lodged deep inside the body's tissues. Ukraine's medical care was far from state-of-the-art before 2022, and the all-out assault on medical infrastructure and the never-ending influx of critically wounded patients has led to a national crisis in medical care. Walking through any polytrauma unit of any hospital in Ukraine are hundreds of soldiers who would never receive the care they needed, in part because there were so many of them and simply not enough qualified doctors, and in part because the time and resources it took to adequately treat such acute wounds was more than any one doctor or any one hospital could afford. Many of these patients would die in the hospital, but if they did not, they would return home maimed and have to learn how to live life in their new bodies. Depending on their wounds, some of them would return again to the front lines.

After three days, Dima was transferred to a recovery ward, and

Anna resolved that she would stick around. "I wanted to convey to him at that moment that he is not alone, that there is a person who will always help. And I myself am this kind of person, who will come running at the first ring."

Even though a few weeks earlier he had hit her, she began going to the hospital, an hour away from their apartment, three times a day to feed him, talk with him, and watch over him. He got tired very quickly, and when he slept, she often stayed, watching him as she had in the early days of the previous fall. The hand that he had raised against her was now gone. She called the nurses to give him more painkillers.

In his calm moments, Dima was grateful she was there. But he also suffered acute pain, and all day he listened as men around him screamed. Dima—who, when Anna had first met him, was funny and sweet and full of ideas and life—had become haunted. He yelled and cried, he suffered nightmares, and just before he was transferred to Kyiv for further care, he told Anna that she should leave and never come back, that there wasn't any future for them, that he had only ever loved her for her looks.

His words scalded Anna, and she walked from the hospital hot, hurt, choking back tears. "He said he didn't need anyone or anything," Anna said. "It hurt me deeply, because I dropped everything, I came and fed him every day at eight in the morning . . . I just felt something that I hadn't felt before. Somehow, I wanted to create a family with him, [I wanted to create] comfort. I waited and worried about him. Well, apparently it wasn't fate."

"You'll be better off without me," he told her.

"He said it out of anger and probably out of despair," Anna said, "because he understood that life would never be like it used to be, and he didn't want to ruin it for me." Weeks later, he asked a friend to write to Anna to thank her for all she had done for him.

Anna knew it was time to move on. She stayed in Kharkiv and got a job at a military supply company. At work, she made a few friends, and she practiced giving manicures, a hobby she'd always enjoyed. She bought a UV light for gel manicures, as well as an electric nail drill and filer. In all her free time, she practiced, gaining expertise in shaping and painting nails, even learning complicated art designs.

"When I was a child, I did manicures for my grandma. I just painted her nails with [regular] polish," she said. "If only there was an opportunity now, I would give her a gel manicure." Anna went on, "I can make a little money on this, but my skills aren't good enough to work in a salon"—not because her work wasn't good but because Ukrainian manicurists are often expertly trained in apprenticeships, a tradition inherited from the Soviet beauty industry.

Someday Anna might become a master manicurist herself. The more she practiced, the more she dreamed that she might one day open her own salon, and all day long she could talk with other girls—far away from the police academy where she began her studies. Perhaps her parents would be proud of that, too. After all, manicurists were in high demand, even during war, and she'd always have a job and, probably, a friend.

Through the spring she became closer with her new group of girlfriends. They talked about the boys they knew from high school who were fighting and dying. Some had boyfriends or even husbands at the front, and when one of their husbands was killed in action, Anna went with her to the funeral. There she saw flags placed at the cemetery marking the losses. "It's very difficult to realize that these people are no longer with us," she said. "It is difficult to see these flags blowing in the wind in the cemetery, hundreds of them. How many more will there be?"

In May, Ukraine neared the surrender of Bakhmut. With every passing month, in every city in Ukraine, people were seeing more and more men without limbs.

As the weather warmed, Anna and her new friends would sometimes go out for picnics and swimming in the river or lake. It was still chilly, but they had all survived the winter, and they waded into the water together, laughing, splashing, shivering, a cohort of girlfriends made in the war.

"Maybe a year from now," Anna wrote, "I'll have forgotten this boy." And maybe, she thought, a few years later she could go back to Luhansk and see her grandma. Maybe by then her parents would be home, and she could tell them about how she did it—survived and made a life for herself. Maybe it would be a story she could tell for the rest of her life, about her wartime love story that was not meant to be, about how she traveled back and forth across the country alone, how she loved a soldier and then fed him in the hospital, how she found a new life in Kharkiv, got a dog and a job, and grew from girl to woman. Even at nineteen years old, Anna tells it that way.

VITALY

Borodyanka, Ukraine

A YEAR AFTER his home and coffee shop were destroyed, Vitaly attended a vigil for his childhood best friend, Serhiy, who had died in the rubble of their apartment building. It had been a year since that explosion and Vitaly's frightening exodus to Artem's house, and in that year, very little had been rebuilt in Borodyanka. The rubble was mostly cleared, but most of the buildings that had been bombed simply sat there, destroyed, through all four seasons.

Movies were now being made in the rubble. On the concrete slabs lying on their sides, crews set up cameras, lights, and reflecting panels. Riding his bike around town, Vitaly stopped on the sidewalk and watched them setting up and filming. He didn't know what the crews had in mind, but along with the Banksy painting on the wall, it seemed that his apartment building had become an iconic image. Vitaly assumed it was because of how the missile strike had split the building cleanly in half, with the right and left sides of the complex still standing.

At the vigil for Serhiy, Vitaly and his friends shared memories of foraging for mushrooms and going to discos. Vitaly chuckled when he remembered how they went to the river every day in the summer and in first grade, when he and Serhiy were trying to learn to swim, the older boys carried them out and then let them go, leaving them to thrash around until they learned to keep their heads above water. Splashing wildly, paddling their arms and kicking their legs in a frantic effort to stay afloat, the two of them emerged on the bank, coughing and gasping for air. The next day they went back and tried to do it again faster.

Once, in the eighties, when Serhiy and Vitaly were seventeen years old, they vacationed in Southern Ukraine at the Sea of Azov, where their families went almost every summer. Vitaly met a girl from another vacation home there, and she invited them to her birthday party. On their way to the party, they realized they had forgotten to buy flowers—an unpardonable social disgrace. Serhiy had a bright idea—he knew where an old woman who sold flowers in the bazaar lived, and they went to her garden, carefully picked a bouquet, and put money in her mailbox—three times more than the flowers were worth. They showed up to the birthday party with the most beautiful bouquet, but in the morning, racked with guilt for picking the flowers without permission, even after paying for them, they went to the market to apologize to the old woman. She laughed and kissed their cheeks, and sent them home with even more flowers for their moms. "I still remember this incident as if it were yesterday," Vitaly said. "The grandmother's name was Mira, and the grandfather was Vasyl."

He and Serhiy watched each other become dads—Vitaly first in his early twenties, and Serhiy a few years later. Vitaly admired Serhiy's parenting—"he was the best father."

A few weeks after the vigil, Vitaly found a scrap of a cement bag in his recycling pile. It wasn't too wrinkled or dirty, and the weight of the paper was substantial. Instead of recycling the scrap, he used it to draw; it was good paper for art.

After he came home from the coffee shop, he sat down at the desk and pulled out the paper. He started sketching one of the last photos he had of himself together with Serhiy, a selfie from a year before the invasion, during Covid, both wearing masks, with Vitaly on Serhiy's left, in a white mask.

His pencil strokes were at first rough and rudimentary, establishing the shapes in the right spot, before he moved on to their faces and eyes, shading and smudging and erasing. Behind them he drew their childhood apartment building after it was bombed. He drew for an hour and didn't look up, hunched over the cement bag, shading in the portion of the picture where their heads rested together.

His eyes became strained from focusing too long in poor lighting. "Soon I'll have to stop drawing," Vitaly said—his eyes got tired now in a way they hadn't before. He was getting older, and he had aged a lot in just over a year of war. Soon he'd need to find other

things to do, he thought, other ways to calm down and other ways to remember.

Vitaly, who loved to ride his bike through the town, sometimes rode to the river and looked across the Zdvyzh—a tiny river that wound through Borodyanka. Sometimes he thought about America. Vitaly, who through his life had a series of lovers and many different jobs and hobbies, claims to have ever had only two real dreams—to be with Natalka, and to see the Statue of Liberty. Somehow that statue had always made him believe in a world where people were free to live as they wanted, where the possibilities were truly endless, where a man could leave his hometown and never look back.

Maybe this was all a fiction, but it made him feel that he wasn't a fool for trying to build a coffee shop and spending every waking moment working with piles of garbage, for sitting on the banks of a tiny river and dreaming of another place.

Would he really go, if he could, and leave Borodyanka behind? When I asked him this question, he hemmed and hawed, eventually saying: "I can't answer this question. I was born and raised here. Every cat and dog knows me here." Even after so much of his town was destroyed and never rebuilt, even though many people left and would never come back, even after he'd seen people killed in the streets and under buildings, he couldn't answer.

Later that week, a little girl from the neighborhood came into the café to buy a treat. Her name was Zlata. He'd written me about her before: she came around often collecting donations for the army. She was still wearing a hat, but it was getting warmer outside, warm enough for an ice cream cone. Watching her sitting on the salvaged couch, Vitaly was pleased that children still came around for ice cream and that his coffee shop in Borodyanka was the one to provide it. Maybe it would be a good memory for her someday.

He sent me the photo later that day. "Spring is coming," he wrote.

Volodymyr—1989

AS THE PLANE touched down in Kyiv, Dmytro Stus prodded Volodymyr awake. They had to hurry from the plane to get to the cargo warehouse where the coffins would be stored. Volodymyr worried that something would happen to the bodies if they dawdled. The warehouse was situated two kilometers from the terminal, and the day was cold and windy. Volodymyr and his team ran the whole way. When they arrived at the warehouse, the manager took Volodymyr's cargo receipt but came back and said that the coffins were gone—somebody else had picked them up.

"I thought I had foreseen everything," Volodymyr said, "and then they stole it from under my nose."

Dmytro's face was blank. He stood silently.

"I tried not to scream," Volodymyr said. He asked the warehouse manager: "So, can you at least tell me who took them? The cops, or the KGB, or the devil?"

The warehouse manager shook his head—it wasn't any of

them—it was a member of Rukh, the People's Movement of Ukraine, who had been helping to organize the reburial on the Kyiv side. Relieved that they hadn't lost the bodies after all, Volodymyr left the warehouse. The poets were now in the hands of the right people, who would make sure they got reburied.

A couple of days earlier, as soon as they received word that the bodies would finally be returned to Ukraine, the reburial team in Kyiv publicized the event widely, inviting as many people as would come to welcome the writers home at the airport and the next day on their procession to the cemetery. Outside Kyiv's Boryspil airport, about six hundred people had gathered, bearing hundreds of Ukrainian flags—a rare sight in the late Soviet Union, when waving the Ukrainian flag was severely restricted or forbidden. One witness of the 1989 reburial commented that it was difficult to get the right shades of blue and yellow fabric needed to make the flags. They simply didn't exist in sufficient supply, because no one was making those flags and no one needed those colors.

"The late 1980s, and especially 1989, were times of heated political debates over the future of a still-Soviet Ukraine, times when the Ukrainian culture and language were neither fully rehabilitated within the ruling structures nor legitimated in the minds of the population, particularly among the Russian-speaking portion," wrote Natalya Shostak, an anthropologist who studied Stus's reburial.

Most of those who gathered had never heard of Vasyl Stus, Yuriy Lytvyn, or Oleksiy Tykhyi. Stus, though he would gain a massive following in the 1990s, was hardly known as a poet or intellectual at the time of his reburial. Shostak recalled her well-read Russian-speaking university friends from Kyiv asking her after news of the poets' reburial spread: "And who actually was that Stus?"

So, the next day, on November 19, 1989, when Volodymyr stepped into the reburial processional and saw thousands of blue-

and-yellow flags waving, his chest tightened: about one hundred thousand people had gathered. It was the largest demonstration in Kyiv since 1917, when Ukrainians had gathered en masse to demand independence from the Russian Empire.

They had heard the news that three martyred Ukrainian writers were returning from Russia and would be reburied in Baikove Cemetery in Kyiv, and they went, overcoming their fear of Soviet authorities, to see Stus, Tykhyi, and Lytvyn laid to rest. The attitude was "If we are arrested, let us be arrested."

That morning, the processional formed in downtown Kyiv was led by a Ukrainian priest, who guided the poets' mortal remains through the city, past cathedrals and apartments, past monuments and parks, past the KGB headquarters where Stus had been held and interrogated years earlier. When they arrived at the cemetery, the families and friends of the writers spoke at the crowded mourning rally.

Volodymyr watched as the three zinc coffins were lowered into the ground. He felt he stood on the precipice of something new, a new era. "A powerful sense of unity pervaded, involving everybody in the same experience of being initiated into the nation," wrote Shostak. "Those who had urged on and supported Stus's symbolic return to Ukraine were people of the new ideology," an ideology based on Ukraine's independence from the USSR as well as its having a distinct identity separate from Russia's.

What would come to Ukraine in the coming years, Volodymyr wondered, standing at the graves. In March of the following year, he ran for a seat in the Ukrainian Soviet Socialist Republic Verkhovna Rada—the parliament of then Soviet Ukraine—and won. It was the first relatively open, free election in Soviet Ukraine's history, and as a member of parliament, Volodymyr served as the chairman of the subcommittee for issues related to the Chernobyl exclusion zone.

In August of the next year, Volodymyr was in France pursuing treatment for a group of 450 children from the Soviet Union who had become ill following radiation exposure from Chernobyl. While he was there, hard-liners attempted a coup in Moscow, effectively stripping Gorbachev of power and propelling the USSR toward collapse. Rushing home to Ukraine, Volodymyr arrived on August 24, 1991—the day Ukraine proclaimed its independence. He recalled: "Before the declaration of independence in August 1991, there was great tension, there were expectations of armed intervention from Russia. But since centrifugal movements began throughout the union republics and movements for independence began, Moscow really did not have the strength to hold everything back."

Parliament scheduled a referendum vote in early December that year to confirm Ukraine's independence. From August 24 to December 1, Volodymyr and other parliament members in favor of Ukraine's independence campaigned throughout the country, agitating for independence. On the night of December 1, Volodymyr and his wife gathered with several other parliamentarians and their families to await the results. "Somewhere around ten p.m., [Ukraine's first vice prime minister, Konstantyn Masyk] called us," Volodymyr recalled. "He knew that we were waiting for the results, and he called us and said: 'I congratulate you! All regions voted for independence, including Donetsk, Luhansk, Crimea, and even the Black Sea Fleet.'

"We were enthusiastic, euphoric. I was afraid that there would not be more than sixty-five percent." But the vote was overwhelming: 90 percent of Ukrainians voted for independence. The twenty-fourth of August was one of the most joyful days many Ukrainians had ever experienced, the dream of generations of Ukrainians. Volodymyr felt fortunate to witness it.

In time, he helped to draft Ukraine's new constitution. "But a lot of people, after a brilliant result of ninety percent, suddenly thought now that we are all independent, rivers of milk and jelly shores will flow, now we will be showered with incredible blessings, wealth, and everything will be great with us, we will work for ourselves. But it turned out a little differently than many thought."

The 1990s and early 2000s proved much more complex for Ukraine than many had anticipated. They underestimated the barriers that would arise in the coming years: the corruption of former Communists and new oligarchs, the dysfunctional legacy of Soviet institutions, the lack of support from the West, and the ferocious lengths to which Russia would go to forestall Ukraine's fledging independence and keep it bound to Moscow politically and economically.

"And immediately," Volodymyr said, "the problem of nuclear weapons loomed over us." Ukraine had the third-largest nuclear arsenal in the world, after America and Russia, and in December 1994, Ukraine entered into an agreement with the United States, the UK, and Russia known as the Budapest Memorandum, which guaranteed Ukraine's security under the condition that Ukraine give up its most powerful weaponry. "Ukraine gave up not only nuclear weapons but also medium-range and longer-range nonnuclear missiles, with which Russia is currently bombarding us," Volodymyr comments. "We gave them because our allies and then guarantors demanded it. But now we are reaping the fruits of our naïveté at that time."

Within a couple of years, Volodymyr lost his bid for reelection to parliament, and he decided to leave politics behind and go back to writing. He struggled throughout the 1990s and 2000s on the educational front. "Ukrainians still had to learn that no one will create a state for us. America will not come to create a state for us, and the Muscovites have already done it to us, and we saw what we got in that empire."

He wrote nearly a dozen books of poetry, short stories, and essays and directed several films. In 2011, Volodymyr started a publishing company called Ukrainian Priority and began publishing books in Ukrainian—poetry, fiction, short stories, history—including the story of how he helped to rebury Stus.

When his body was reburied in the late eighties, hardly anyone knew of Stus. And yet, more than three decades after Stus's reburial, as Ukrainians' belief in their own free destiny grows stronger while the outcome of the war becomes increasingly uncertain, Stus's story feels more familiar. It all seemed to happen just as Stus had written: *in death I will return to you in life.*

Stus's poetry, which he had composed in the isolation of the gulag, hoping it might be read by some future Ukrainian, had now reached them: in the months before and after the full-scale invasion, people graffitied Stus's poetry on the sides of buildings in the Donbas and tattooed Stus's words on their bodies. In May, after the theater in Mariupol was bombed, the troupe that had performed there put on a show in Western Ukraine dedicated to the life and work of Vasyl Stus. Stus's introduction into the Ukrainian consciousness brought forward a clear precedent. Soldiers made videos reciting Stus's poetry in trenches, under shelling, not far from where Stus was born: "Suffer, suffer on, because the suffering strengthens you," they quoted. "Highway to hell or stairway to heaven, you've got to stand, you've got to soldier on. The path chose you and it's forever: it started when you were a young boy, God himself made you for it."

Through the first year of the war, millions of Ukrainians chose that path, and Volodymyr's words—"Heroes are born on the graves of heroes"—seemed to have become true, too.

Volodymyr, now an old man, volunteered with Ukraine's Territorial Defense Forces on February 24, 2022, and his two sons and one son-in-law joined the army. Volodymyr was issued a machine gun and assigned—along with other volunteers—to stand at checkpoints to monitor the flow of cars to and from Kyiv.

As he did this work, in early April of the first spring, a modest order for books came in to his publishing company. The order was from a man in the Kharkiv region, which was, at the time, subjected to near-constant artillery fire. The city was being decimated, and the order for books perplexed Volodymyr. Certainly there were more pressing concerns. He called the phone number on the order and reached the man, who assured that he meant to place it.

"Do you know what the *rashisty* do when they enter our villages?" the man asked. "They destroy our Ukrainian books." In all occupied regions, books by Stus and other Ukrainian authors have been destroyed, replaced in libraries and schools by titles meant to manipulate how children understand history.

In an attempt to right this wrong as best he could, the man ordered a few copies of some of the books Volodymyr published: biographies of repressed Ukrainian writers, histories of the varied Ukrainian guerrilla fighters who battled the Soviet Army, new colonial interpretations of Ukraine's relationship with Russia.

At the time, all the employees of Volodymyr's publishing house had evacuated or were serving in the military, which left Volodymyr to manage operations more or less on his own. He rushed to their warehouse in Kyiv, found the books, packed them up, and shipped them to Kharkiv. A few days later, he received an order from someone in Borodyanka, and then an order from Bucha, then Irpin— towns that had been ravaged and occupied in the first days of the invasion. He again went to the warehouse, rifled through piles of books, and sent them off in various directions.

For months, as the fighting went on, and as his sons learned to fly drones and operate complex antiaircraft systems, Volodymyr shipped books to all corners of Ukraine, and later he began driving across the country to give talks to educators and distribute works on

Ukraine's history. As Vitaly had found while rummaging through piles of wastepaper, people were tired of reading books in which Ukraine was always Russia's younger brother. In the war, they came increasingly to abandon those reading lists in favor of literature in which Ukrainians pursued or attempted to pursue their own destiny apart from Russia's. Such books—scarce a generation ago—now proliferate in free Ukraine and are burned in bonfires in its occupied territories. As Volodymyr travels the country to give talks in small local libraries and school classrooms and book fairs, people come to listen, and many go home with something new to read.

By the second spring, both of Volodymyr's sons, who'd been children at Chernobyl, now fought in Bakhmut. Volodymyr's publishing manager, with whom he'd worked for nine years, was killed there. No one was able to collect the body, and by the end of May, that city would be captured by the Russians, ending a bloody monthslong slog that claimed tens of thousands of lives and left hundreds of thousands wounded.

A couple of weeks after Bakhmut fell, Russia blew up the Kakhovka dam in the Kherson region, flooding an area of almost six hundred square kilometers in Southern Ukraine, including Tania's village. Water, which had been scarce for months, spread widely, eventually destroying many homes throughout Mykil'ske and drowning hundreds of thousands of chickens, cows, horses, and pigs, their bodies consumed by the water and left to rot. Hundreds more people left Mykil'ske, and finally, in December of that year, so, too, would Tania and Viktor, who set out for Odesa.

Volodymyr's sons were transferred to other areas with intense fighting—Avdiivka, Zaporizhzhya, Kharkiv, Sumy—where they flew drones and engaged in reconnaissance and bombing. In late summer 2024, his son Georgiy was killed in combat, while through it all Volodymyr continued shipping out his books, believing that the written word wields its own power in war. Perhaps if he sent enough books out into Ukraine, he hoped, they might galvanize readers to believe in their country—perhaps they could build a defensive line of their own, perhaps they would reach the hands of some young person who might someday change the course of history. After all, nothing had ever been the same for Volodymyr since the night in 1989 when he first held that rare foreign edition of *Palimpsests*.

"I was and still am an optimist about the future of Ukraine," Volodymyr said. "I believe that Ukraine will win. We have no other option—we will either disappear or win. And we will win," he said, packing his car full of books to drive those long stretches of land that have belonged to different empires in different times and where the blurry line between nations is still being decided by force of arms. In the years yet to come, only his children will know which books survived to be read—and which did not.

A NOTE ON SOURCES

The material in this book comes primarily from the interviews I conducted with the Ukrainians featured in the book, as well as interviews with their families and friends. I am especially grateful to them— Anna, Vitaly, Maria, Yulia, Oleg, Polina, John, Tania, and Volodymyr— for sharing their lives so generously, sparing few details and allowing me to observe from my perspective so much of what they experienced. I have done my best to represent them as accurately as possible; any imperfections in the telling of their stories are my own. Many of them are not accustomed to speaking or writing about their lives, but they were motivated to do so, even when it was uncomfortable or inconvenient. I hope this book honors their lives and experiences.

A note on method: I was introduced to Vitaly, Maria, Yulia, and Anna through the aid project I participated in during the first months of the war. The project was funded by the Dell Loy Hansen Family Foundation and run by the Leavitt Institute for International Development, founded by my parents in the early 2000s. I had only a small role in the aid project. Under my father's direction, the staff of the Leavitt Institute set up and ran the diary project that stemmed from the aid project, and I assisted in explaining the purpose of the diaries to participants in the aid program as well as in communicating with diarists.

I met Tania and Volodymyr through introductions made by friends, and I have known Polina since the early 2000s, when my family first moved to Kyiv and attended her and her family's church for a time. Except for Polina, I established communication with each of the people in this book through WhatsApp or Viber—messaging apps—asking if I could interview and feature them in a book on Ukrainians in the war. They agreed to answer my questions, provide details of their experiences, and allow me to correspond with them for many months, often several times a week. I communicated with Polina and John primarily in one long in-person interview, which we added to over time in several shorter exchanges. The subject of my conversations with each of my interlocutors began more or less at the beginning of the full-scale invasion, moving backward and forward in time to build a robust context for their experiences in 2022. Many shared old family photos, and some introduced me to family members and friends, with whom I also corresponded.

In my communications with the people in this book, we spoke Ukrainian, Russian, and English, sometimes switching back and forth between languages as my subjects saw fit. In general, I let my interlocutors choose the tongue, especially as many of them were experiencing new emotional reactions to language, especially Russian. Where appropriate, I tried to corroborate the statements and narratives of those featured in this book with additional material, usually scholarly.

I am also grateful to the many other Ukrainians who provided details and anecdotes for this book, many of them participants in the Leavitt Institute's diary project established in the first months of the war. Their stories and experiences helped me more fully understand the complexities and nuances of living in this war.

I consulted many valuable written sources. First and foremost was a pamphlet written by Volodymyr Shovkoshitny titled *Heroes Are Born on the Graves of Heroes* (*Герої народжуються на могилах героїв*, Ukrainian Priority, 2012). In this pamphlet, Shovkoshitny tells the story of reburying Vasyl Stus, which I have featured in the interludes and postlude of this book. In personal interviews, he provided additional details pertaining to the reburial story, as well as his own biographical details that are related throughout the book. Vasyl Stus's advice to his son, as remembered by Dmytro Stus, comes from Dmytro Stus's book *Vasyl Stus: Zhyttya Yak Tvorchist* (Duh i Litera, 2015). Additionally, on the life of Vasyl Stus, I consulted the recollections and writings of Vasyl Ovsiyenko.

Among the other insightful written sources I consulted, some of which I quoted throughout, were works by Serhii Plokhy (*The Gates of Europe*; *Chernobyl*; *The Cossacks and Religion in Early Modern Ukraine*; *The Origins of the Slavic Nations*), Timothy Snyder (*The Reconstruction of Nations*; *Bloodlands*; *Black Earth*), Yaroslav Hrytsak (*A Brief History of Ukraine: The Forging of a Nation*; "The Postcolonial Is Not Enough," *Slavic Review* 74, no. 4 [Winter 2015]), Willard Sunderland (*Taming the Wild Field: Colonization and Empire on the Russian Steppe*), Oxana Shevel and Maria Popova (*Russia and Ukraine: Entangled Histories, Diverging States*; "Ukraine Belongs in the EU," *Journal of Democracy*, March 2022), Terry Martin (*The Affirmative Action Empire*), Lewis Siegelbaum and Daniel Walkowitz (*Workers of the Donbass Speak: Survival and Identity in the New Ukraine, 1989–1992*), Catherine Wanner (*Burden of Dreams: History and Identity in Post-Soviet Ukraine*), Mitchell Orenstein and Kristen Ghodsee (*Taking Stock of Shock: Social Consequences of the 1989 Revolutions*), Jeffrey Veidlinger (*In the Midst of Civilized Europe*), Anne Applebaum (*Red Famine*; *Gulag: A History*; *Iron Curtain: The Crushing of Eastern Europe, 1944–1956*), Andrey Kurkov (*Ukraine Diaries: Dispatches from Kyiv*), Marci Shore (*The Ukrainian Night: An Intimate History of Revolution*), Serhiy Yekelchyk (*Ukraine: The Birth of a Modern Nation*; *Stalin's Empire of Memory*), Paul Robert Magocsi (*The History of Ukraine*), Dominic Lieven (*Empire: The Russian Empire and Its Rivals*), Mark Mazower (*Hitler's Empire: How the Nazis Ruled Europe*), Kate Brown (*A Biography of No Place*), Mark Beissinger (*Nationalist Mobilization and the Collapse of the Soviet Union*), Roman Szporluk (*Russia, Ukraine, and the Breakup of the Soviet Union*), Stephen Kotkin (*Uncivil Society*; *Armageddon Averted: The Soviet Collapse*),

Simon Clarke ("Privatization and the Development of Capitalism in Russia," *New Left Review* 196 [Nov./Dec. 1992], Andrej N. Lushnycky and Mykola Riabchuk (*Ukraine on Its Meandering Path Between East and West*), Mykola Riabchuk (in his *New Yorker* interview with Isaac Chotiner, "The Soft Politics That Exploded into War," March 24, 2022), Natalya Shostak ("To Whom Does a Poet Belong? The Reburial of Vasyl' Stus (1989) as a Ritual of Cultural Appropriation," *spacesofidentity.net*, 2[3)], 2002), and Bohdan Tokarskyi ("Thriving in Isolation and Beyond: The Empowering Poetry of Vasyl Stus," *Los Angeles Review of Books*, June 9, 2020).

My comments on Ukraine's underground music scene in part 4 are informed by an article written by Max Hunder and Stefaniia Bern titled "Kyiv Ravers Escape Horrors of War Through Music," Reuters, August 30, 2022. I consulted articles from *The New York Times* on the Kherson counteroffensive, including "Russian Officials Flee Kherson as Russian Troops Dig In for a Battle," by Marc Santora and Eric Nagourney (October 24, 2022), as well as "Ukrainian Forces Enter Kherson, a Strategic Prize, in a Blow to Putin," by Andrew E. Kramer and Marc Santora (November 11, 2022). On the siege of Azovstal, I consulted "Russia Says the Long-Besieged Azovstal Steel Complex in Mariupol Has Fallen," by Ivan Nechepurenko and James C. McKinley Jr. (May 20, 2022). Many details on the trials of Vasyl Stus came from the *Chronicle of Current Events.* I'm indebted to the excellent reportage of Stanislav Aseyev, which was collected in his book *In Isolation: Dispatches from Occupied Donbas,* as well as that of Christopher Miller, Yaroslav Trofimov, Simon Shuster, Maria Varenikova, and many others who have documented the daily movements of this war so well.

I also consulted the transcripts of several talks that took place at the Harvard Ukrainian Research Institute (HURI) in 2023–2024 as I wrote this book, especially those by Yevhen Hlibovytsky, Oxana Shevel, Maria Popova, and Bohdan Tokarskyi.

ACKNOWLEDGMENTS

I have many people to thank for their support and expertise, which brought this book to life. My first thanks go to the seven Ukrainians and their families and friends, who spent hundreds of hours in conversation with me. Their generosity, strength, and spirit inspired me again and again. I hope this book can, in its own small way, bring to light what they've endured and garner support for them and the millions of other Ukrainians like them.

Serhii Plokhy advised all along the way on matters big and small, and I'm grateful for his mentorship, guidance, and kindness. His perspectives on Ukraine have shaped mine more than any other. The Harvard Ukrainian Research Institute was my intellectual home while I wrote this book, and I am grateful to the wonderful staff at HURI who made that time productive and comfortable: Megan Duncan Smith, Emily Channel-Justice, Tymish Holowinsky, and others.

Thank you to the Dell Loy Hansen Family Foundation, which funded the fellowship year I took to write this book. The Hansen Family Foundation in partnership with the Leavitt Institute for International Development aided dozens of families in displacement, four of whom are featured in this book. That aid helped hundreds to survive the first brutal months of the war and opened a door for many to tell their stories.

I am grateful to the entire production and editing staff at Farrar, Straus and Giroux, and especially to my editor, Alexander Star, whose insight has been unparalleled and whose intuition shaped this book from the beginning. An additional thanks to Ian Van Wye for his helpful work on the manuscript and maps.

Early readers of my manuscript offered productive comments and critiques, and my thanks go to Aden Knaap, Bohdan Tokarskyi, Jonathon Palmer, Hannah Shepley, Rachel Ruekert, and my grandmother Anne Leavitt. Erin Hutchinson and Anna Whittington answered various queries and provided astute historical takes. Yana Skorobogatov gave, as always, great advice. Natalia Formanchuk assisted with transcription. Britta Elwanger's unmatched understanding of Ukrainian communities and civilian and soldier life near the front lines was invaluable. Thank you.

For those who cared for my children while I wrote this book—Luiselena Rubio Peraza, Kamian Coppins, Paula Bardhan, Alison Fenske, Olivia Crowley, Alicia Eagles, Tyra Prepetit, Yordanos Berhe, and Fei Wang—thank you. I could not have written it without you; your help and kind care were instrumental in this process.

Thank you to good friends who cheered for me along the way: Rose Allen, Caitlin Carr, Lindsey Encinas, Brianna Cragun Greenhalgh, Sarah Hogan, Katie Jepson, Natalie Marsh, Tess Maxwell, Tatiana Leavitt Messersmith, Deborah Palmer, Rachel Farnsworth Pierce, Natania Quist, and Katie Stevenson.

I am grateful to my agent, Lucy Cleland, who saw the potential in this book long before it was a book and fought hard for it. Additionally, I thank the many teachers whose influence I felt as I wrote this book: Pat, Mark, Matt, Justin, and many others.

My family has encouraged me all along the way, and I am grateful to each of them: Adam, Mary, Hannah, Parker, Eliza, Caitlin, Daniel, Seth, Brayden, Ethan, Emma, Eric, Mindy, Britton, Kirsten, Brady, Natania, Abbie, Bobby, Troy, and Hannah. Curtis and Lisa Quist have supported me consistently with profound kindness.

I am especially thankful to my parents, David and Chelom Leavitt, who have read, edited, and supported my writing longer than anyone else. Thank you for taking us to Ukraine all those years ago. I've always felt your belief in me—and I do not take that for granted.

To my daughters, Camilla and Greta, who do not yet even know that I wrote this book: I carried you in my heart as I wrote every word.

Finally, Kramer Quist, my husband and best friend, believed in this project even before I did and read each page from start to finish—multiple times. Your faith in this book and in my ability to write it has sustained me from the start. I am grateful to have my own story, with you.

A Note About the Author

Danielle Leavitt holds a PhD in history from Harvard University, where she has been a fellow at the Ukrainian Research Institute. She grew up in both Ukraine and the United States and currently lives in Ann Arbor, Michigan. *By the Second Spring* is her first book.